D0953421

The New American Economy

The New American Economy

The Failure of Reaganomics and a New Way Forward

Bruce Bartlett

palgrave
macmillan

THE NEW AMERICAN ECONOMY
Copyright © Bruce Bartlett, 2009.

All rights reserved.

First published in 2009 by
PALGRAVE MACMILLAN®
in the United States—a division of St. Martin's Press LLC,
175 Fifth Avenue, New York, NY 10010.

Where this book is distributed in the UK, Europe and the rest of the world, this is
by Palgrave Macmillan, a division of Macmillan Publishers Limited, registered in
England, company number 785998, of Houndmills, Basingstoke, Hampshire
RG21 6XS.

Palgrave Macmillan is the global academic imprint of the above companies and
has companies and representatives throughout the world.

Palgrave® and Macmillan® are registered trademarks in the United States, the
United Kingdom, Europe and other countries.

ISBN: 978–0–230–61587–8

Library of Congress Cataloging-in-Publication Data is available from the
Library of Congress.

A catalogue record of the book is available from the British Library.

Design by Newgen Imaging Systems (P) Ltd., Chennai, India.

First edition: October 2009

10 9 8 7 6 5 4 3

Printed in the United States of America.

Contents

INTRODUCTION

Back in the 1970s, I had a front-row seat to the disintegration of Keynesian economics and the rise of supply-side economics. As a staffer for Congressmen Ron Paul and Jack Kemp, I was involved in an important national debate on what to do about inflation and how to get the American economy moving again.

At that time, Keynesian economics had been distilled into the simple ideas that budget deficits stimulated growth and inflation was caused by low unemployment. The supply-siders' contrary view was that slow growth resulted mainly from high tax rates and inflation was caused by the Federal Reserve creating too much money. At that time, the top income tax rate was 70 percent and inflation was rapidly pushing workers up into tax brackets originally reserved for the rich.

Supply-side economics was highly successful in addressing these problems, both politically and substantively—just as Keynesian economics had been when it was credited with ending the Great Depression. After Ronald Reagan implemented supply-side policies in 1981, inflation came down rapidly and growth was restored. By 1986, supply-side ideas were so popular that Republicans and Democrats joined together to lower the top income tax rate to just 28 percent.

But just as Keynesian economics went off on the wrong track and became discredited, I think supply-side economics has also reached the end of its useful life. What is still right about it has been completely integrated into mainstream economics. What remains when people think of "supply-siders" is a caricature—that there is no problem that more and bigger tax cuts won't solve. Talk radio and groups such as the Club for Growth and Americans for Tax Reform ruthlessly enforce this view among Republicans, even though it is obvious that the tax cuts of the George W. Bush years were not especially successful, and that the economy's problems today are due primarily to a lack of demand, not supply.

I know how rigidly the party line on taxes is enforced. In 2003, I became convinced that our budgetary problems were so severe that a major tax increase was inevitable. I wrote a book on the subject that was published in 2006: *Impostor: How George W. Bush Bankrupted America and Betrayed the Reagan Legacy.* As a result, I was fired from my job at a think tank closely aligned with the Republican Party, and since then have been treated as something of a pariah by every group similarly aligned with the GOP.[1]

The deterioration of the economy and the budget since 2006 has, of course, only reinforced my conviction that tax cuts are no longer a viable means of dealing with the problems facing us today. President Barack Obama has already started the process of raising taxes by permitting the Bush tax cuts to expire at the end of 2010 and by asking Congress to impose a huge new tax on energy in the form of a cap-and-trade program for carbon emissions.

These actions are far from the best ways of raising federal revenues. They will damage growth and incentives more than is necessary. I remain convinced that a value-added tax (VAT), a type of national sales tax, would be a much better method of raising additional revenue. But it seems that there is no one in American politics willing to say so publicly, although high-ranking members of both parties have told me privately that I am right.

When this book was originally conceived, the economic crisis of 2008–2009 was nowhere on the horizon. But by the time I was finished, I felt like I was reliving much of the history I had been writing about. Not only are economic conditions almost identical to those in the early 1930s, but many of the debates among economists are eerily similar as well. It was as if we had learned nothing about the economy in the intervening 75 years.

Introduction

The current crisis is the greatest the world has seen since the Great Depression. While no two crises are ever the same, we can nevertheless learn from the failures and successes of the past. For one thing, many current policymakers are known to have studied the Great Depression intensively—Federal Reserve Board Chairman Ben Bernanke and Council of Economic Advisers Chair Christina Romer in particular. It is useful to know what they know about the Great Depression to anticipate how they will react to current economic developments.

It is also clear that we need to draw upon the greatest thinkers of the past to guide us though today's difficulties. The economist of the past who thought most deeply about precisely the problems we confront today is John Maynard Keynes. Although he and his ideas continue to be hated by those on the right, I argue that he was in fact a conservative whose main concern was preventing the rise of socialism.

One motivation for writing this book was to resolve in my own mind a concern I have long had about the length and depth of the Great Depression. I learned early in my career that the Federal Reserve, our nation's central bank, had allowed the money supply to decline by a third between 1929 and 1933. All other things being equal, such a decline would force the price level to fall by about an equal amount. This deflation was at the heart of the Great Depression.

I always had difficulty understanding why this happened. Surely, I thought, economists of the 1930s were not ignorant of Federal Reserve policy. They couldn't have been blind to the downward pressure on prices and the economic consequences of it. Nor could they have been so unsophisticated as to not understand that an expansive Fed policy was the key to solving the economic problem.

As I came to understand, Keynes, Irving Fisher, and many others perfectly well understood the monetary origins of the Great Depression virtually from day one. They tried to explain this fact in many forums—books, academic papers, congressional testimony, op-ed articles, newspaper interviews, etc.—but to no avail. The problem was that they simply could not get through to the policymakers with the power to make a difference. Even in the face of the greatest

3

economic crisis of modern times, policymakers and politicians found it easier to keep policy on automatic pilot rather than admit that they might be responsible for it.

This fact became clear to me when I took advantage of now easily searchable newspaper databases. I went back through the *New York Times, Wall Street Journal, Washington Post,* and other popular publications of the 1930s to see what economists like Keynes were saying to policymakers in real time. Too many economists today rely exclusively on their predecessors' writings in books and academic publications, which were necessarily too technical for policymakers to grasp or even know about, and were often published long after they had made their points in other forums.

Consequently, contemporary economists' understanding of the policy implications of historical figures like Keynes is incomplete. He used a wide variety of means to reach policymakers, including meetings and correspondence as well as interviews with and writings for popular publications, to try and get his message through. It's essential to be aware of this work to understand where the fault lies in terms of the government's failure to either grasp or devise appropriate solutions for the economic crisis.

Once I learned what economists were saying and doing in real time, it was clear that there was no essential difference between Keynes, the arch fiscalist, and Fisher, the arch monetarist and the Milton Friedman of his day. Their positions reinforced each other and both were needed to deal with the Great Depression. While the basic problem was monetary, Fed policy was impotent because the economy was at a dead stop. Money was unable to circulate and the Fed's efforts to expand the money supply were like pushing on a string. Fiscal stimulus was necessary to compensate for the collapse of private spending in the economy, and thereby mobilize monetary policy. Once fiscal policy got the economy off dead stop, monetary policy would again become effective, ending the deflation and the depression.

I think we entered into the same basic situation in 2007. The Fed had been too easy for too long, creating a bubble in the housing market and threatening price stability. In the words of Columbia University economist Jeffrey Sachs, "The U.S. crisis was actually made by the Fed, helped by . . . none other than Alan Greenspan."[2] When it began to tighten monetary policy in 2004, it deflated the housing bubble, dragging down the entire financial sector, which was more heavily dependent on housing than anyone realized. Changes in Fed policy take about two years to impact the economy. Thus housing prices peaked in mid-2006, fell modestly in 2007 and sharply in 2008.

As housing prices fell, consumer spending fell. The converse of the well-known tendency for people to spend $5 to $10 of each $100 increase in their wealth occurred.[3] Spending fell $5 to $10 for every $100 decrease in wealth. As housing losses ran into the many trillions of dollars, spending fell by hundreds of billions of dollars per year.

The result was a situation not unlike that in the early 1930s, but with one difference. What was collapsing wasn't the money supply but something called velocity—the ratio of the money supply to the gross domestic product; that is, the number of times money turns over in a year. When velocity falls, its impact on the economy is identical to a decline in the money supply. Nominal GDP must fall and results in declining prices and declining output, two prominent features of the 2008–2009 crisis.

While the Federal Reserve attempted to staunch the decline by increasing the money supply, it ran into the same problem that it had back in the 1930s—it couldn't get the money to circulate. Consumers cut back on spending, businesses cut back on investment, and banks cut back on lending faster than the Fed could pump money into the economy.

So once again the burden fell on fiscal policy to jump-start the economy. Only when aggregate spending in the economy was again rising would monetary policy become effective. Neither monetary nor fiscal policy was effective by itself; they needed each other to pull the economy out of depression. While monetary policy provides the primary stimulus, it simply doesn't work except in conjunction with fiscal policy under severe deflationary conditions. This was the basic rationale for the $787 billion stimulus package enacted by Congress in early 2009.[4]

There was considerable debate among economists over the size, shape, and timing of the stimulus, with a number of prominent economists arguing against any stimulus at all. But the opponents missed the point. Stimulus should not be viewed in isolation or compared to fiscal actions in normal times. Fiscal policy is needed because it is the only means possible for mobilizing monetary policy, which is at the root of the economy's problem.

In the course of the debate over Barack Obama's stimulus package, Republicans insisted that the only fiscal policy effective in raising growth was cutting taxes. Increased government spending, they argued, was ineffective because the increased borrowing simply took out of the economy what the spending put back in. For reasons that were unclear, Republicans said that tax cuts would have a different impact and be more stimulative.

If Republicans had looked at interest rates on Treasury bills, which were close to zero and even turned negative for a brief period, they would have realized that federal borrowing was not preempting any private uses of saving.[5] The federal government was borrowing money that was earning nothing, not being used at all. Nor did Republicans explain how tax cuts would stimulate growth when growing numbers of people had no income because they had been laid off, when businesses had no profits because they had no sales, and investors had no gains to realize.

Republicans explained that they were basing their proposals on supply-side economics. But they never understood the essential differences in the economies of 1981 and 2009. In particular, the role of the Fed was completely different. In the early 1980s it was fighting inflation; in 2009 it was fighting deflation. Fiscal policy has a completely different role to play under each of these circumstances.

Without the inflation of the 1970s it is doubtful that supply-side economics would ever have come into existence. Economist Robert Mundell, one of its originators, argued that one of the main reasons why inflation had a negative effect on the economy is because it caused taxes to rise. Workers got pushed up into higher tax brackets when they only got cost of living pay raises, corporations paid taxes on illusory inventory profits, and investors paid taxes on capital gains that represented nothing but inflation.

For this reason, Mundell said, tax rate reductions were critical to getting the economy moving when it was suffering from slow growth and inflation—dubbed "stagflation"—as was the case in the 1970s. There was no need for fiscal policy to mobilize monetary policy; indeed, the cause of inflation was that money growth and spending were too large, not too small, as was the case in the 1930s and is today.

Consequently, tax cuts would have been a highly inappropriate response to the problems of 2009. Republicans pushed them only out of dogma and not because they had any rational reason to believe that they would improve the economy. If they had been serious about using tax policy to stimulate growth they would have proposed the sorts of tax cuts that would have increased spending. One such tax cut is the Investment Tax Credit, which would have encouraged business spending on capital equipment.[6] But this idea was never considered. Instead, Republicans simply repackaged the same old tax cuts they had been promoting for years under completely different economic conditions.

One theme of this book is that ideas such as Keynesian economics and supply-side economics came into being to deal with major problems that the existing consensus could not fix. When these new ideas are successful there is a tendency for them to be treated as all-purpose answers for every economic problem, despite the fact that they may be applicable only under a particular set of circumstances. When they became misapplied in inappropriate circumstances and therefore failed, this set in motion the development of new theories or the rediscovery of old ones that had been previously discarded.

Keynesian economics worked in the 1930s because it was designed for deflationary conditions. But applied when deflation wasn't a problem, it stimulated inflation. And for the same reason, there wasn't much in Keynesian economics that was helpful to ending inflation. This led to the abandonment of Keynesian theories in the 1970s when inflation was the primary problem.

Supply-side economics was an appropriate response to stagflation. Tight money and tax rate cuts were a policy mix that worked very well in the early 1980s, helping to bring down double digit inflation at far less economic cost than most economists thought possible. Supply-side policies also laid the foundation for higher real growth well into the 1990s. But in the first decade of the twentieth century, many policies were implemented in the name of supply-side economics that bore no resemblance to those of the Reagan era.

For example, supply-side economics said that only permanent tax cuts caused people and businesses to change their behavior, yet all of George W. Bush's tax cuts were enacted on a temporary basis. Supply-side economics said that only reductions in marginal tax rates had meaningful incentive effects, yet the bulk of Bush's tax cuts consisted of tax rebates and tax credits with no incentive effects. Nevertheless, Bush and his advisers continued to claim that his policies were based on supply-side economics.

The failure of Bush's policies discredited supply-side economics just as inflation had discredited Keynesian economics. The recent economic crisis has given Keynesian economics a new lease on life, but if history is a guide it will continue to be applied long past the point where it is valid. It is almost a certainty that monetary and fiscal stimulus will continue to be applied in large doses well after the economy has turned the corner. Neither the Obama administration nor the Federal Reserve will want to risk tightening until they are absolutely certain that the economy is on a solid footing once again. There is no possibility that they will come to this conclusion until after the 2012 election.

Excessive monetary and fiscal stimulus means that inflation will once again be a serious problem in the not-too-distant future. At that point, supply-side economics may experience a revival. But it will have to cope with a different fiscal environment than Reagan had to deal with. He had the benefit of being in office during a fairly benign demographic period. The baby boom generation was entering its peak earning years, while there were relatively few retirees because birth rates were low during the 1930s and war years. But now the baby boomers are set to retire—the first ones turns 65 in 2011. This is going to put massive pressure on the federal government to increase spending for Social Security and Medicare just at the point when fiscal policy will need to be tightened to reduce the inflation and higher interest rates that will inevitably follow today's stimulus.

Many critics have long argued that the main weakness of the originators of supply-side economics is that they focused only on reducing taxes, not on reducing the size of government. There's truth in this. Supply-siders took the view that the absolute size of government is not important economically. Moreover, they saw that there was no political support for the sorts of spending cuts that would even keep the size of government from growing, let alone cutting its size. The supply-siders took the view that the size of government was meaningful only relative to the size of the economy. Therefore, if policies could be adopted that would cause GDP to grow at a faster rate than spending, then the size of government as a share of GDP would have to fall as a matter of simple math. In short, it wasn't necessary to cut spending, only to restrain its growth to a rate less than that of GDP.

This view was unsatisfactory to many conservatives at the time who wanted the budget to be balanced and spending cut. They reconciled themselves to supply-side economics only by convincing themselves that cutting taxes would deny revenue to the government and thereby put downward pressure on spending. This came to be called "starving the beast." It had plausibility in an era when the deficit was seen as a serious economic problem because it raised inflation and interest rates. Pressure to reduce the deficit could realistically be channeled into spending cuts.

But as inflation faded and interest rates fell to historically low levels, political support for reducing the deficit evaporated. Yet Republicans continued to push tax cuts as if they were the height of fiscal responsibility. During the George W. Bush administration Republicans deluded themselves into believing that cutting taxes was the *only* thing they had to do to be fiscally responsible. This allowed them to rationalize a vast increase in spending at the same time they cut taxes. Instead of cutting taxes to hold down spending, Republicans increased both simultaneously. This left them with nonexistent credibility when they complained about Obama's spending.

Eventually, fiscal retrenchment will return as the top item on the political agenda. Obviously, we cannot continue to spend as we are today without suffering catastrophic consequences in the form of inflation, a collapsing dollar, and double-digit interest rates. While the Obama administration hopes that most of the temporary stimulus spending will simply expire as the emergency passes, the growth of entitlement spending caused by the aging of the baby boomers means that we face a fiscal crisis even if that happens as hoped.

I believe that when this second fiscal crisis hits sometime in the next few years, it is inevitable that higher revenues will be needed to plug much of the fiscal hole. Unfortunately, both parties are in denial about this; Republicans still delude themselves that tax cuts starve the beast and that tax increases feed it, while Democrats are so afraid of being seen as tax increasers that they simply refuse to acknowledge reality. Obama's proposed tax increases were all carefully packaged with tax cuts in order to counter the charge that he was a tax increaser.

But the reality is that even before spending exploded to deal with the economic crisis, the government was set to grow by about 50 percent of GDP over the next generation just to pay for Social Security and Medicare benefits under current law. When the crunch comes and the need for a major increase in revenue becomes overwhelming, I expect that Republicans will refuse to participate in the process. If Democrats have to raise taxes with no bipartisan support, then they will have no choice but to cater to the demands of their party's most liberal wing. This will mean higher rates on businesses and entrepreneurs, and soak-the-rich policies that would make Franklin D. Roosevelt blush.

Such taxes will be highly detrimental to the economy—certainly more so than other forms of taxation, such as a VAT, that can raise a lot of revenue at a very low cost in terms of lost output. But conservatives oppose it for this very reason. They fear that the VAT is a money machine that will lead to bigger government than we would have with less efficient forms of taxation.

That argument may work when the federal government is only taking 20 percent of GDP in revenue, but it doesn't when revenues rise to 30 percent of GDP, as they will absent massive and politically impossible cuts in spending. At that point, the structure of our tax system will be costing the country 10 percent to 15 percent of GDP in lost output that could be saved if we simply raised the same revenue more efficiently.

Eventually, Republicans will get over their VAT phobia and realize that it would allow for a significant reduction in marginal tax rates. Ironically, many Republicans already support such a reform without realizing it. The flat tax supported by many of them is essentially a subtraction-method VAT on all businesses with a deduction for cash wages paid.

In the midst of a crisis unlike the world has seen for three quarters of a century, worrying about the next one may seem like something that can wait. But this sort of myopia is exactly what created the current crisis. Congress, the White House, and the Federal Reserve all overreacted to the 2001 recession and kept pouring on additional stimulus long past the point when fiscal and monetary tightening was needed, thereby creating a bubble that finally burst with tragic consequences. It is a near certainty that they will overreact even more strongly following the current recession, which more closely resembles the Great Depression than any other downturn in history.

It's essential that we learn from the past and try to avoid making the same mistakes all over again. At least those who can see what is coming will be better able to protect themselves from the consequences.

CHAPTER 1

THE GREAT DEPRESSION
Misunderstanding Deflation

The economic crisis of 2009 has only one precedent in modern history: the Great Depression of the 1930s. The similarities are not only their depth and breadth, but their origins as well. Both resulted from an excessively easy monetary policy by the Federal Reserve that created economic distortions in both financial markets and the real economy. In each case, when the Fed tried to fix its mistake by tightening monetary policy, it went too far and created deflation—a falling price level, the opposite of inflation—that was most evident in the collapse of stock prices but was also seen in business bankruptcies and widespread unemployment.

Policymakers of the 1930s misunderstood the nature of the economic problem and were slow to pinpoint the Federal Reserve's policy as the primary source. By the time they did the economy had declined too much for an expansive monetary policy alone to turn it around. Simply lowering interest rates was not enough to encourage borrowing and spending, as it usually is during moderate economic downturns. Only by coupling an easy monetary policy with an aggressive fiscal expansion through federal spending and deficits was it possible to get the economy off a dead stop, end the deflation, and end the depression.

Unfortunately, it took Franklin D. Roosevelt and his advisers a long time and a lot of trial and error before the proper set of policies were in place. Many mistakes were made and setbacks suffered. Since history's errors often teach us more valuable lessons than its successes, knowledge of the Great Depression is essential if we are to avoid repeating those mistakes and get today's economy moving again.

As the nation coped with its second greatest economic crisis in early 2009, analogies to New Deal policies were common.[1] The Obama administration was explicit in its belief that the mistakes that caused the Great Depression to be so long and so deep would not be repeated. Thus, Barack Obama's first major action in office was to ask for a huge stimulus bill that was enacted less than a month later. The Fed was also extremely aggressive in pursuing unorthodox policies of previously unthinkable magnitude, such as its announcement on March 18, 2009 that it was prepared to add an additional $1.2 trillion to the nation's money supply to unlock credit markets.

Throughout the 2008–2009 crisis, echoes of identical debates from the 1930s were common. Did low interest rates indicate a sufficiently easy Fed policy or did one also have to look at the money supply and pursue what the Fed calls "quantitative easing"? Was a stimulative fiscal policy essential to economic recovery or was it only necessary to wait for monetary policy to do its job? Was deflation the central economic problem or something inherent in the nature of financial markets?

I believe that revisiting the experience of the Great Depression—especially the arguments among top economists about its fundamental causes and the reactions of politicians and policymakers to the circumstances they faced as they faced them—can help us more clearly understand the nature of today's problem, avoid the errors that made the Great Depression so severe, and help restore prosperity as quickly as possible.

THE CRASH OF '29

In the popular imagination, the stock market crash that began on October 24, 1929, known as "Black Thursday," was the cause of the Great Depression. It is thought that it mainly resulted from a speculative bubble—excessive buying of stocks, pushing them to prices that were unjustified by economic fundamentals—not unlike those that had led to spectacular market crashes over the centuries.

Some saw it coming. One famous example is banker Paul M. Warburg, a founder of the Federal Reserve, who said in March 1929, "If orgies of unrestrained speculation are permitted to spread too far . . . the ultimate collapse is certain not only to affect the speculators themselves, but also to bring about a general depression involving the entire country."[2]

Perhaps even more famous were the comments by Yale University economist Irving Fisher in September 1929 denying the possibility of a stock market collapse. Responding to a prediction by statistician Roger Babson that a sharp decline was imminent, Fisher said, "Stock prices are not too high and Wall Street will not experience anything in the nature of a crash." As late as mid-October, Fisher asserted that the market had reached "a permanently high plateau" and would move higher in coming months. Even after the market started to break, Fisher remained optimistic, citing the economy's underlying strength.[3]

In truth, Fisher's analysis of the stock market was not unreasonable. Many studies have found that only a few stocks making up the Dow Jones Industrial Average had price-to-earnings ratios that appear to have been unsustainable. Most of the stocks were trading at very conservative ratios, and in fact could be considered undervalued based on earnings growth.[4] This suggests that the market collapse was not the result of errors by investors but some change in the economic environment that fundamentally changed the rules of the game. Investors don't all make the same mistake at the same time otherwise.

As soon as the market broke, analysts immediately began searching for deeper causes. As with all major historical events, it was hard for those living through it to see all the pieces and their interrelationships. Even with the benefit of historical perspective, there are many details that remain contentious, and probably always will. That is why events like the Great Depression need to be studied and reexamined by each new generation in light of their own experience and the knowledge gained from subsequent events.

On November 11, 1929, Frank Kent, a director of Bankers Trust, fingered the Smoot-Hawley Tariff, which was then making its way through the Senate, as a prime factor. He declared that growing support for the tariff had created unrest, fear that industry would be injured, prospects for higher unemployment, and general unease in the business community.[5]

Senator Reed Smoot of Utah and Representative Willis Hawley of Oregon, both Republicans, had initiated their tariff legislation in April. It proposed higher duties on a wide variety of industrial and agricultural products, and many products would have tariffs assessed on them for the first time. In those days, most Republicans were strong supporters of trade protection and believed that high tariffs were needed to insulate American farms and factories from cheap foreign imports. In May, Smoot-Hawley passed the House of Representatives, where Republicans had a large majority, by a wide margin. But free-traders held out hope that the legislation could be derailed or modified in the Senate, where a coalition of Democrats and liberal Republicans threatened passage. By October, however, it was clear from test votes that there was very little likelihood that Smoot-Hawley would fail to get majority support. This led Kent and other analysts to conclude that it was a central factor in triggering the Great Depression.[6]

Rather than respond to the substance of Kent's assessment, tariff supporters instead attacked Kent for lying about the cause of the market crash. Senators William E. Borah, Republican of Idaho, and Harry Hawes, Democrat of Missouri, demanded a congressional investigation of Kent and other tariff opponents. Senator Thaddeus Caraway, Democrat of Arkansas, called Kent's statement "propaganda" and said it was caused by "arrested mental development." But Kent refused to back down.[7]

On November 19, Babson added his voice to those blaming the tariff for the market's malaise. He pointed out that if Congress was in effect going to prohibit nations heavily indebted to the United States from selling their goods here, then they would have no way of servicing their debts. Moreover, they would have no earnings with which to buy American goods, leading to reduced output and employment in exporting industries. Babson suggested that the best thing Congress could do to restore confidence would be to adjourn indefinitely.[8]

Some analysts maintain that Smoot-Hawley couldn't have been a factor in the stock market crash because it wasn't enacted into law until June 1930. However, financial markets routinely discount the impact of future actions, incorporating their effects into prices well before an action becomes effective. Economist Alan Reynolds carefully tracked movement of the tariff bill through Congress and observed that every time there was a legislative setback the market rallied, and whenever the prospects improved it fell.[9]

As to the tariff's economic effects, it has been argued that trade protection was already quite severe owing to the Fordney-McCumber Tariff enacted in 1922. Therefore, the additional Smoot-Hawley duties were not quantitatively significant. However, studies have shown that the marginal impact of Smoot-Hawley was in fact quite considerable and sharply reduced trade. It also led to a large decline in investment and a rise in trade protection among our trading partners, which further reduced exports.[10]

By itself, the Smoot-Hawley Tariff probably wouldn't have had that much impact on either the stock market or the economy. But monetary forces had already made the economic and financial environment very vulnerable to any shock. The tariff may have been the last straw, a trigger that pushed the stock market and the economy into a major downturn.

ROLE OF THE FED

The Federal Reserve, our nation's central bank, had long been concerned about the outsized gains in the stock market in the 1920s that appeared to be potentially destabilizing. But it had to contend with the fact that its policy levers, mainly changes in short-term interest rates, were incapable of targeting just that one sector of the economy without spillover effects elsewhere. In other words, the price for bringing the stock market down to earth was that healthy sectors would also be brought down, creating unnecessary suffering for those not even involved in the market. As Yale University economist Robert Shiller explains:

> One thing we do know about interest rate policy is that it affects the entire economy in fundamental ways, and that it is not focused exclusively on the speculative bubble it might be used to correct. It is whole-body irradiation, not a surgical laser. Moreover, the genesis of a speculative bubble...is a long, slow process, involving gradual changes in people's thinking. Small changes in interest rates will not have any predictable effect on such thinking; big changes might, but only because they have the potential to exert a devastating impact on the economy as a whole.[11]

Benjamin Strong, president of the Federal Reserve Bank of New York and the Fed's dominant figure through most of the 1920s, was deeply concerned about what he viewed as a stock market bubble but didn't know how to deal with it without bringing the whole economy down. As he put it in a 1927 letter, "I think the conclusion is inescapable that any policy directed solely to forcing liquidation in the stock loan account and concurrently in the prices of securities will be found to have a widespread and somewhat similar effect in other directions, mostly to the detriment of the healthy prosperity of this country."[12]

By 1928, however, the Fed felt that it had to take some action to prick the stock market bubble and let some air out before it burst and brought the whole economy down. It began tightening monetary policy by raising the discount rate—the interest rate at which private banks borrow directly from the Fed. In February, it raised the rate from 3.5 percent to 4 percent. In May the rate was raised again to 4.5 percent and to 5 percent in July. There were concerns within the Fed that its monetary policy was endangering the economy as a whole—a cure worse than the disease. But the feeling seems to have been that the Fed could reverse course quickly if necessary.[13]

Unfortunately, Strong took ill and died in October 1928. This created a massive power vacuum at the Fed and left it effectively leaderless at a critical moment in time. Lacking anyone with the ability to change its direction, the Fed basically continued on automatic pilot. Seeing the stock market continue to rise in 1929, despite a tighter monetary policy, the Fed concluded that stronger action was needed. In February, it issued a statement warning against stock market speculation. Frustrated by the lack of impact from its jawboning, the Fed raised the discount rate to 6 percent in August. This proved to be one rate hike too many. Instead of cooling the stock market's speculative fever, the Fed induced a case of pneumonia that became evident a few months later on Black Thursday.[14]

Almost immediately some economists pointed their fingers at the Federal Reserve for causing the stock market collapse. Fisher said that the Fed had created the stock market bubble in the first place by running a monetary policy that was too easy during the mid-1920s.[15] Columbia University economist H. Parker Willis, who had been deeply involved in creation of the Federal Reserve, said this was caused by two factors: first, an overreaction to the brief deflation resulting from the recession of 1920–1921; and second, a desire to help Great Britain get back on the gold standard by encouraging the outflow of gold from the United States. The Fed also hoped to shed what it viewed as excessive gold stocks, which had flowed into the country in search of a safe haven during and after the First World War. Ironically, the Fed viewed the excess gold as dangerously inflationary.[16]

In a classical gold standard, such as that which existed before the First World War, the money supply is tied directly to the quantity of gold reserves. Money in circulation automatically rose or fell as gold moved in or out of the country in response to changes in interest rates and inflationary expectations. If there were signs of inflation, gold flowed out, automatically shrinking the money supply and stopping the inflation. Deflation would draw gold inward, expanding the money supply and easing that problem. But after the war, this largely automatic mechanism was replaced by one that was more managed, giving central banks additional latitude to expand or contract the money supply while maintaining a linkage to gold. This is usually called a gold-exchange standard. While the gold-exchange standard did not provide as much monetary flexibility as exists today, there was much more central bank maneuvering room than is commonly believed.[17]

DEFLATION

As a result of the sharp decline in stock prices and the growing slowdown in economic activity that was exacerbated by increased tariffs on imports, the demand for money fell and the supply of money contracted as banks folded, causing bank deposits to evaporate.[18] (There was no deposit insurance in those days.) But the Fed allowed the money supply to shrink too much, bringing on a general deflation. Economists have long believed that there is a relationship between the quantity of money times its turnover, on the one hand, and the general level of prices times the quantity of goods and services, on the other. Thus, a shrinkage in the money supply necessarily requires either a decline in prices or a cutback in the production of goods and services.

Another important factor was a decline in the speed at which people were spending their money, which economists call velocity. When velocity increases, less money is needed for economic transactions; when it falls, more money may be needed. Indeed, because velocity is the ratio of the money supply to the gross domestic product, changes in velocity affect the economy exactly the same way changes in the money supply do. Since velocity also fell during this period, as families and businesses hoarded cash and held off making purchases or investments, it exacerbated the deflationary impact of the shrinking money supply.[19]

The impact of the money supply shrinkage was almost instantaneous. Dun and Bradstreet's commodity price index peaked in October 1929 at a level of 192.204 and fell almost continuously thereafter. By April 1930 the index was down to 179.294 and by December had fallen to 163.20—a decline of 15 percent in a little over a year.[20] Changes in the general price level always show up first in sensitive commodity prices. Therefore, such a sharp decline in a broad range of commodities should have been a signal to the Fed that downward price pressure would soon be felt among industrial goods, real estate, and other sectors of the economy. However, the Fed took no action to add liquidity to the economy.

Economist Virgil Jordan of McGraw-Hill condemned the Fed for standing by passively while the money supply fell, thus bringing on a deflation that was paralyzing economic activity. Consumers were holding off making purchases while they waited for prices to drop further, he said, and businesses were incurring huge losses as they were forced to sell products for less than they cost to produce, which brought investment to a standstill. Jordan urged the Fed to immediately inject $250 million into the economy by buying Treasury securities.[21] This would be about $34 billion in today's economy.

One problem is that the Fed was a relatively new institution in 1930, having only been created in 1913. The idea of using open-market operations, as Jordan suggested, to expand money and credit was not yet well developed and was resisted by key members of the Fed's leadership.[22] In such an operation, the Fed buys and sells U.S. Treasury securities. When they are bought, the Fed creates the money itself, thus expanding the money supply. When it sells securities, money flows into the Fed and the money supply contracts. In this way, the Fed can offset changes in the money supply resulting from changing economic and financial conditions. The Fed can also influence the money supply by changing the amount of reserves banks must hold as backing for deposits and by changing the discount rate.

The economy itself causes the bulk of changes in the money supply because most money is not in the form of cash (notes and coin), but bank deposits (checking accounts) and other forms of near-money. Depending on reserve requirements, every dollar deposited in a bank can be loaned out four or five times, thus expanding the money supply. Conversely, withdrawals force banks to cut back on lending and shrink the money supply. There is no formula that tells the Fed exactly how much money the economy needs at any given moment in time, so the Fed must use its judgment. When it is wrong and too much money is created, the result is inflation—a rise in the general price level. Too little money leads to deflation—a fall in the price level.

As an example of how poor the Fed's leadership was after the death of Benjamin Strong, Irving Fisher later recounted a discussion he had with Federal Reserve Board chairman Eugene Meyer in the summer of 1931 about shrinkage of the money supply. According to Fisher, Meyer had no idea that bank deposits constituted the bulk of the nation's money supply or that they had contracted sharply until Fisher brought this to his attention. In Fisher's words, Meyer "was like a chauffeur going blindfolded and running into the curb because he could not see the direction in which he was driving."[23]

The continuation of deflation into 1931 brought forth additional calls for the Fed to ease monetary policy. By September, the commodity price index had fallen to 141.724—down 16 percent over the previous year and 26 percent from its October 1929 peak. This led University of Wisconsin economist John R. Commons to call upon the Fed to inject $1 billion of new money into the economy by purchasing Treasury securities (about $137 billion today). He said that it should have as a goal restoration of the general price level to its 1926 level.[24]

Other economists echoed Commons. On January 31, 1932, 24 prominent economists wrote a letter to Herbert Hoover recommending that the Federal Reserve "systematically pursue open-market operations with the double aim of facilitating necessary government financing and increasing liquidity of the banking structure." That same month, a group of Harvard economists circulated a memorandum criticizing the Fed for effectively forcing a contraction in the money supply.[25]

RISING REAL DEBT

Fisher was especially concerned that deflation had the effect of increasing the burden of debt because borrowers were forced to repay loans in dollars worth more than those they had borrowed. This rise in the real burden of debt discouraged new borrowing and prevented business expansion and credit circulation.

Under the procedures followed by the Fed in those days, it paid little attention either to prices or the quantity of money. Operationally, its main focus was on the stability of interest rates. If member banks were not borrowing at the discount window, the Fed assumed that credit conditions were adequate. Furthermore, because its focus was on market rates rather than real rates, the Fed was blinded to the massive rise in rates resulting from the deflation in commodity prices. Although market interest rates on short-term Treasury securities fell from 4.42 percent in 1929 to 2.23 percent in 1930, to 1.15 percent in 1931, and to 0.78 percent in 1932, the real (deflation-adjusted) rate actually rose sharply to 10.95 percent in 1932.[26]

In a period of inflation, interest rates can rise to whatever level is necessary to compensate for the decline in monetary value. If the natural rate of interest would be, say, 5 percent in a period of price stability and something changed that caused lenders to believe that prices would rise by 10 percent over the coming year, then market interest rates would likely jump to 15 percent. This way, lenders would still get 5 percent in inflation-adjusted terms. But with a large deflation, the reverse is not possible. If prices were expected to fall by 10 percent, the market interest rate would have to fall to negative 5 percent to compensate for the deflation. But lenders are never going to lend money at a negative nominal rate; they would instead just hold onto their cash and in effect make 10 percent by doing nothing. Because prices were falling by 10 percent, they would be able to buy 10 percent more in a year, the equivalent of getting 10 percent interest.

In this way, deflation becomes self-reinforcing beyond a certain point. The more people think prices will be lower in the future, the more they hoard cash and hold off making purchases. This causes velocity to fall, thus exacerbating the deflation and encouraging still more cash hoarding and so on. This was essentially the economy's problem in 2008 and 2009. Although the Fed tried to raise the money supply, people held off spending and investors parked their cash in Treasury bills even though the interest rate was barely above zero. The continuing decline in velocity counteracted the Fed's money supply increases, leaving the economy suffering from deflationary conditions.

Congress at least recognized the monetary roots of the economy's weakness in 1932, even if the Federal Reserve didn't, and enacted the first Glass-Steagall Act, which reduced the amount of gold the Fed was required to hold as backing for the dollar. This freed the Fed to inject about $1 billion of new money into the economy during the spring of 1932.[27] This would be about $212 billion in today's economy.

This had an immediate effect in halting the slide in commodity prices. Dun and Bradstreet's index bottomed at 125.316 in July—a decline of 14.5 percent from the previous year and 35 percent from its peak. But during the balance of 1932, the index moved upward as the increased liquidity bid up commodity prices. By October, the index was up 9 percent to 136.555, an impressive increase in a short time. At a meeting of the American Statistical Association in September, economists praised the Fed's action and gave it full credit for halting and reversing the crippling deflation that was paralyzing industry.[28]

Unfortunately, the Fed prematurely halted its efforts to increase the money supply in June 1932, which ended the upward movement in prices a few months later. The Fed may have stopped the policy of injecting money into the economy because interest rates were falling too much for banks to make any money. Rates on 90-day commercial paper in New York fell from 2.88 percent in January 1932 to 0.38 percent by December. This led banks to exert intense pressure on the Fed to halt the monetary easing so that interest rates would rise and bank profits would be restored.[29] By November the commodity index was again moving downward, and by March 1933 it was down 6.5 percent from its October 1932 high.

The Fed's easing in early 1932 might have been enough to turn the economy around had it been taken earlier. But more than two years into the deflation, it was too little, too late.[30] The deflationary momentum was too strong at that point and required much more aggressive action to reverse its course. As Yale University economist James Harvey Rogers explained:

> Taken in their incipient stages, both rises and falls—inflation and defla-
> tion—can even with mild measures apparently be checked.... When,
> however, the movement in either direction has gained momentum, not
> only is it much more difficult to check, but—what is apparently even
> more important—other problems ... appear with such overwhelming
> impressiveness as to occupy the entire center of the stage. Thus when
> bold and vigorous action has become increasingly imperative, actual
> policies are apt to become confused and based much too largely upon
> relatively insignificant, though seemingly much more important,
> considerations.[31]

Rogers's point here is one also made by economists in 2008—the longer an economic downturn progresses without vigorous action to reverse its course, the harder it becomes to do so. A small amount of properly designed stimulus early in a downturn might be enough to arrest the decline, but may be grossly insufficient at a later date. It's possible that relatively modest action by Congress and the Fed in 1930 could have turned the economy around and made the Great Depression just a run-of-the-mill recession. But when no meaningful action was taken throughout the Hoover administration, the downward momentum by 1933, when Franklin D. Roosevelt took office, was very deep and required actions of greater orders of magnitude than what might have sufficed earlier.

So, too, many economists argued that had Congress enacted a stimulus package in the fall of 2008, it might have forestalled the need for a much bigger one in February 2009. Even after passage of the $787 billion fiscal stimulus in February, many economists continued to argue for more because the economic downturn had festered too long before the federal government took meaningful action.[32]

CONGRESS TRIES TO
MAKE MONETARY POLICY

The fight over the Goldsborough bill in 1932 illustrates how difficult it was to focus the attention of key policymakers on the critical issue of monetary policy and its relationship to the deflation at the heart of the Great Depression. The bill was opposed not only by the Federal Reserve and the Hoover administration but also by the mainstream media. The fight shows that three years into the Great Depression there was still a widespread lack of understanding of its basic cause.

In early April 1932 Representative Thomas Goldsborough, Democrat of Maryland, got a subcommittee of the House Banking Committee to endorse a bill that would have required the Fed to add as much liquidity to the banking system as necessary to raise the general level of commodity prices to their previous level as quickly as possible. Federal Reserve Board chairman Meyer and George Harrison, president of the Federal Reserve Bank of New York, denounced the legislation in the strongest terms. The Treasury Department also voiced opposition and a veto by Hoover was promised.[33] They all felt that maintaining the independence of the Federal Reserve, even in the face of its manifest failure, was more important than solving the nation's economic crisis.

Nevertheless, on April 22 the full Banking Committee reported the Goldsborough bill to the House of Representatives. The next day, the *New York Times* attacked the proposal as "prosperity by fiat." Echoing the Fed, it said that such an effort would be futile, likening it to a hypothetical law requiring the Secretary of Commerce to double foreign trade.[34] But the newspaper's analogy was totally inappropriate. The Commerce Department didn't have the power to double trade, but the Federal Reserve was in fact the only institution capable of stopping the deflation.

The House of Representatives voted in favor of the Goldsborough bill on May 2 by a remarkable vote of 289 to 60. Despite opposition from a Republican administration, a majority of Republicans joined virtually every Democrat in supporting the measure. Speaking in favor of his legislation, Goldsborough emphasized that deflation increased the real burden of debt, forcing individuals and businesses to repay loans in dollars that had far greater purchasing power than the dollars they borrowed. It was like having to pay back $1.60 for every dollar someone had borrowed, he said, plus interest.[35]

The *Washington Post* sharply criticized the Goldsborough bill, calling it "a cheap political move." *Barron's* and the *Wall Street Journal* vigorously attacked the bill as dangerously inflationary. Their view seems to have been that it was perfectly all right for prices to fall drastically, but under no circumstances were they ever to rise from wherever they happened to be.[36]

Fisher tried to explain that there is a conceptual difference between "inflation" and "reflation." The former indicates a rise in the price level from a position of stability. The latter refers to raising the price level back to its previously stable position after a period in which the price level had fallen. Deflation, Fisher said, was the central cause of the depression, mainly because it had the effect of magnifying debts. For example, farm mortgages were larger in terms of the fallen prices for wheat and cotton.[37]

On May 5, 1932, Hoover attacked the Goldsborough bill directly. The problem, he said, wasn't monetary, but fiscal. Hoover demanded a sharp reduction in government spending and a large increase in taxes in order to balance the federal budget. This would restore confidence, he said, and thereby lead to economic recovery.[38] This was, of course, exactly the opposite of what the economy needed. Every economist today recognizes that raising taxes in the middle of an economic depression is insane and that Hoover's policy made a bad situation much worse.

In July 1932, the Senate effectively killed the Goldsborough bill by substituting a Fed-approved measure sponsored by Senator Carter Glass, Democrat of Virginia and former Secretary of the Treasury under Woodrow Wilson, that made it easier for banks to borrow from the Federal Reserve.[39] While a useful measure, it was thin gruel compared to Goldsborough.

OPPOSITION TO REFLATION

From the beginning of the Great Depression there were those who refused to see any governmental errors behind the calamity. Instead, they blamed workers and businessmen for excesses that needed to be purged before economic health could be restored. As Treasury Secretary Andrew Mellon famously remarked when Hoover asked him what should be done, "Liquidate labor, liquidate stocks, liquidate the farmers, liquidate real estate.... It will purge the rottenness out of the system. High costs of living and high living will come down. People will work harder, live a more moral life. Values will be adjusted, and enterprising people will pick up the wrecks from less competent people."[40]

Among the strongest opponents of reflation were economist Benjamin M. Anderson of the Chase National Bank and Henry Hazlitt, an editor at the *Nation* magazine. Both repeatedly insisted that *any* effort to raise prices from where they were constituted inflation and nothing but inflation. Like a number of other economists and commentators during the early years of the depression, they felt that deflation was a nonproblem; if wages would simply fall by the same amount that commodity prices had fallen, then equilibrium would be restored and economic growth would resume. Workers would be no worse off because they would still be able to buy the same bundle of goods and services since their prices had fallen to the same degree.[41]

There was certainly truth in this argument. Where it went wrong was in thinking that labor is a commodity like wheat or copper, which are easily traded on exchanges and can fall in price very rapidly. But workers don't like pay cuts and employers don't like making them. Thus cuts in wages are much more difficult and more protracted than reductions in commodity prices.

The anti-reflation zealots also forgot that debts were fixed in nominal dollars. There was no easy mechanism for renegotiating them except through extremely time-consuming and painful bankruptcies. Although interest rates had fallen, debtors still had to pay off their debts with dollars that were worth much more than the dollars they had borrowed. Also, interest rates could not fall by enough to compensate for the deflation because they could not go below zero.[42]

Thus it is a mistake to view an equivalent inflation and deflation as symmetrical—as having equal and opposite economic effects. Because of the problem of debt, deflation is far worse. Small deflations can be offset by reducing market interest rates. But once the rate of deflation is greater than the rate of interest, as was the case in the early 1930s, the zero-percent floor becomes a huge barrier to readjustment. The only way out is to raise the price level. This approach was naturally opposed by bankers, who liked getting repaid in dollars worth more than those they had lent, and also by hardliners who saw every whiff of inflation as the first step toward hyperinflation and complete economic collapse, as occurred in Germany in the mid-1920s.[43]

The Fed faced precisely the same dilemma in 2008–2009 as it cut the interest rate it charged banks almost to zero, and rates on Treasury securities also approached zero. Under normal circumstances, giving banks access to virtually free money would have caused them to make new loans that would have led to increased buying, investment, and growth. But because of deflation, the real rate of interest was still quite high and the Fed was blocked from reducing rates further because it is impossible to reduce nominal rates below zero.[44]

The interaction between debt and deflation formed the core of Fisher's theory of the Great Depression, and it is why he thought that reflation was the best path to recovery. Since the Federal Reserve had the ability to increase liquidity and thereby raise the price level, responsibility for causing and curing the economic malaise basically belonged to the Fed alone. As Fisher put it, "If the debt-deflation theory of great depressions is essentially correct, the question of controlling the price level assumes a new importance; and those in the drivers' seats—the Federal Reserve Board and the Secretary of the Treasury...will in [the] future be held to a new accountability."[45]

Fisher was aggressive in bringing his theory to the attention of Franklin D. Roosevelt, who defeated Hoover in the 1932 election. On February 25, 1933, Fisher wrote to the president-elect and explained how deflation was at the root of the economy's problems. "What we are fighting now is deflation. It needs to be stopped and reversed," he stated. "We need a rise in the price level by the only means it can be raised...an increase in the quantity or velocity, or both, of the circulating medium whether credit, paper, or gold, or all three," he said. Failure to act, Fisher continued, would be "ruinous economically, politically, socially."[46]

Shortly after taking office on March 4, 1933, Roosevelt received a remarkably sophisticated memorandum from a lawyer named Benjamin Henry Inness-Brown that precisely outlined the monetary nature of the deflation underlying the economic crisis. Dated April 25, 1933, and transmitted to him through Col. Edward M. House, a former adviser to Woodrow Wilson and a close family friend of Roosevelt's, the memo noted that although the amount of currency in circulation had risen from $3.9 billion in June 1931 to $6.3 billion by March 1933, the collapse of demand deposits such as checking accounts was much greater. These had fallen from $25.2 billion to just $13 billion over the same period. The economic impact of this monetary contraction was all the greater because velocity had also declined sharply, reducing the effective money supply by $126.2 billion since 1929, according to the memo.[47]

Another sophisticated analysis of the economic situation was produced by University of Chicago economist Jacob Viner in April. He correctly identified the Federal Reserve as the source of the deflation that was at the root of the problem, observing that there had been a steady contraction of bank credit since 1929. Anticipating Keynesian economics, Viner pointed out that simply printing money might not do much good because it would likely be hoarded or substitute for bank credit. To really bring about the increase in the money supply that was essential to recovery, he said it was necessary for the federal government to greatly increase the budget deficit by increasing spending or reducing taxes and to finance the deficit with new money creation. Moreover, it might be necessary to engage in such an inflationary policy for some time in order to bring about a sufficient increase in liquidity, Viner said.[48]

Unfortunately, Roosevelt's recovery program failed to get at the root of the problem. His initial plan for staunching the deflation mainly involved price fixing and limitations on production. The regulatory system established by the National Industrial Recovery Act, enacted on June 16, 1933, prohibited businesses from lowering wages or prices. But by preventing prices from adjusting, which would have restored equilibrium, Roosevelt's effort actually inhibited recovery rather than fostering it.[49]

Roosevelt was not unaware of the monetary underpinnings of the deflation, but he thought the whole problem related to the price of gold. Both Roosevelt and Treasury Secretary Henry Morgenthau were strongly influenced by an economist named George F. Warren who had carefully studied the correlation between gold and commodity prices.[50] Roosevelt and Morgenthau concluded from Warren's research that if the price of gold rose, then this alone would automatically raise prices for other commodities.

Roosevelt ordered the Reconstruction Finance Corporation, a government agency established by Hoover, to buy gold on the open market in order to raise its price. This policy didn't work very well for a variety of reasons, the main one being that the RFC had to borrow the money it used to buy the gold. Consequently, there was no net increase in liquidity—the borrowing took out of the financial system exactly what the gold purchase put in. While the price of gold increased, it was only a relative price change resulting from increased demand for that one particular commodity and did not have any effect at all on the general price level. This point was made to Roosevelt and Morgenthau when the Treasury's principal monetary economist, O.M.W. Sprague, resigned on November 16, 1933, to protest the gold-buying policy. In his letter of resignation, Sprague said it would neither induce greater demand for materials and labor nor increase domestic consumption.[51] Sprague's point was seconded by University of Missouri economist Harry Gunnison Brown:

> I insist that gold purchases, taken alone and without increase of circulating medium, cannot be counted on either to stimulate business or to raise the level of prices.... The fact is that the purchase of gold by the government has in itself no more tendency to raise the general price level or to promote recovery than would have the purchase of building or building stone or the purchase of rolltop desks. The truth is that our problem centers in the securing of expanded bank credit or additional money.[52]

Nevertheless, despite the fact that Roosevelt's gold-buying plan had absolutely no inflationary potential—and no inflationary impact— it was condemned in some quarters for being the first step in a total breakdown of the monetary system. Fifteen members of the Yale University economics department signed a letter attacking Roosevelt for attempting to secure an "artificially higher level of prices." Among those not signing the letter was Fisher, who correctly noted that there is no level of prices that isn't inherently artificial.[53]

In November 1933 Harvard economist Lauchlin Currie published the best data to date on the decline of the money supply. Using a more comprehensive definition of money that included demand deposits and other financial instruments for which data was not generally available in those days, he found that the money supply had fallen from $26.7 billion in 1929 to $20.8 billion in 1932, a decline of 22 percent. Like the memo Roosevelt received in April, Currie's paper showed that cash in circulation had risen, from $3.9 billion in 1929 to $4.9 billion in 1932. But demand deposits held at banks fell sharply from $22.7 billion in 1929 to $15.9 billion in 1932, a 30.2 percent shrinkage.[54]

KEYNES'S CRITIQUE

British economist John Maynard Keynes was among those who thought the Roosevelt program was on the wrong track because it did not get at the root cause of deflation.[55] He outlined his objections in an open letter to the president that was published in the *New York Times* on New Year's Eve 1933. Regarding the National Recovery Administration, which administered the price-fixing arrangements at the base of Roosevelt's strategy, Keynes saw little value. "I cannot detect any material aid to recovery in the NRA," he wrote. It "probably impedes recovery . . . in the false guise of being part of the technique of recovery."

Keynes correctly observed that "output depends on the amount of purchasing power." Rising prices were to be welcomed because they were normally a consequence of faster growth. But it was essential that additional output be accompanied by an increase in the money supply, he said. Without that, forcing up prices artificially only raised business costs without doing anything to stimulate growth. "Thus rising prices caused by deliberately increasing prime costs or by restricting output have a vastly inferior value to rising prices which are the natural result of an increase in the nation's purchasing power," Keynes emphasized. He concluded that "national recovery as a whole will be retarded" by the Roosevelt plan.

A better approach, Keynes suggested, was to prime the pump by increasing government spending that should be financed by borrowing and accommodated by an easier monetary policy. This was necessary to mobilize money creation. Just adding new money to a destitute economic system was like trying to get fat by buying a larger belt, Keynes said. The additional government borrowing in financial markets caused by budget deficits would put upward pressure on nominal interest rates, but the Federal Reserve would be able to keep the rates down by buying the additional government bonds on the open market and paying for them with new money. In this way, the additional purchasing power would be induced to circulate and thereby jump-start the recovery. "The object is to start the ball rolling," Keynes explained.[56]

Fisher quickly endorsed Keynes's analysis. The artificial price rise engineered by the NRA was retarding recovery, Fisher said. What was needed was monetary expansion. "A rise of prices at the expense of output, which practically means at the expense of the national income, is a different matter from a rise of the price level through monetary and credit reflation," he emphasized. Economist Willford I. King of New York University agreed and added that it was critical for policymakers to understand that simply increasing the federal budget deficit was not expansionary unless accompanied by an increase in the money supply, because government borrowing alone would simply withdraw purchasing power from the economy to the same extent that government spending expanded it.[57]

In 2009 the debate on this point resurfaced as a number of conservative economists similarly argued against the Obama stimulus package on the grounds that fiscal stimulus was inherently ineffective. The government, they said, would just be taking with the one hand by running bigger deficits what it would be handing out with the other in the form of tax cuts and spending for various programs. The result would be a wash and that would fail to raise total spending or growth.[58]

Obama administration economists responded that there was ample empirical evidence in the historical record to show that budget deficits were stimulative. Perhaps for fear of appearing to speculate about Fed policy, however, they never drew a connection between fiscal expansion and monetary expansion. Nevertheless, it was clear from Federal Reserve statements that it viewed fiscal stimulus as critical to its efforts to expand liquidity.[59]

ROOSEVELT ACTS

Among the most perceptive members of Congress in the early 1930s was Senator Elmer Thomas, Democrat of Oklahoma, who clearly saw monetary policy at the root of the nation's economic problems. As he explained:

> The record before us demonstrates that we have but two possible roads open to travel. One is a continuation of deflation leading to bankruptcy and repudiation of debts, public and private. The other road is an expansion of the currency leading to more money; hence, cheaper money, higher prices for commodities, higher wages and salaries, and therefore added buying power for the people. More money means the payment of taxes, interest, and debts. More money means the saving of homes, farms, and factories. More money means the restoration of personal, corporate, city, county, state, and national solvency.[60]

The farm bill enacted in May 1933 included an amendment offered by Senator Thomas that gave the president the power to expand Federal Reserve credit by $3 billion, issue up to $3 billion in new Treasury notes (greenbacks), reduce gold backing for the currency by up to 50 percent, and monetize silver.[61] These would have been helpful measures, but by the end of 1933, none of them had been utilized by Roosevelt.

Roosevelt finally acted on January 3, 1934, arbitrarily raising the official price of gold from $20.67 to $35 per ounce. But this action had essentially no monetary effect at all. Since, under previous laws and executive orders, the Treasury had come to own virtually all of the nation's monetary gold, its only effect was to create a paper profit for the Treasury of $2.8 billion (about $528 billion today). This money wasn't spent, however, but mostly retained by the Treasury. The net result of all this gold maneuvering, therefore, had virtually no economic effect in terms of stemming deflation or stimulating growth because it did nothing to increase the volume of money and credit. Economist H. Parker Willis tried to explain this to the Senate Banking Committee on January 20, 1934:

> I refuse to accept the idea at all that a change in the theoretical weight of the dollar would have any effect whatever on prices....I submit, with all due respect, that there is nothing in recent statistics or statistical experience in this country or abroad to show that the changing of the price of gold would also change at the same time, or shortly, the price of commodities. I believe that the expectation that this kind of stabilized dollar will bring a higher level of prices is entirely unwarranted, and I say with the utmost earnestness that I believe those who look forward to that will be seriously disappointed in the results.[62]

When George Warren testified before the same committee two days later, he insisted that the linkage between the price of gold and those of other commodities was direct and had nothing to do with the volume of money and credit. When asked why prices had fallen after 1929 despite no change in the price or volume of gold, Warren gave this incoherent response: "For some reason the gold-using world had a high price level, and having it, it could do nothing else than become adjusted to it. For some reason prices in gold-using countries collapsed."[63]

A few days later on January 25, several Harvard economists including Currie sent a letter to Roosevelt agreeing with the necessity for ending a formal gold-dollar link, but at the same time confirming Willis's view that this action by itself would have no effect on the problem of deflation. Said the economists, "We do not believe there is any exact relationship between the price of gold and the prices of commodities and that a policy acting on such a belief is based on error."[64]

In February, an exasperated Fisher suggested that monetary policy be taken away from the Federal Reserve altogether and placed in the Treasury Department. The Fed, by virtue of its governance by a committee structure and separate regional banks, was perpetually rife with "dissension and vacillation," he said.[65]

In March, Russell Leffingwell, a partner at J. P. Morgan, gave one of the clearest explanations that appeared throughout this period on the true path to recovery. Unlike so many other analysts who were confused by gold, exchange rates, and other extraneous matters, he precisely fingered Federal Reserve policy as the central issue. As Leffingwell explained in a speech to the Academy of Political Science:

> The future technique of dollar revaluation should follow the course of an orthodox cheap money policy: the expansion of credit and currency through the Federal Reserve banks; the purchase of government securities by them in the market, or even as ways and means advances to the Treasury if need be; the purchase by them of longer government bonds as well as short; and the maintenance by them of discount rates favorable to the borrower upon such securities. The Federal Reserve banks should be prepared to enlarge their portfolio of government securities, and of loans on government securities, at low rates of interest; to make credit cheap, and to finance at least a part of the government's deficit; until the stimulus of cheap money raises prices, and restores a profit to business, so that business can reemploy labor and will have more taxes to pay on increased incomes.[66]

A VISIT FROM KEYNES

In June 1934 Keynes visited the United States and met with Roosevelt and many of his advisers. Reiterating the views he expressed in his open letter six months earlier, Keynes urged abandonment of the NRA's price-fixing because it was only raising business costs without getting at the root of the deflation problem. He said that if government relief spending rose from $300 million per month to $400 million per month for a year it might be enough to end the depression ($100 million of extra spending would be equivalent to about $19 billion in today's economy, or about $220 billion per year). For his plan to work, however, Keynes said, it was essential that "continuous pressure" be brought upon the Treasury and Federal Reserve to monetize the deficit spending and to hold down interest rates.[67]

According to updated figures compiled by Currie, the narrow money supply fell to $19.9 billion in 1933, mainly owing to a further decline in bank deposits. Finally in 1934 came indications of improvement. The money supply jumped to $22.9 billion, almost all of it in bank deposits.[68] Not surprisingly, the economy began to show the first real signs of recovery. According to current Commerce Department data, real GDP fell 8.6 percent in 1930, 6.4 percent in 1931, 13 percent in 1932, and 1.3 percent in 1933, but showed impressive growth of 10.8 percent in 1934.

Nevertheless, few economists felt that the country had turned a corner. In any case, a great deal of ground needed to be made up; real GDP would not achieve its 1929 level again until 1936. Fisher believed that the NRA was a key factor holding back the economy because it relied on restricting output to raise prices rather than on expanding liquidity—in effect destroying wealth to create wealth, a policy at war with itself. As he explained:

> We may raise prices by making goods scarce or by making money abundant. The first way is followed when cotton fields are plowed up, wheat acreage limited, pigs slaughtered to reduce the food to be made of them, business paid to induce people not to produce. All of these and like measures reduce the national income, for that income consists of these very goods—bread from wheat, pork from hogs, clothes from cotton, and so on. Our income is our "daily bread"—our "bread and butter"—and we cannot get more of this real income by producing less of the elements of which it consists. Such a New Deal is a raw deal, however good the intentions and however it may relieve certain classes at the expense of other classes.
>
> But putting more money into circulation to replace the $9 billion of checking deposits destroyed in the banks raises prices in a total opposite way, for it leads to more production, not less. Wherever such correct monetary policies have been tried . . . profit and so production and employment have increased. There is more, not less daily bread, more bread and butter and clothing.[69]

Although economists like Keynes, Fisher, Currie, and others had done yeoman work in explaining that the fundamental cause of the Great Depression was a deflation caused by inept Federal Reserve policy, five years into the economic malaise this fact was still only dimly understood. Furthermore, the length and depth of the depression meant that much more effort was needed to get the economy moving again than would have been required in the early years. Think of trying to push a car over a small rock. When it has even a little bit of momentum, you can push it over the rock easily. But if the car is at a dead stop, that small rock is a very difficult obstacle to overcome.

Across the Atlantic Ocean in England, Keynes pondered this problem as well. Looking at the growing problem of Nazi Germany, he knew that it was essential for the United States to pull itself out of its lethargy, which would be critical to England's survival in the event of war. In 1935, he finally figured out how to do it.

CHAPTER 2

THE TRIUMPH OF KEYNESIAN ECONOMICS

When I first began studying economics in 1969 I was quickly attracted to economists with a free-market perspective. In those days, almost all of them were affiliated with either the Austrian school of Ludwig von Mises and F. A. Hayek or the Chicago school of Frank Knight and Milton Friedman. While superficially similar, these two schools of economic thought had too many methodological disagreements to ever really be allies.[1] But they did share a common view that John Maynard Keynes was a man of the far left whose theories were primarily responsible for inflation and most of the other economic ills of society at that time.

I got to know many of the most prominent anti-Keynesian economists of the 1970s, including Mises, Hayek, Friedman, Murray Rothbard, Henry Hazlitt, Gottfried Haberler, W. H. Hutt, James Buchanan, and Allan Meltzer, and felt comfortable among those of any school that was opposed to Keynesian economics. One of the first articles I ever published was an attack on Keynes that appeared in the Rutgers College newspaper. Some of my earliest academic works were attacks on Keynesian economics.[2]

Eventually I fell in with some economists trying to develop an explicit alternative to Keynesian economics that came to be called supply-side economics, which I will discuss in chapter 4. Ironically, even as supply-side economics achieved ascendancy in the 1980s and Keynesian economics seemed thoroughly discredited, I found myself mourning its passing. It had been the glue that united the left on economic policy for a long time. But once Keynesian economics fell from grace, I saw it being replaced by industrial policy: the idea that the government needed to directly guide the economy with subsidies, regulations, and trade protection. In the 1980s many on the left viewed these sorts of policies as the keys to Japan's incredible economic success.[3]

I suddenly realized that Keynesian economics was far preferable to the quasi-socialist policies that seemed to be replacing it on the left. It was then that I understood that Keynes had developed his theories in large part to save the free market from Marxism and various socialisms of the left and right that were highly popular in the depths of the Great Depression, which was widely viewed as representing the ultimate failure of capitalism. I saw that complete rejection of Keynes had created a vacuum that was being filled by something far worse. I began an effort to rehabilitate Keynes and eventually came to have a great deal of respect for his ideas.[4]

This respect grew as I read Keynes himself, rather than relying on the interpretations of his followers or his critics. Especially valuable in understanding him and what he was trying to accomplish in the 1930s are his early works. Everything he wrote before *The General Theory of Employment, Interest and Money* in 1936 tends to be ignored by economists and historians alike. But it is critical to see how Keynes thought his way through economic problems very similar to those we are suffering today. He was such a prolific writer and commentator, and his collected works are so well organized and indexed, that it is possible to see the evolution of his thinking in real time.

I believe it's time to rehabilitate Keynes. His theories provide the best guide that economics has to offer to the problems we face today. As the previous chapter shows, many economists had concluded well before 1936 that the fundamental economic problem was deflation and that an expansive fiscal policy was necessary to mobilize monetary policy to stop prices from falling. But they were unsuccessful in getting policymakers adopt the right policies or be bold enough to offset the economy's downward momentum. Keynes succeeded where they failed. This chapter explains how.

KEYNES: ENEMY OF
INFLATION *AND* DEFLATION

Since Keynes is still often condemned as a crude inflationist, it's important to understand that he always held price stability to be among the most important prerequisites for economic progress. As he wrote in 1919:

> [Russian Revolution leader Vladimir] Lenin is said to have declared that the best way to destroy the capitalist system was to debauch the currency. By a continuing process of inflation, governments can confiscate, secretly and unobserved, an important part of the wealth of their citizens. By this method they not only confiscate, but they confiscate *arbitrarily;* and, while the process impoverishes many, it actually enriches some. The sight of this arbitrary rearrangement of riches strikes not only at security, but at confidence in the equity of the existing distribution of wealth. Those to whom the system brings windfalls, beyond their deserts and even beyond their expectations or desires, become "profiteers," who are the object of the hatred of the bourgeoisie, whom the inflationism has impoverished, not less than the proletariat. As the inflation proceeds and the real value of the currency fluctuates wildly from month to month, all permanent relations between debtors and creditors, which form the ultimate foundation of capitalism, become so utterly disordered as to be almost meaningless; and the process of wealth-getting degenerates into a gamble and a lottery. Lenin was certainly right. There is no subtler, no surer means of overturning the existing basis of society than to debauch the currency.[5]

For many years, it was thought that Keynes was mistaken because there was no record of Lenin having said what Keynes quoted.[6] But

Keynes was proved correct by a quote recently unearthed by economist Kurt Schuler: Lenin indeed did believe that inflation would destroy capitalism. As Lenin said in 1919:

> Hundreds of thousands of ruble notes are being issued daily by our
> Treasury. This is done not in order to fill the coffers of the state
> with practically worthless paper, but with the deliberate intention of
> destroying the value of money as a means of payment. There is no jus-
> tification for the existence of money in a Bolshevist State, where the
> necessities of life shall be paid by work alone. . . .
>
> Already even the hundred ruble note is almost valueless in Russia.
> Soon even the simplest peasant will realize that it is only a scrap of
> paper not worth more than the rags from which it is manufactured.
> Men will cease to covet and hoard it so soon as they discover it will
> not buy anything, and the great illusion of the value and power of
> money on which the capitalist state is based will have been definitely
> destroyed.
>
> This is the real reason why our presses are printing ruble bills day
> and night without rest. But this simple process must, like all the mea-
> sures of Bolshevism, be applied all over the world in order to render
> it effective. Fortunately, the frantic financial debauch in which all the
> governments have indulged during the war has paved the way every-
> where for its application.[7]

Keynes thought it was a terrible mistake for the Versailles Treaty,
which ended World War I, to force Germany to pay huge reparations
to the war's victors. They would cripple Germany's economy and make
it fertile ground for revolution. Keynes's fears were soon realized when
Germany tried to inflate its way out of its debts by just printing money.
At the peak of the resulting hyperinflation in 1923 even the largest bank
notes were barely worth the paper they were printed on; a wheelbarrow
full of money was needed just to buy a loaf of bread. And, as Keynes
predicted, the result was to impoverish the middle class while enrich-
ing the wealthy, who borrowed heavily, bought gold and foreign cur-
rencies, and repaid their debts in money that was virtually worthless.

It is generally agreed that the social unrest created by the German
hyperinflation was central to the rise of Adolf Hitler and the Nazi

Party. As economist Lionel Robbins put it in 1937, "Hitler is the foster-child of the inflation." In a 1942 lecture, the great German novelist Thomas Mann agreed: "A straight line runs from the madness of the German inflation to the madness of the Third Reich." Historians Niall Ferguson and Brigitte Granville concur: "By discrediting free markets, the rule of law, parliamentary institutions, and international economic openness, the Weimar inflation proved the perfect seedbed for national(ist) socialism."[8]

Keynes was keenly aware of events in Germany. His 1919 book, *The Economic Consequences of the Peace,* had made him well known as an expert on the subject and he was in regular contact with German economists and businessmen during the early 1920s. In his *Tract on Monetary Reform,* published in 1923, Keynes often referred to the disastrous effects of inflation in Germany. Indeed, the *Tract* is one of the strongest anti-inflation polemics ever written. Its basic theme is that price stability is essential to the operation of capitalism. Keynes even suggested that capitalism could not survive in its absence. And opposition to inflation wasn't just a public posture for Keynes. In private communications with British Treasury officials he was quite adamant about the need to fight inflation with the strongest possible measures.[9]

Keynes's opposition to inflation flowed from his belief in the importance of stable money—he was equally opposed to inflation *and* deflation. Many so-called hard-money people today adamantly oppose inflation but don't complain about the problems of deflation, and often view it positively.[10] Keynes was not one of these. In his view, the main effect of inflation was to impose a *de facto* tax on capital—which in practical terms meant on the wealthy, whom he called the *rentier* class, those who didn't work for a living and lived off income from capital. But at the same time, inflation benefited the business class, which was able to increase prices faster than costs rose, leading to higher profits.[11]

Deflation, on the other hand, mainly hurt workers because it led to unemployment as real wages increased, forcing employers to lay off employees in order to reduce labor costs. Eventually, the unemployment would force employers to cut nominal wages by the amount of the deflation, but this was a very painful and prolonged process. Thus, although inflation and deflation were both bad, deflation was the bigger problem distributionally in Keynes's view, because it was worse to raise unemployment than to harm the *rentiers*.[12] That is why he was so opposed to the British government's policy of intentionally deflating the pound after World War I to restore the prewar exchange rate.

The deflation in Britain began in 1920 when the government committed itself to raising the value of the pound back up to $4.86 from $3.66. This required a shrinkage of the money supply in order to make the pound scarcer vis-à-vis the dollar. The British government considered it important both economically and morally to restore the prewar parity lest all of those who had bought British bonds suffer a de facto 30 percent loss. It was also thought that failure to repay its debts at the prewar parity would raise interest rates by adding a risk premium to British bonds, making them less attractive to foreign investors.[13]

Shrinking the money supply causes prices to fall, which puts downward pressure on wages. But producers can't very well cut prices unless their costs also fall and labor is the largest expense for any business. As Keynes explained in 1925:

> Our problem is to reduce money wages and, through them, the cost of living, with the idea that, when the circle is complete, real wages will be as high, or nearly as high, as before.... The object of credit restriction, in such a case, is to withdraw from employers the financial means to employ labor at the existing level of prices and wages. The policy can only attain its end by intensifying unemployment without limit, until the workers are ready to accept the necessary reduction of money wages under the pressure of hard facts.[14]

In the past, workers had been disorganized and less able to resist demands by employers for lower wages when the Bank of England tightened money to protect the pound. But by the 1920s unionization had become widespread and workers were in a better position to resist wage cuts. The institution of welfare programs also made it easier for workers to survive without working, thus prolonging strikes and raising unemployment.[15] In 1926 a massive general strike against wage cuts convinced Keynes that offsetting an inflation with a deflation as a means to maintain average price stability was no longer a viable option. Since workers would strenuously resist the wage cuts that were a necessary consequence of a deflation, British businesses would be compelled by market forces to cut prices yet be stuck with high labor costs that would cripple them.

The first effect of deflation, Keynes believed, was felt by entrepreneurs because they were forced to reduce market prices for their output while their costs were largely unchanged. In the initial phase of this development they simply absorbed the losses and reduced their profits. In the second phase they cut back on their least profitable lines of business. Only after this process had continued for some time did employers finally feel compelled to force wage cuts. Thus the full implementation of a deflationary program was very protracted and therefore inefficient.[16]

By contrast, the process of inflation was relatively smooth. Entrepreneurs could raise their prices as soon as they sensed increased demand. Since their costs were largely fixed in the short-run, the price increases raised profits and encouraged capital investment. Although workers suffered from a fall in real wages as prices rose while their wages were unchanged, they also benefited from a rise in employment as businesses expanded production in response to higher profits. Thus while inflation and deflation each had their negative consequences, Keynes saw some benefits to inflation while deflation essentially had none. Given a choice, therefore, a modest inflation was much to be preferred over the equivalent deflation.[17]

In the post–World War II era, most U.S. recessions took place under inflationary conditions. This greatly aided economic readjustment by, for example, reducing real wages when nominal wage rates were unchanged. But the recession of 2008–2009 created deflationary conditions like those of the 1930s. Unless workers were willing to accept actual pay cuts there was no way businesses could avoid massive layoffs and bankruptcies—a situation most evident in the problems of the auto industry, which had the highest wages and benefits in the manufacturing sector and suffered the brunt of the deflationary pressure, hastening a collapse in sales and profits.

THE GREAT DEPRESSION

When the Great Depression began, Keynes opposed the traditional cure for economic downturns—price and wage cuts that would restore equilibrium. It wasn't that this cure wouldn't work, he thought, it's that the social cost of this policy was so great that it would threaten the maintenance of liberal democracy, leading to an authoritarian state such as that in the Soviet Union. As Keynes explained to an American audience in a 1931 lecture:

> Will not the social resistance to a drastic downward readjustment of salaries and wages be an ugly and dangerous thing? I am told sometimes that these changes present comparatively little difficulty in a country such as the United States where economic rigidity has not yet set in. I find it difficult to believe this. But it is for you, not me, to say. I know that in my own country a really large cut of many wages, a cut at all of the same magnitude as the fall in wholesale prices, is simply an impossibility. To attempt it would be to shake the social order to its foundation. There is scarcely one responsible person in Great Britain prepared to recommend it openly.[18]

Instead of forcing wages and prices to adjust to a monetary deflation, Keynes thought it made much more sense to readjust the currency. Better to raise prices back up to where they were previously than endure the pain of vast unemployment and huge wage cuts, he argued. This would restore equilibrium without the necessity of reducing wages by the same percentage that the price level had fallen. As Keynes put it, "The cumulative argument for wishing prices to rise appears to me . . . to be overwhelming."[19]

Shortly after giving this lecture, Keynes wrote an article for the American magazine *Vanity Fair* in which he explained his point further. The decline in prices, he said, was so severe that it threatened the whole financial structure. Eventually the economy would recover on its own, but without governmental action the result would be "a period of waste and disturbance and social injustice." Keynes viewed this forced rearrangement of wealth as utterly unnecessary and feared that its capriciousness would reinforce the idea that capitalism had no redeeming moral foundation.[20]

In early 1933 Keynes published a short pamphlet, *The Means to Prosperity*. In it he expressed growing frustration with the inability of policymakers to understand the nature of the economic problem and to take sufficiently bold actions to deal with it. He was especially critical of the large tax increase enacted by the United States in 1932, which Keynes felt was totally counterproductive. In the process, he even developed a version of what later became known as the Laffer curve—the idea that tax rates may be so high as to reduce revenue. As Keynes explained:

> Nor should the argument seem strange that taxation may be so high as to defeat its object, and that, given sufficient time to gather the fruits, a reduction of taxation will run a better chance than an increase of balancing the budget. For to take the opposite view today is to resemble a manufacturer who, running at a loss, decides to raise his price, and when his declining sales increase the loss, wrapping himself in the rectitude of plain arithmetic, decides that prudence requires him to raise the price still more—and who, when at last his account is balanced with naught on both sides, is still found righteously declaring that it would have been the act of a gambler to reduce the price when you were already making a loss.[21]

Keynes tried as hard as he could to get Franklin D. Roosevelt and other American policymakers to understand that the issue was one of deflation. But as the previous chapter recounts, his efforts were largely futile. By the end of 1934, meaningful understanding of the fundamental economic problem was still limited to a few isolated individuals like

Irving Fisher who seemed to have little influence with those in power at the White House, Treasury, or Federal Reserve. This led Keynes to conceive of a new approach to the problem designed to get around the institutional resistance to a monetary and fiscal policy sufficiently expansive to get the job done.

THE GENERAL THEORY

By 1935, Roosevelt was still pursuing ad hoc stimulus policies. Although the overall size of the U.S. economy had grown 10.8 percent in 1934, it was still a third below its potential based on pre-depression growth rates.[22] The administration and Congress seemed unwilling to pursue aggressive stimulus policies and instead reacted halfheartedly to minicrises as they occurred. Many economists were equally frustrated in 2009 as the very justification for *any* stimulus was hotly debated even as the economy continued to deteriorate.

Keynes decided that he needed to make the argument for stimulus much more systematically and in much more detail than he had done previously. During 1935 he worked on a new book, *The General Theory of Employment, Interest and Money*. Published the following year, its basic argument was that it was impractical to reduce unemployment by forcing down money wages to adjust for a monetary deflation.[23] It was vastly preferable, Keynes explained, to simply reduce real (inflation-adjusted) wages by offsetting the deflation with a compensating inflation. As he put it early in the book:

> Whilst workers will usually resist a reduction of money-wages, it is not their practice to withdraw their labor whenever there is a rise in the price of wage-goods. It is sometimes said that it would be illogical for labor to resist a reduction of money-wages but not to resist a reduction of real wages.... But, whether logical or illogical, experience shows that this is how labor in fact behaves.[24]

Further on Keynes was even more explicit about using inflation to reduce real wages in order to raise employment. "A movement by employers to revise money-wage bargains downward will be much more strongly resisted than a gradual and automatic lowering of real wages as a result of rising prices," he wrote.[25]

Keynes's argument basically boiled down to practicality. "A flexible wage policy and a flexible money policy come, analytically, to the same thing," he explained, "inasmuch as they are alternative means of changing the quantity of money in terms of wage-units." Keynes conceded that governments could theoretically force down wage rates by decree but that only authoritarian states had such power. Every nation, however, had the power to alter the value of its currency and thus the price level through monetary policy. As he put it:

> A change in the quantity of money...is already within the power of most governments by open-market policy or analogous measures. Having regard to human nature and our institutions, it can only be a foolish person who would prefer a flexible wage policy to a flexible money policy, unless he can point to advantages from the former which are not obtainable from the latter. Moreover, other things being equal, a method which it is comparatively easy to apply should be deemed preferable to a method which is probably so difficult as to be impracticable.... It can only be an unjust person who would prefer a flexible wage policy to a flexible money policy.[26]

Part of the problem, however, was getting money out into the economy where it could do some good. Lower interest rates by themselves would not bring forth additional investment because of a liquidity trap that results when market rates are so low that money and bonds become virtually interchangeable. When this happens, open market operations by the central bank, which involves buying bonds and paying for them with newly created money, become impotent. It would simply be exchanging one asset for another that is virtually identical because money is really just a perpetual bond that pays no interest.[27]

Getting the money moving, so to speak, requires the government to engage in deficit financing precisely for the purpose of increasing market interest rates, which would get the economy out of the liquidity trap and make an expansive monetary policy effective once again. It didn't really matter what the money raised by borrowing was spent on as long as it involved the purchase of goods and services. Income transfers and tax cuts were less effective because much of the money would be saved, thus frustrating the need to raise interest rates. It would be best for governments to finance the construction of socially beneficial public works, such as roads and buildings.[28] But for macroeconomic purposes it was not necessary that the construction be inherently productive, because the primary purpose of the effort was to create a mechanism for making monetary policy effective.

Toward this end, Keynes suggested that pyramid-building, earthquakes, and even wars might serve an economically useful purpose when the economy was stuck in a liquidity trap, because they forced governments to spend funds rapidly and run deficits. He jokingly proposed that governments might even bury cash in old mine shafts that had been filled with rubbish. The resources expended by entrepreneurs to dig up the money would make the scheme economically productive to society by employing workers, creating incomes, and mobilizing capital.[29]

It must be emphasized that Keynes was being facetious. He understood that societies could not enrich themselves in the long run through such wasteful projects. They were applicable *only* during times when deflation had brought on an economic slowdown that reduced interest rates to the point where a liquidity trap existed. These were extremely special circumstances that occurred only very, very rarely; in normal times, Keynes knew perfectly well, such schemes would be economically counterproductive.

The Obama administration tried to make this point as well in early 2009 in trying to get a massive stimulus bill enacted. It was more important to do something quickly, it explained, even if it meant wasting a lot of money on programs of dubious value. Growth would not come from the programs themselves but from the overall impact of the deficit on the economy. But because it did not explain the Keynesian argument very well, the Obama administration left itself open to easy attack by Republicans who ridiculed the stimulus as a grab bag of spending with no inherent logic.

REACTION TO THE GENERAL THEORY

The initial reaction to *The General Theory* among professional economists was quite modest. They recognized very quickly that Keynes wasn't really saying anything much different than he had been saying all along. Among those who were initially less than enthusiastic were many who would later be among the strongest supporters of Keynesian economics. For example, one of the first reviews of *The General Theory* was by economist Alvin H. Hansen, who became Keynes's number one advocate in the United States during the early postwar era. Writing in the *Yale Review,* Hansen saw little, if anything, in *The General Theory* that was inconsistent with mainstream economics, given Keynes's assumption of relatively inflexible wages and prices. A few months later, writing in the *Journal of Political Economy,* Hansen reiterated his view that there was nothing new in *The General Theory:*

> The book under review is not a landmark in the sense that it lays a foundation for a "new economics." It warns once again, in a provocative manner, of the danger of reasoning based on assumptions which no longer fit the facts of economic life.... The book is more a symptom of economic trends than a foundation stone upon which a science can be built.[30]

Shortly thereafter, Wassily Leontief, winner of the Nobel Prize in economics in 1973, was equally dismissive. "The difference between Mr. Keynes' new theory of economic equilibrium and the 'orthodox' classical scheme is fundamentally a difference in assumption," he wrote in the *Quarterly Journal of Economics.*[31] In that same issue, economist Jacob Viner, one of the greatest of the twentieth-century economists, also saw no meaningful difference between Keynes's theory and the traditional view except in terms of his preference for inflation over wage cuts as a cure for unemployment: "Keynes' reasoning points obviously to the superiority of inflationary remedies for underemployment over money-wage reductions.... The only clash here between Keynes' position and the orthodox one is in his denial that reduction of money wage rates is a remedy for underemployment."[32]

Later economists came to the same conclusion—Keynes had simply assumed "sticky" wages and adapted a theory around that assumption.[33] This was not nothing in the days of the Great Depression, but hardly earth shattering. Indeed, it didn't have any effect whatsoever on economic policy in the near term.

Consequently, the Roosevelt administration was unmoved by Keynes's new argument for stimulus. Indeed, it went in the opposite direction, raising taxes and tightening fiscal policy rather than expanding it. In 1937 Treasury Secretary Henry Morgenthau even convinced Roosevelt that balancing the budget was what was needed to restore growth. At the same time, passage of the Social Security Act increased taxes by imposing a payroll tax for the first time. Since benefits weren't paid out until 1940, for the first three years of the program Social Security took more out of the economy than it put in.[34]

At the same time, the Federal Reserve unwisely tightened monetary policy because it was becoming concerned about inflation, which rose from 1.4 percent in 1936 to 2.9 percent in 1937. The result was a severe recession in 1937 following three years of fairly robust growth. After growing at an average rate of almost 10 percent per year between 1934 and 1937, real GDP fell 3.4 percent in 1938.[35]

The economic downturn was deeply frustrating to Roosevelt. It called into question the whole rationale for the New Deal to date, but finally made him and his advisers sympathetic to the Keynesian idea of pumping up spending despite the political risks. As historian Charles A. Beard explains:

> In its range the shock of the economic collapse was startling to President Roosevelt and his advisers. Unemployment continued to be alarming in amount and effects. Labor agitation grew more turbulent. The hostility of the financial community was aggravated. To

the administration, an enlargement of federal spending seemed again necessary as a stimulus to business recovery, and that meant an extension of the "deficit financing" which had for a time been regarded, even by many New Dealers, as a temporary and deplorable expedient. Doubts came to the President and his counselors: perhaps they had been wrong in seeking recovery through specific measures they had espoused and were at the end of their improvisation.[36]

There was still strong resistance to the idea of intentionally running deficits because balancing the budget annually had been considered the norm since the time of the Founding Fathers. The deficits to date had been only reluctantly been tolerated. Therefore, to get Congress and the American people to support a sufficiently large-scale spending program, it had to be for something everyone viewed as absolutely necessary and legitimate. A military buildup fit the bill nicely. But first the American people had to be convinced that it was justified by national security. Here, Roosevelt's growing concerns about impending war dovetailed with the Keynesian approach to economic stimulus.[37]

A shift in focus also helped Roosevelt with some of his political problems following the Democrats' big loss in the 1938 elections. As historian Basil Rauch explains, "The president effectively checked the growth of opposition by reducing domestic affairs to secondary position and working for party and national unity on a program of foreign policy."[38] Those on the left immediately recognized the political and economic shift. Writing in the liberal *New Republic* magazine in November 1938, columnist John T. Flynn made this observation:

> Well, it looks as if the United States was going to have its war scare and of course its battle implements to match the degree of our fright. The President of the United States has set out as the drummer of fear and is deliberately selling to our people the baleful notion that some enemy is about to assail us and that we are defenseless against the coming attack.... The next phase, of course, is the President's current, still undisclosed, plans for the greatest peacetime rearmament of both the army and the navy in our history.... We are now to attempt

to make a great arms program the basis of our recovery effort instead of depending on consumer-goods production.[39]

The clouds of war were gathering in Europe and Roosevelt was increasingly convinced that American intervention was inevitable. But neutrality laws enacted to keep America out of another European war blocked direct action by the United States. They grew from a wide-spread belief that British pressure and lobbying by arms manufacturers had maneuvered the United States into a war in 1917 in which it had no vital interests. In a January 1937 poll 64 percent of Americans agreed that it was a mistake for America to have entered the First World War.[40] An intense desire for isolation from the problems of Europe, therefore, prevented Roosevelt from taking preparatory measures for another war, which simultaneously inhibited defense spending on the scale Keynes thought was necessary for his theory to work.

The outbreak of World War II in Europe in September 1939 increased Roosevelt's conviction that America would eventually have to join the fighting. At the same time, it was increasingly evident that national defense was the only purpose for which he might be able to get sufficient support to raise spending and deficits enough to make a real impact on the economy. The conservative congressional coalition of Republicans and southern Democrats, which had gained great strength after the 1938 elections, vigorously advocated economy in government expenditures, but was willing to make an exception for military spending. In a 1939 column Flynn identified this tendency: "I find among conservative groups a phenomenon which is worth noting. It is that while there is a growing feeling against the use of deficit financing for recovery or relief purposes, there is a very strong feeling in favor of spending money for national defense, despite the fact that it must be done with borrowed funds."[41]

By mid-1940, Keynes was lamenting that the federal government had still not done nearly enough to raise spending by an amount sufficient to really make a difference, economically. In a *New Republic* article, he complained that spending was "hopelessly inadequate." Keynes speculated that only "war conditions" would bring forth expenditures "on the scale necessary to make the grand experiment which would prove my case."[42]

DEPRESSION'S END

World War II finally did what the New Deal couldn't do and ended the Great Depression. It forced the federal government to run deficits on an unprecedented scale, while the Federal Reserve fixed interest rates and provided as much liquidity to the banking system as necessary to keep them from rising.[43] Economists concluded that the war brought about the ultimate success of Keynesian economic theory, and they all adopted the new approach en masse. Within a few years, it was hard to find any economist who was not essentially a Keynesian.

Ironically, at the very moment of his greatest triumph, Keynes himself was backing away from his own program. In 1944, economist F. A. Hayek published *The Road to Serfdom,* a book that was highly critical of the growth of government, partly as the result of the widespread adoption of Keynesian economic theories. Nevertheless, in a June 1944 letter to Hayek, Keynes proclaimed himself to be largely in agreement with his argument. Indeed, not only in agreement with it, "but in a deeply moved agreement."[44]

In the last article he ever wrote, Keynes tried to turn the clock back toward the classical economics that had been thoroughly discredited by the length and depth of the Great Depression and ultimately superseded by Keynesian economics. Keynes warned that the baby had been thrown out with the bathwater and economists needed to appreciate the enduring truths of classical economics. As he put it:

> I find myself moved, not for the first time, to remind contemporary economists that the classical teaching embodied some permanent truths of great significance, which we are liable today to overlook because we associate them with other doctrines which we cannot now accept without much qualification. There are in these matters deep undercurrents at work, natural forces, one can call them, or even the invisible hand, which are operating toward equilibrium. If

it were not, we could not have got on even so well as we have for many decades past.[45]

Through the years, many economists have puzzled over the contradictions in Keynes's work. But there is one thing that ties it all together: his intense desire to influence public policy. As Keynes biographer Robert Skidelsky put it, "He invented theory to justify what he wanted to do." If one goes through the 30 volumes of his collected works, the vast bulk of the material is not technical economics, but articles for newspapers and popular magazines, as well as memoranda and policy papers for government officials. "He was an opportunist who reacted to events immediately and directly, and his reaction was to produce an answer, to write a memorandum, and to publish at once," economist Elizabeth Johnson explains.[46] In this respect, economist Don Patinkin believes that Keynes and his ideological opposite, Milton Friedman, were really two of a kind:

> For both of these men the purpose of economic analysis is not only to construct theoretical models, but to lead to policy recommendations— and accordingly both had a continuous and detailed concern with the current empirical data on the workings of the economy. Furthermore, both regarded as an essential part of their task as economists not only to formulate policy positions, but to generate public opinion in support of them. And both sedulously exploited all means of communication for this purpose: articles in leading newspapers and magazines; books and pamphlets; participation in radio and television programs (of course, there was no television in Keynes' day; but can anyone doubt he would have been a television personality if there had been?); appearances and testimony before government committees and bodies; and personal contacts with leading government officials responsible for formulating and carrying out policy, while at the same time eschewing (except in wartime) official government positions.[47]

It is clear that Keynes would often put forward proposals because he thought they would be helpful at a particular moment in time, knowing full well that it would be highly undesirable for them to be maintained for the long term. Perhaps the best example of this expediency was Keynes's proposal for national self-sufficiency. Before the Great Depression, he was a conventional free trader. But then he got the idea that it might be economically beneficial if nations could avoid international trade as much as possible. This would insulate them from economic and financial problems imported from abroad. When Keynes first put forward this idea in 1930, his friend Roy Harrod expressed concern. Keynes told him not to worry: "When this phase is past, we can reverse the process." Unfortunately, when Keynes actually tried to do this at the end of World War II, he found it harder to undo what he had done than he thought it would be. The problem was, as Harrod explained, "the autarkists and trade controllers were now in the saddle."[48]

Keynes had enormous confidence in his ability to manipulate public opinion and this had a great deal of impact on the nature of his work. For one thing, it obviated any necessity for consistency; he would say what needed to be said one day and if it needed to be changed the next day, then he would simply make it happen. Hayek thought this was the key to understanding Keynes, as he explained in a review of Harrod's biography of Keynes in 1952:

> Perhaps the explanation of much that is puzzling about Keynes's mind lies in the supreme confidence he had acquired in his power to play on public opinion as a supreme master plays on his instrument. He loved to pose in the role of a Cassandra whose warnings were not listened to. But, in fact, his early success in swinging around public opinion about the peace treaties had given him probably even an exaggerated estimate of his powers. I shall never forget one occasion—I believe the last time that I met him—when he startled me by an uncommonly frank expression of this. It was early in 1946, shortly after he had returned from the strenuous and exhausting negotiations in Washington on the British loan.... A turn in the conversation made me ask him whether he was not concerned about what some of his disciples were making of his theories. After a not very complimentary remark about the persons concerned, he proceeded to reassure me by explaining that those ideas had been badly needed at the time he had launched them. He continued by indicating that I

need not be alarmed; if they should ever become dangerous I could rely upon him again quickly to swing round public opinion—and he indicated by a quick movement of his hand how rapidly that would be done. But three months later he was dead.[49]

Other economists have expressed similar views of Keynes. For example, in his presidential address to the American Economic Association in 1951, Harvard economist John H. Williams said that Keynes "started with what he regarded as the policy requirements of the time and built his theory around them." Keynes himself probably would have agreed with this assessment. He once explained that his policy prescriptions were often unrelated to their apparent theoretical underpinnings. In discussing *The General Theory,* Keynes said: "I consider that my suggestions for a cure, which, avowedly, are not worked out completely, are on a different plane from the diagnosis. They are not meant to be definitive; they are subject to all sorts of special assumptions and are necessarily related to the particular conditions of the time."[50]

Keynes fully understood that his theory would have different applications at different times. As he told economist Gardner Means in 1939, "I would emphasize again the distinction between my *General Theory,* regarded as a more or less all-embracing theory, and the applications of it which can be made in different circumstances according to the different sets of realistic assumptions." This, Skidelsky believes, was the real beauty of the Keynesian system: it could easily be used to support a variety of actions that governments wanted to take for other reasons.[51]

Of course, Keynesian economics fit in nicely with liberal political views about the need for government to be more deeply involved in the economy, which were dominant among the intelligentsia of the 1930s and 1940s. As economist Joseph Schumpeter explained, "Whatever its merit as a piece of analysis may be, there cannot be any doubt that it [*The General Theory*] owed its victorious career primarily to the fact that its argument implemented some of the strongest political preferences of a large number of modern economists."[52]

In short, Keynesian economics was a brilliant synthesis of both the theoretical and the practical. It was primarily a theory for the times that also made some important contributions to economic science. But it was mainly a rationale for things governments everywhere wanted to do anyway—such as break free of the balanced-budget constraint—that they would have done with or without Keynes. His theories, however, made them seem scientific rather than merely opportunistic.

KEYNES AS A CONSERVATIVE

One thing that is a constant in Keynes's efforts is that they were consistently motivated by a desire to maintain the liberal capitalist order. Honest conservatives have always understood this. In 1945 economist David McCord Wright noted that a conservative political candidate could easily run a campaign "largely on quotations from *The General Theory*." The following year, economist Gottfried Haberler of the conservative Austrian school conceded that the specific policy recommendations of Keynesian economics were not at all revolutionary. "They are in fact very conservative," he admitted.[53]

In 1981 *Wealth and Poverty* author George Gilder said that Keynes's works "are far more favorable to supply-side economic policy than current Keynesians comprehend." He thought that Keynes deserved special credit for restoring "to a position of appropriate centrality in economic thought the vital role and activity of the individual capitalist." Peter Drucker, another conservative admirer of Keynes, viewed him as not merely conservative but ultraconservative:

> He had two basic motivations. One was to destroy the labor unions and the other was to maintain the free market. Keynes despised the American Keynesians. His whole idea was to have an impotent government that would do nothing but, through tax and spending policies, maintain the equilibrium of the free market. Keynes was the real father of neoconservatism, far more than Hayek![54]

John Kenneth Galbraith, whose politics were well to the left of Keynes, not to mention Drucker, agreed with this assessment. "The broad thrust of his efforts, like that of Roosevelt, was conservative; it was to endure that the system would survive," he wrote. But, Galbraith added, "such conservatism in the English-speaking countries does not appeal to the truly committed conservative."[55]

Keynes's friend and biographer Harrod tells us that underneath his veneer of trendy liberalism, Keynes was always deeply conservative.[56]

> He valued institutions which had historic roots in the country; he was a great upholder of the virtues of the middle-class which, in his view, had been responsible for all the good things that we now enjoy; he believed in the supreme value of intellectual leadership, in the wisdom of the chosen few; he was interested in showing how narrow was the circle of kinship from which the great British leaders in statesmanship and thinking had been drawn; and he was an intense lover of his country....He was not a Socialist. His regard for the middle-class, for artists, scientists and brain workers of all kinds made him dislike the class-conscious elements of Socialism. He had no egalitarian sentiment; if he wanted to improve the lot of the poor...that was not for the sake of equality, but in order to make their lives happier and better....He did not think it would be beneficial for the State to run industry and trade. He considered the doctrine of State Socialism to be quite obsolete.[57]

As Keynes himself explained, "the class war will find me on the side of the educated *bourgeoisie*." Conservative icon Edmund Burke was one of his political heroes. Keynes expressed contempt for the British Labor Party, calling its members "sectaries of an outworn creed mumbling moss-grown demi-semi Fabian Marxism." He also termed the British Labor Party an "immense destructive force" that responded to "anti-communist rubbish with anti-capitalist rubbish."[58]

It was obvious to those on the political left and in the Soviet Union that Keynes was one of socialism's greatest enemies, even if some on the right still view Keynes as a crypto-communist.[59] State socialism, he said, "is, in fact, little better than a dusty survival of a plan to meet the problems of fifty years ago, based on a misunderstanding of what someone said a hundred years ago." Indeed, Keynes told George

Bernard Shaw that the whole point of *The General Theory* was to knock away the Ricardian foundations of Marxism.[60]

Keynes often expressed disdain for Soviet Communism. "Red Russia holds too much which is detestable," he wrote, terming Communism "an insult to our intelligence." Communists, Keynes believed, were people who produced evil in the hope that good may come of it. And he had little respect for Karl Marx, calling him "a poor thinker," and *Das Kapital* "an obsolete economic textbook which I know to be not only scientifically erroneous but without interest or application for the modern world." Keynes went on to say:

> On the economic side I cannot perceive that Russian Communism has made any contribution to our economic problems of intellectual interest or scientific value. I do not think that it contains, or is likely to contain, any piece of useful economic technique which we could not apply, if we chose, with equal or greater success in a society which retained all the marks, I will not say of nineteenth-century individualistic capitalism, but of British bourgeois ideals. Theoretically at least, I do not believe that there is any economic improvement for which revolution is a necessary instrument. On the other hand, we have everything to lose by the methods of violent change. In Western industrial conditions the tactics of Red revolution would throw the whole population into a pit of poverty and death.[61]

Keynes understood completely the central role of profit in the capitalist system. This is one reason why he was so strongly opposed to deflation and why, at the end of the day, his cure for unemployment was to restore profits to employers. He also appreciated the importance of entrepreneurship, which he called "animal spirits": "If the animal spirits are dimmed and the spontaneous optimism falters . . . enterprise will fade and die." And he knew that the general business environment was critical for growth; hence business confidence was an important economic factor. As Keynes acknowledged, "Economic prosperity is . . . dependent on a political and social atmosphere which is congenial to the average businessman."[62]

OPPOSITION TO PLANNING

A major theme of Keynes's *General Theory* is the importance of maintaining the freedom for prices to adjust, which is essential for the proper functioning of the economy. This made Keynes a strong opponent of national economic planning, which was much in vogue after the Second World War. "The advantage to efficiency of the decentralization of decisions and of individual responsibility is even greater, perhaps, than the nineteenth century supposed; and the reaction against the appeal to self-interest may have gone too far," he wrote.[63]

Indeed, the whole point of his *General Theory*, Keynes felt, was about preserving what was good and necessary in capitalism as well as protecting it against authoritarian attacks by separating microeconomics, the economics of prices and the firm, from macroeconomics, the economics of the economy as a whole. In order to preserve economic freedom in the former, which Keynes thought was essential for efficiency, increased government intervention in the latter was unavoidable. While pure free marketers might lament this development, the alternative, as Keynes saw it, was the complete destruction of capitalism and its replacement by some form of socialism. As he explained:

> Whilst...the enlargement of the functions of government...would seem to a nineteenth century publicist or to a contemporary American financier to be a terrific encroachment on individualism, I defend it...both as the only practicable means of avoiding the destruction of existing economic forms in their entirety and as the condition of the successful functioning of individual initiative....The authoritarian state systems of today seem to solve the problem of unemployment at the expense of efficiency and of freedom. It is certain that the world will not much longer tolerate the unemployment which...is associated—and, in my opinion, inevitably associated—with present-day capitalistic individualism. But it may be possible by a right analysis of the problem to cure the disease whilst preserving efficiency and freedom.[64]

In Keynes's view, it was sufficient for government intervention to be limited to the macroeconomy—that is, to use monetary and fiscal policy to maintain total spending (effective demand), which would both sustain growth and eliminate political pressure for radical actions to reduce unemployment. "It is not the ownership of the instruments of production which is important for the State to assume," Keynes wrote in *The General Theory*. "If the State is able to determine the aggregate amount of resources devoted to augmenting the instruments and the basic rate of reward to those who own them, it will have accomplished all that is necessary." As he explained more clearly in a letter to the *Times* of London in 1940:

> If the community's aggregate rate of spending can be regulated, the way in which personal incomes are spent and the means by which demand is satisfied can be safely left free and individual. Just as in the war the regulation of aggregate spending is the only way to avoid the destruction of choice and initiative ... through the complex tyranny of all-round rationing, so in peace it is only the application of this principle which will provide the environment in which the choice and initiative of the individual can be safely left free. This is the one kind of compulsion of which the effect is to enlarge liberty. Those who, entangled in old unserviceable maxims, fail to see this further-reaching objective have not grasped, to speak American, the big idea.[65]

One of Keynes's students, Arthur Plumptre, explained his philosophy this way. In Keynes' view, Hayek's "road to serfdom" could as easily come from a lack of government as from too much. If high unemployment was allowed to continue for too long, Keynes thought the inevitable result would be socialism—total government control—and the destruction of political freedom. This highly undesirable result had to be resisted and could only be held at bay if rigid adherence to laissez-faire gave way, but not too much. As Plumptre put it, Keynes "tried to devise the minimum government controls that would allow free enterprise to work."[66]

Keynes died at the age of 63 on April 21, 1946, shortly after returning from an arduous visit to the United States where he had participated in negotiations relating to postwar economic institutions such as the International Monetary Fund. He did not live to see the final triumph of his ideas, which really reached their pinnacle in the 1960s. But just over a decade later the word "Keynesian" would become a hostile epithet, as Keynes's theories were widely blamed both for causing the inflation of the 1970s and for lacking any means to deal with it.

CONTEMPORARY RELEVANCE

I was completing this book just as the economic crisis hit with severity in the fall of 2008, and was very grateful for having finished the research because it greatly clarified in my mind what needed to be done for the economy.

The parallel to the Great Depression seemed clear to me. The key difference was that the Federal Reserve didn't allow the money supply to shrink as it did in the 1930s. However, velocity—the speed at which money turns over as people spend it—fell so much in 2008 and 2009 that it had economic effects identical to a sharp decline in the money supply. The decline in spending—and hence velocity—resulted from the collapse in wealth that in turn resulted from a sharp fall in housing and stock prices. According to the Fed's flow of funds statistics, net household wealth fell to $51.5 trillion in the fourth quarter of 2008 from $64.3 trillion in the third quarter of 2007, which reduced aggregate spending by at least $600 billion per year and perhaps twice that—more than enough to create a severe recession.[67]

The Fed tried to compensate for the fall in velocity by virtually doubling the monetary base from $90 billion in September 2008 to $170 billion in January 2009. But rather than lead to a doubling of the money supply, banks simply sat on the money because there was no demand for loans. Excess reserves—deposits private banks hold at the Federal Reserve as backing for their deposits over and above what the Fed requires—rose from less than $2 billion in August 2008 to $80 billion in January 2009. It was as if an individual took savings out of an interest-earning account and deposited them all in a checking account earning no interest.

In short, money was immobilized and simply piled up in ultra-safe Treasury bills instead of financing consumption and investment. Indeed, at one point yields on T-bills actually fell to zero.[68] This was classic evidence of a liquidity trap just like the one in the 1930s. Under such circumstances, it seemed to me that the federal government had no choice but to try and compensate for the fall in private spending by increased government spending.[69] Only when aggregate spending increased would money begin to circulate, making Federal Reserve policy effective again, thereby relieving the deflation at the heart of the nation's economic problem.

This view put me very much in the minority among conservatives, virtually all of whom felt that fiscal stimulus was useless and that the Fed had gone overboard in trying to stimulate money growth. But they had made the same arguments in the early 1930s. Now, as then, I think Keynes was right and the conservatives were wrong.

CHAPTER 3

INFLATION

The Downfall of Keynesian Economics

Sustained inflation proved to be the downfall of Keynesian econom-ics, which was blamed for both causing the great inflation of the 1970s and having no viable plan to deal with it. In truth, Keynes had a clear theory of inflation and inflation control, but he never emphasized it or developed it. By the time inflation became a serious problem his analysis had mostly been forgotten.

A key factor leading to the extremely rapid and widespread adop-tion of Keynesian economics after World War II was the fear that war spending had only temporarily ended the Great Depression. Consequently, people were concerned that the end of the war would bring on an economic collapse as growth and unemployment would abruptly return to their prewar levels.

As it turned out, the cold war picked up right where the Second World War left off, and within a few short years the United States was again involved in a shooting war in Korea, followed not too many years later by the Vietnam War. Although it would be wrong to imply that

Keynesian economic theories encouraged the waging of wars just to maintain domestic prosperity, there is no question that war spending did have a Keynesian impact. It helped maintain total spending in the economy and thereby reduced the severity of postwar recessions.[1]

Keynesian theories had a more direct impact on macroeconomic policy. At the first sign of recession it became common for Congress to enact a public works jobs program. Unfortunately, there are important institutional reasons why they never work very well. Forecasters almost never see recessions coming far enough in advance for Congress to act in a timely manner.[2] And even if they could, it takes a long time to implement a public works program and it is almost impossible to target it to areas of the greatest need. The result is that countercyclical stimulus invariably impacts the economy long after recessions are over and seldom offers much aid to the unemployed.

The biggest long-term problem for Keynesian economics was that those who followed John Maynard Keynes overgeneralized his policy prescriptions.[3] As previous chapters have shown, his policies were always intended to have an inflationary impact, but this was only to get the economy out of a deflationary depression. Once this phase was past, Keynes fully expected them to be reversed; instead of running budget deficits, he expected governments to run budget surpluses to soak up excess purchasing power and keep inflation in check. As economist Robert Leeson put it, "Keynes was a *re*flationist, but not an *in*flationist."[4]

This flip side of Keynesian theory did not prove to be as popular as his prescription for recession: government spending, deficits, and easy money. Governments have almost never made any effort to run budget surpluses during boom times. This built an inflationary bias into Keynesian economics.

When budget surpluses emerged during the Clinton administration, they were not justified on Keynesian grounds as a means of dampening demand in order to prevent inflation, but rather as a means to reduce real interest rates and thereby stimulate growth and investment. Whatever else one may think of this policy, it was definitely not Keynesian economics.[5]

Inflation was a problem for Keynesian economics because it is fundamentally a theory of how to stop deflation, which necessitated inflationary policies to combat it. After the death of Keynes in 1946, his followers increasingly forgot that his policies presupposed deflationary conditions. They mistakenly applied them in every economic slowdown and as a general means of raising the basic growth rate in the economy—something Keynes had never intended.

Keynesian economists also forgot that fiscal policy for Keynes was largely a means to an end—the end being an effectively expansive monetary policy. They came to think that fiscal policy alone was sufficient to stimulate growth and monetary policy was viewed as essentially passive. One consequence of this was to leave neo-Keynesians without an adequate theory of inflation.

By the 1970s, inflation and unemployment were both rising together—something that neo-Keynesians said wasn't supposed to happen. Because governments were already running historically large budget deficits, it wasn't realistic to increase them further to reduce unemployment. The result was to utterly discredit Keynesian economics for the next several decades.

KEYNES ON INFLATION

Although Keynes correctly advocated reflation as the best cure for unemployment caused by a monetary deflation, his analysis in *The General Theory of Employment, Interest and Money* left the impression that he thought inflation was a cure for unemployment at all times. Economist Jacob Viner was among those who recognized that this was a highly undesirable policy if that's what Keynes meant. As Viner put it, "In a world organized in accordance with Keynes' specifications there would be a constant race between the [money] printing press and the business agents of the trade unions, with the problem of unemployment largely solved if the printing press could maintain a constant lead and if only volume of employment, irrespective of quality, is considered important."[6]

Many economists still argue that Keynesian economics is nothing but a prescription for inflation. This conclusion, however, can be sustained only by ignoring everything Keynes wrote after *The General Theory*. Almost immediately after he finished that work, he started writing about the need to reverse the policy of running deficits as soon as the economy was expanding solidly. In a neglected essay, "How to Avoid a Slump," published in January 1937, Keynes said it was already time for the government to start reversing its deficit policy and begin paying down debt. Despite the fact that the unemployment rate in Britain was still high at 12½ percent, it was necessary to begin cutting back on stimulus. The boom, he said, "is the right time for austerity at the Treasury."[7]

In March 1937 Keynes reemphasized his concern that inflation was starting to rear its ugly head. He feared that unless action were taken to cut nondefense spending to reduce demand and free up industrial capacity for rearmament, the government would be forced to resort to rationing and price controls, which he strongly opposed. During the First World War the British government had largely dealt with inflation by means of rationing and price controls, both of which Keynes rejected as inefficient and distortionary. As he wrote in *The Economic Consequences of the Peace*, "The preservation of a spurious value for the currency, by the force of law expressed in the regulation of prices, contains in itself...the seeds of final economic decay, and soon dries up the sources of ultimate supply." Price controls, he explained, would be ineffective when the nature of the problem was that demand exceeded the available supply of goods.[8]

The outbreak of World War II in Europe in September 1939 made the problem of keeping inflation under control more acute. War inevitably meant increased demand for goods and services and the diversion of production into areas required by the military rather than the satisfaction of consumer needs. Keynes believed that the most efficient means of controlling demand and keeping inflation under control was to increase aggregate taxation. But there were two problems with this approach. First, income tax rates were already so high they were having a detrimental effect on economic incentives. Second was figuring out how to make sure that everyone, including those with low incomes, curbed their consumption during a period of scarcity of consumer basics and contributed to the financing of the war effort. A sales tax might achieve this purpose, but Keynes thought it would be too difficult and take too much time to introduce an entirely new tax when the government bureaucracy was already severely strained.[9]

Keynes was also concerned about permanently enlarging the government with new methods of taxation to deal with the temporary problem of fighting and financing a war. "There is a fatal family resemblance between the bureaucracies in Moscow, Berlin and Whitehall; and we must be careful," Keynes cautioned.[10] It would be better, he thought, to use temporary measures to deal with a temporary problem and do so in a way that preserved individual initiative and incentives.

In a newspaper article in November 1939, Keynes first laid out his scheme for dealing with all these problems at once through forced saving. Every worker would be required to contribute a portion of his wages, with the percentage rising with income levels. The money would be deposited in the worker's name in an account at the Post Office Savings Bank and earn interest. In general, the money could not be withdrawn or borrowed against until after the war. This would simultaneously accomplish the goals of reducing demand and keeping inflation under control, financing the war effort, and preserving incentives. The scheme would also provide a boost to spending after the war as the blocked accounts were gradually opened. Even F. A. Hayek, who was probably Keynes's greatest intellectual opponent, thought the plan was brilliant and said so publicly.[11]

But those on the political left in Britain strenuously opposed Keynes's plan. They were adamant that financing for the war should come mainly from taxing the rich. If this was insufficient, the left was prepared to accept a considerable amount of inflation. If it got out of control, they saw price controls and rationing as tolerable responses. In short, leftists rejected Keynes's proposal from beginning to end.[12]

Keynes was equally unsuccessful in getting his American followers to accept his anti-inflation program. They were too concerned about maintaining growth and believed that supply was expanding rapidly enough to offset the increased demand resulting from deficits and easy money.[13] In the end, the United States followed Britain and used price controls to keep wartime inflation in check.

It's important to emphasize that Keynes's approach to the economic problems of war was very consistent with his general approach to the Great Depression. He wanted to preserve political and economic freedom to the greatest extent possible, strongly opposed direct planning and price controls, and viewed macroeconomic policy as the only way of doing both. As Keynes biographer Robert Skidelsky explains:

> Since Keynes is so often unthinkingly placed in the *dirigiste* camp, it is important to insist that he favored the fiscal theory of war control. More importantly, he *invented* the fiscal theory, precisely in order to avoid "totalitarian" planning. He did not see demand management as a useful adjunct to planning, price fixing, rationing, bureaucratic controls and so on, but as an alternative to them, in war as in peace.... Keynes's fiscal theory was an alternative to inflation as well as to physical planning. Indeed, he believed that the first would inevitably lead to the second. What he called "totalitarianism" was an inevitable outcome of failing to control inflation in a modern economy—a conclusion strikingly similar to that of Hayek in his *Road to Serfdom*, published in 1944.[14]

It's worth remembering that during the Second World War even hard-core free-marketers, like economist Lionel Robbins, felt that there was no alternative to controls. But rejecting Keynes's free-market approach and accepting the necessity of controls was to have long-term consequences, just as Keynes feared. Controls were maintained long after the end of the war lest all the pent-up inflation cause a price explosion. As time went by, people became accustomed to the controls and offered little resistance to comprehensive economic planning, the nationalization of industry, and other aspects of quasi-socialism. Eventually, this heavy state control of industry led to misallocation and inefficiency that slowly impoverished the British people until their economy's ills were too obvious to ignore in the 1970s.[15]

OUTLAWING DEPRESSIONS

Although people were very grateful for the end of the depression after the outbreak of World War II, they knew that the war was eventually going to end. If, as was widely believed, war was the *only* thing that had ended the depression, it followed that the depression would likely start right up again where it left off as soon as hostilities ended and defense spending fell. As Harvard economist Alvin Hansen wrote in 1943:

> The fact is that many people dread to think of what is coming. Businessmen, wage earners, white-collar employees, professional people, farmers—all alike expect and fear a postwar collapse: demobilization of armies, shutdowns in defense industries, unemployment, deflation, bankruptcy, hard times.... Everywhere one hears it said that, when this war is over, all countries including our own will be impoverished.[16]

Hansen and many other economists shared a belief that capitalism had matured to the point where secular stagnation—permanently low growth—had set in. This resulted, they thought, from declining population growth, a dearth of new inventions, closing of the frontier, and the declining rate of profit on capital investment.[17] It also followed from Keynes's theory of underemployment equilibrium.[18] In short, depression-like conditions might be the economic norm in the future once the temporary stimulus of war was past.

American policymakers were deeply concerned about this possibility and did everything in their power to maintain economic growth after the war and prevent a return to depression. Unquestionably, this was the highest priority of postwar planning from the moment war began. As historian Gabriel Kolko explained American thinking:

> The impact of the prewar world depression and the experience of the 1930's profoundly colored United States planning of its postwar peace aims. [Secretary of State Cordell] Hull...and the other leaders in Washington were determined to undo its still pervasive consequences to the world economy, and perhaps above all, to prevent its

recurrence. For this reason the United States did not simply wish to repair the prewar world economy, but to reconstruct it anew. There was a remarkable unanimity in Washington on this objective, and it was by far the most extensively discussed peace aim, surpassing any other in the level of planning and thought given to it.[19]

Thus economic reconstruction meant opening foreign markets to U.S. exports, rehabilitating the economies of nations battered by war as quickly as possible so that they would have the means to buy those exports, and establishing a stable international monetary system to facilitate trade and capital flows. There would be no Versailles Treaty requiring the payment of reparations by Germany and Japan, no hyperinflations or ruinous deflations to reestablish prewar exchange rates, and no Fordney-McCumber Tariff to prevent foreigners from selling to us—in other words, no repeat of the errors that followed World War I, which were widely viewed as having sown the seeds of World War II.

This perspective complemented Keynesian theory, as Keynes himself well understood, and explains his efforts to have his vision incorporated into postwar economic institutions such as the International Monetary Fund, which would manage and stabilize world exchange rates; the World Bank, which would provide capital for growth in war-torn nations in return for opening their economies to trade and foreign investment; and the General Agreement on Tariffs and Trade (now known as the World Trade Organization), which would establish free trade as a basic principle of international relations. Other institutions such as the Marshall Plan and the Organization for European Economic Cooperation (now known as the Organization for Economic Cooperation and Development) reinforced these goals. For example, Marshall Plan aid was conditioned upon the adoption of open trade among all aid recipients.[20]

Policymakers had every reason to think this would work and did not need to create an artificial enemy to justify keeping defense spending at a high level after the war. But at the same time, there is no question that the emergence of the Soviet Union as a threat was extremely convenient from the point of view of Keynesian economics. The Keynesian model does not differentiate between government spending on defense and government spending on domestic programs. Spending is spending in the model, and total spending (public and private consumption and investment spending plus net exports) is what determines the size of the economy.[21]

It wasn't long after the war that Keynesian economists were praising defense spending for underpinning the postwar boom. The popular press also saw the importance of defense spending to national prosperity. For example, in 1950 the "Newsgram" columnist for *U.S. News & World Report* said, "Business won't go to pot so long as war is a threat, so long as every alarm can be used to step up spending—lending for defense at home and for aid abroad. Cold war is almost a guarantee against a bad depression."[22]

As recently as 2008, President George W. Bush extolled the virtues of war spending in Keynesian terms. When asked whether the Iraq war was a drag on the economy, Bush replied, "Actually the spending in the war might help with jobs...because we're buying equipment and people are working." Liberal economist Paul Krugman agreed: "It's just wrong to blame the war for our current economic mess; in the short run, wartime spending actually stimulates the economy." Conservative economist Martin Feldstein suggested that increased defense spending would be an ideal means of getting the economy out of recession.[23]

BROADENING GOVERNMENT INVOLVEMENT

Another way policymakers hoped to prevent a recurrence of the Great Depression was by passing the Employment Act of 1946, which legally mandated the federal government to use every means at its disposal to maintain full employment.[24] To monitor economic conditions and advise on how to accomplish this goal, two organizations, the Council of Economic Advisers and the Joint Economic Committee, were created. The former was part of the White House and the latter a congressional committee. The CEA has three members appointed by the president and confirmed by the Senate. The JEC has twenty members, ten each drawn from the House and Senate. Both groups have professional staffs to aid them in their work.

The CEA and JEC played a critical role in the transformation of economic policy during the coming four decades. In the 1960s, they helped institutionalize Keynesian economics. In the 1970s, they supported the rise of monetarism, which essentially killed Keynesian economics. And in the 1980s, they were critical to the development of supply-side economics, which replaced Keynesian economics as the federal government's dominant economic policy framework from the 1980s through the early 2000s. As executive director of the JEC in the early 1980s, I played an active role in the latter development.

In the 1950s, the JEC was the more significant institution. It held numerous hearings and issued many reports and studies emphasizing the importance of fiscal policy and strongly supported the Keynesian view. The committee was greatly aided by the presence of Senator Paul H. Douglas, Democrat of Illinois, among its members. Before his election to Congress in 1948, he had been a prominent professor of economics at the University of Chicago, where he was among the few Keynesians in the economics department. The CEA, however, was dominated by economist Arthur F. Burns, whose view of Keynesian economics bordered on the hostile.[25]

Among the JEC's important early efforts under Douglas's leadership was a series of hearings in 1955 on the impact of taxation on economic growth. Directed by staff economist Norman Ture, more than 80 of the top tax economists and lawyers in the United States contributed papers on the topic. Based on these hearings, the JEC urged greater attention to the aggregate level of taxation as a factor in economic growth and increased use of tax policy for economic stabilization. A similar set of hearings in 1957 focused on federal expenditures, with many witnesses expressing Keynesian views on the evils of a rigid balanced budget requirement and the virtues of spending as an economic stabilizer.[26]

Dwight D. Eisenhower, however, steadfastly followed orthodox policies, resisting calls for antirecession programs and tax cuts, and favoring a balanced budget at all times. When the Eisenhower administration's first recession began in July 1953 there is no evidence that he or his advisers were even aware of it until long afterward. In his January 1954 economic report, Eisenhower said, "The year just closed was very prosperous with record output.... Our economic growth is likely to be resumed during this year." Later, when signs of a slowdown were unmistakable, he supported a small increase in highway spending. But basically no action was taken to counteract the recession, which ended in May 1954.[27]

Eisenhower confronted a second recession in August 1957. Again, there is no indication that he saw it coming. In July, Treasury Secretary George Humphrey told the Senate Finance Committee, "I don't see any significant recession or depression in the offing."[28] Although the administration did not put forward any specific antirecession legislation, neither did it oppose congressional efforts to act. Eventually, Eisenhower signed legislation increasing grants to states for highway construction and raising federal spending on rivers and harbor projects. The highway bill became law on April 16, 1958, and the rivers and harbors bill was signed on July 3. The recession ended in April.

An uptick in inflation in the late 1950s was alarming to Eisenhower, but Keynesians saw it as not much of a problem. Economist Franklyn Holzman probably expressed their commonly held view when he said, "The output effects of mild inflation are, of course, negligible and may even be positive."[29]

Moreover, a growing view among Keynesians was that prices were largely administered by big corporations, which charged pretty much whatever they could get away with. Consequently, macroeconomic policy was a very ineffective tool for moderating inflation. This was especially the case with monetary policy, which Keynesians tended to see purely in terms of the interest rate. They viewed this as essentially an administered price set by the Federal Reserve that was disconnected from the quantity of money, just as administered prices were set without regard to supply and demand. The only effect of raising interest rates, Keynesians argued, was to slow growth by reducing investment without doing anything meaningful to reduce inflation.[30]

KENNEDY GOES FOR GROWTH

In early 1960 Arthur Burns informed the White House that another recession was coming. Vice President Richard Nixon begged Eisenhower to take action. Nixon, the putative presidential nominee of the Republican Party that fall, knew too well how badly a weak economy could impact the election. Largely because of recessions, Republicans lost control of Congress in 1954 and relinquished a further 48 seats in the House and 12 in the Senate in 1958. Nevertheless, Eisenhower sided with those in his cabinet who did not share Burns's bearish forecast. In the end, however, Burns was right. A recession began in April and undoubtedly contributed to Nixon's defeat by John F. Kennedy in November.[31]

The recession was only one reason why Kennedy came into office determined to raise the economic growth rate as quickly as possible. At this point in the cold war there were many people convinced that the Soviet Union had found a better growth model. Economists widely believed that the Soviet economy was growing at least as rapidly and probably more rapidly than the U.S. economy even if one discounted the official Soviet data.[32] Unless the United States could clearly demonstrate the superiority of capitalism, some nations might be inclined to adopt socialism or communism in a mistaken belief that this was the best way to enrich their people.

Another problem was a growing fear of permanent job losses from automation, which Kennedy had often talked about during the 1960 campaign. As the computer age began to emerge there were many workers alarmed that their jobs would be taken over by machines and there would be nothing for them to do. This is an area where Keynesian economists were right on the mark. Kennedy's economic advisers assured him that automation was a non-problem and that adoption of the proper macroeconomic policies could maintain full employment regardless of how many jobs were lost due to automation. Growth would simply produce new jobs in new industries.[33]

Shortly after the election, Kennedy appointed an economic task force to advise him on what actions he should take to stimulate growth once he took office. Norman Ture was among the economists recruited for this effort and he drew heavily on the many JEC studies he had overseen during the previous five years. Among the task force recommendations was institution of an Investment Tax Credit, which Kennedy proposed in 1961 and was enacted by Congress the following year. It reduced the cost of new investments in capital equipment by seven percent.[34]

At the same time, Kennedy proposed a more conventionally Keynesian public works program. A key element was the Area Redevelopment Act, which directed federal aid to areas with high unemployment. It was signed on May 1, 1961, although the recession had ended in February. An assessment of the program found that 40 percent of its funds simply went to reimburse other government agencies. Almost any project undertaken in a depressed area was eligible for ARA funding even if it would have been undertaken anyway. Economist Sar Levitan found that 7,100 miles of roads in depressed areas were funded by ARA, but the Federal Highway Administration "could not point to a single mile of road which was constructed as a result of priorities accorded to depressed areas."[35]

In 1962, Congress passed further antirecession legislation in the form of the Accelerated Public Works program. Subsequent analysis showed that the peak employment created by it did not come until June 1964–39 months after the end of the recession. In fact, spending on this program was so drawn out that expenditures were still being made on projects as late as 1971.[36]

A General Accounting Office (now known as the Government Accountability Office) report found that the number of jobs created by the Area Redevelopment Administration, which administered both programs, was overstated by 128 percent. Another study found the number of jobs created was overstated by 94 percent. The GAO also found that only 55 percent of jobs created by the APW program went to workers living in the areas where the projects were located. Most of the jobs went to contractors' regular employees, not to locally unemployed persons.[37] Partially as a result of such criticism, Congress abolished the Area Redevelopment Administration in 1965.

KENNEDY AND KEYNES

Kennedy is often said to have been thoroughly Keynesian in his economic thinking. As John Kenneth Galbraith put it, "The policy in the Kennedy years was openly, unapologetically Keynesian." But this is clearly an overstatement. Kennedy often expressed sympathy for a balanced budget and in 1961 even suggested raising taxes to pay for a defense build-up before being talked out of it by his staff. He also tended to be very conservative when it came to international financial policy. Kennedy was deeply concerned about the balance of payments deficit and increasing demands for American gold by foreign countries.[38] This severely constrained his ability to push for growth-oriented policies.

Foreign exchange rates were more or less fixed at this time and changing them was difficult and painful. In the absence of exchange rate adjustment, a balance of payments deficit led to the outflow of gold as foreigners cashed in their excess dollars. But the price of gold was fixed at $35 per ounce, which led the United States to hemorrhage gold reserves, putting downward pressure on the dollar.

The fix for a balance of payments problem consisted of nothing but unpalatable options: higher interest rates to attract foreign capital would slow growth; trade protection to reduce the trade deficit would lead to foreign retaliation that would reduce U.S. exports, which would also reduce growth; capital controls to prevent money from leaving the country would be difficult to enforce and make trade more costly.[39]

The dilemma Kennedy faced in the early 1960s was how to raise growth, lower unemployment, reduce inflation, and stabilize the dollar simultaneously. His economic advisers told him this wasn't possible; that he needed to choose between raising growth and reducing unemployment, on the one hand, and price and exchange rate stability on the other. Only Galbraith, whom Kennedy appointed ambassador to India, said Kennedy could do both by imposing wage and price controls, thus permitting an expansive fiscal policy to stimulate growth without inflation.[40]

Kennedy's approach was to do a little bit of everything. Capital controls were imposed in the form of an interest equalization tax that discouraged foreign borrowing. Corporations, especially the steel industry, were browbeaten into holding down prices despite rising labor costs. Calls from liberals for new social programs were rebuffed, and the White House reluctantly supported the Federal Reserve when it raised interest rates.[41] While these measures were moderately successful, they clearly did not constitute a permanent solution and left the economy growing sluggishly, which threatened Kennedy's re-election in 1964.

Kennedy was therefore receptive when on August 6, 1962, Wilbur Mills, Democrat of Arkansas and chairman of the House Ways and Means Committee, suggested the idea of a permanent income tax cut rather than the temporary tax cut to ward off a recession that Kennedy had been contemplating. (At his press conference on June 7, 1962, Kennedy had requested authority for standby tax reduction authority that could be used "instantly and effectively should a new recession threaten to engulf us.") As Mills explained, "to give the economy this temporary injection, it may have some effect, but the minute that injection wears off, it's just like medicine." Kennedy liked the idea of a permanent tax cut, but was concerned that congressional conservatives wedded to the balanced budget would block him.[42]

The way Kennedy dealt with conservative opposition to a big tax cut that would unbalance the budget was by devising an unusually conservative tax plan. He knew that Keynesian economics operated through the budget deficit and it didn't matter that much whether the deficit increased due to higher spending or lower revenues. The only thing that mattered was the deficit, because that is what stimulated growth in the Keynesian model. So Kennedy's idea was to reduce the high World War II tax rates, which were still in effect and went as high as 91 percent. This appealed both to conservatives and liberal Keynesians.

Like Franklin D. Roosevelt, Kennedy also got conservatives to support increased defense outlays despite their general aversion to government spending. It greatly amused Galbraith that so many conservative businessmen would routinely rail against government spending and Keynesian economics without realizing how dependent they were on both. As he wrote in 1967, "Not for many years has any important business executive condemned the prodigality of expenditures on defense. From all pleas for public economy, defense expenditures are meticulously excluded.... Those who have thought it suspicious of Keynesian fiscal policy have failed to see how precisely it has identified and supported what is essential for that policy."[43]

Kennedy argued that a permanent tax rate reduction could provide a Keynesian boost to growth without stimulating inflation or endangering the dollar the way an equal rise in spending would. In other words, he believed that the same dollar increase in the deficit resulting from a permanent tax cut was less inflationary than an equal rise in the deficit resulting from an increase in spending. As Kennedy explained:

> The most direct and significant kind of federal action aiding economic growth is to make possible an increase in private consumption and investment demand—to cut the fetters which hold back private spending. In the past, this could be done in part by the increased use of credit and monetary tools, but our balance of payments situation today places limits on our use of those tools for expansion. It could also be done by increasing federal expenditures more rapidly than necessary, but such a course would soon demoralize both the government and our economy. If government is to retain the confidence of

the people, it must not spend more than can be justified on grounds of national need or spent with maximum efficiency.[44]

Kennedy also believed that a rise in spending resulting from higher defense outlays would be less inflationary than an equal rise in domestic spending. Thus, tax cuts and defense spending became the foundation of Kennedy's growth policy—just as they would under Ronald Reagan 20 years later.

INFLATION FESTERS

The emphasis on growth left the problem of inflation festering. Fortunately, the immediate problem of gold outflow moderated as the balance of payments improved. Moreover, when the cold war heated up after the Berlin crisis, Kennedy was able to convince America's allies to, in effect, finance its trade deficit as a way of helping share the burden of defense at a time when only the United States had the means to counter Soviet aggression. But this merely put off the day of reckoning by exporting inflation. As long as all major countries inflated simultaneously, exchange rates could remain fixed, thus avoiding a financial crisis.

At a theoretical level, American Keynesians were strongly influenced by a 1958 paper by British economist A. W. Phillips showing that, historically, the unemployment rate was closely correlated with the rate of change in money wages. When unemployment was low wages tended to rise faster and higher unemployment rates slowed the growth in wages.[45] This became known as the Phillips curve and it eventually evolved into the idea that there was a conceptually simple trade-off between inflation and unemployment—more of one would cure the other.

Key to advancing the Phillips curve thesis was a 1960 paper by two economists who both went on to win the Nobel Prize in economics, Paul A. Samuelson and Robert M. Solow. They hypothesized that wages overreacted to changes in prices and rose faster than justified by macroeconomic conditions, thus leading to cost-push inflation as workers demanded excessive wage increases and employers tried to stay ahead by raising prices more than necessary to keep pace with underlying inflationary forces.[46]

The Samuelson-Solow formulation was extremely important in making the Phillips curve operational in terms of policy. All policymakers had to do was figure out which problem, inflation or unemployment, was more serious and then apply the appropriate remedy. As Federal Reserve economist Thomas Humphrey explains, "By providing a ready-made justification for discretionary intervention and activist fine tuning, this interpretation helped make the Phillips curve immensely popular among Keynesian policy advisers."[47]

Almost immediately, some Keynesians recognized that the Phillips curve had no basis in anything Keynes said, and was in fact contrary to what he believed. In the words of economist Sydney Weintraub, "If unemployment is the answer to the inflation problem, then Keynesianism as a social philosophy is dead, literally interred by Keynesians and, curiously, all in the name of the mentor."[48]

A seminal event in unleashing inflation in the 1960s was the 1966 credit crunch. The Federal Reserve had become concerned about inflation and felt that it needed to raise interest rates to keep it in check. But Lyndon Johnson and his economic advisers were convinced that inflation was largely a fiscal problem and promised to raise taxes in return for an easier monetary policy.[49] The Johnson administration got a 10 percent income tax surcharge enacted and the Fed reduced interest rates. But inflation did not fall—it got worse, and heavily contributed to Richard Nixon's election in 1968.

Unfortunately, Nixon's economic advisers were also largely Keynesian in orientation and continued the Johnson administration's policy of maintaining high taxes and a loose monetary policy. The surtax was extended despite Nixon's promise to let it expire and the Federal Reserve, now chaired by Arthur Burns and under heavy White House pressure, kept monetary policy expansive even as inflation rose. But by 1971 inflation was so severe that Nixon was forced to impose comprehensive wage and price controls to keep it contained long enough for him to get reelected in 1972.[50]

It is in the nature of price controls that they break down after a short time. One reason is that basic commodities like oil and agricultural output can't really be controlled. And eventually the bureaucracy controlling prices simply ceases to be effective. By 1974 Nixon's price controls were breaking down rapidly, allowing pent-up inflation to explode.[51] At the same time, the most severe recession of the postwar era began. This is when Keynesian economists who had adopted the Phillips curve really lost credibility, because they said that a recession and the higher unemployment arising from it should bring down inflation rapidly. When inflation got worse, the Keynesians really had nothing to offer.

THE FAILURE OF COUNTERCYCLICAL POLICY

By the mid-1970s it was also clear that the Keynesian medicine was no longer working. A recession began in November 1973 and anti-recession legislation—a tax rebate—was enacted in March 1975, the very month that the recession officially ended. This $22.8 billion bill ($184 billion in today's economy) gave taxpayers a 10 percent rebate on their 1974 tax payments up to $200 per taxpayer ($1,700 today), payable in the second quarter of 1975. The legislation also extended unemployment benefits, increased the ITC from seven percent to 10 percent, and made various other tax changes. The purpose of the legislation was to pump up demand by putting dollars into peoples' pockets. However, most of the money was saved and thus had a negligible effect on spending.[52]

The following year, Congress believed that the aftereffects of the recession, especially on state and local governments, justified further antirecessionary action. Over Gerald Ford's veto, it enacted the Antirecession Fiscal Assistance Program in 1976. Also enacted was the Public Works Employment Act of 1976, which established the Local Public Works Program. The ARFA program increased revenue sharing to the states by $1.25 billion ($9.5 billion today) and the amount of aid was dependent on the local unemployment rate. The LPW program increased funding to state and local governments for public works projects by $2 billion ($15 billion today).

As late as 1977, Congress was still enacting legislation to deal with the aftermath of the recession. This came in the form of the Local Public Works Capital Development and Investment Act of 1976, which was passed early in the Carter administration. This legislation added another $4 billion ($26 billion today) to the LPW program. The ARFA program was also extended for another year and its funding increased by another $1.75 billion ($11 billion today).

Subsequent analysis showed that these programs utterly failed in their purpose. A Treasury Department study of the ARFA program found that because the funds were not disbursed until well after the end of the recession, the program failed to provide assistance when it was most needed, and probably contributed to inflationary pressures during the economic expansion. It also found that rather than spend the federal money immediately, state and local governments tended to save it. State and local government budget surpluses increased during this period, thereby mitigating the stimulative effect of the federal program. The GAO found that ARFA grants often went to governments not affected by the recession, and concluded that the program was not particularly effective as a countercyclical tool.[53]

The LPW program also was ineffective. Although the recession ended in March 1975, 20 percent of the expenditures occurred in 1977, 61 percent in 1978, 18 percent in 1979, and 1 percent in 1980. It was estimated that the cost per direct job created was $95,000 (over $300,000 today). Federal funds substituted for 25 percent to 30 percent of state and local funds that would have been spent anyway, and 9 percent of funds crowded out private expenditures that otherwise would have been made. Only 12 percent of workers on LPW projects were previously unemployed and half of them had been unemployed less than five weeks. The average job lasted just 2.6 months. Also, due to the Davis-Bacon Act, which requires prevailing (essentially union) wages be paid on federally-funded projects, some workers on LPW projects were paid more than they had previously received for the same work, thus reducing the number of jobs created per dollar of spending.[54]

The most severe criticism of the LPW program came from University of Michigan economist Edward Gramlich, who argued in 1978 that because it had no allocation formula, required no matching funds, and funded only projects that could be started within 90 days, it virtually guaranteed that the only projects funded were those that would have been built by state and local governments anyway. He further noted that since the Commerce Department received some $22 billion worth of project applications for just $2 billion in federal funds, this suggested that the LPW program had postponed $22 billion worth of construction spending, thus reducing GNP by $30 billion ($195 billion today). Consequently, rather than stimulating the economy, the LPW program actually was contractionary.[55]

Despite the fact that the first phase of the LPW program, which was enacted in mid-1976, had yet to create any jobs at all six months later, one of Jimmy Carter's first actions upon taking office in 1977 was to push for an expansion of the program. The CBO argued that it would have no impact on the economy for at least a year, but this had no effect on Carter's thinking. The legislation was signed on May 13, 1977.[56]

Another recession occurred in 1980 as the result of Carter's ill-considered imposition of credit controls. Although it was over by midyear, after the controls were lifted, Carter asked for more money for public works to deal with the recession. It was then revealed that some $100 billion ($500 billion today) was already available for public works from previous programs—50 times more than he was asking for. According to analyst Pat Choate, these projects were being held up by a combination of incompetence at the state and local level and federal regulations that made it difficult to get money released.[57]

Despite its general aversion to government spending, even the Reagan administration adopted two programs specifically designed to attack the recession that began in July 1981 and ended in November 1982. The first was the Surface Transportation Assistance Act of 1982, which raised the gasoline tax by five cents and increased spending for highways and mass transit by $33.5 billion over five years ($136 billion today). The second was the Emergency Jobs Act, which increased spending by $9 billion ($37 billion today) for 77 different programs.

Reagan predicted that the transportation bill would create 320,000 jobs. But it actually created far fewer. Employment in highway construction increased less than total employment in the year following passage of the legislation, but wages for highway construction workers rose sharply.[58]

Interestingly, at the very time Reagan was pressing hard for passage of the transportation bill as a jobs program, his Office of Management and Budget was producing a study showing that increased federal aid for public works actually caused an overall reduction in public works because it led state and local governments to cut back on their own public works spending. Of course, these and other studies showing the perverse effects of such jobs programs did nothing to even slow down passage, because both Congress and the administration were under irresistible political pressure to appear to be doing something about the recession even though it ended in November 1982, before the transportation bill was signed into law and long before any spending resulted from it.[59]

The ink was barely dry on the transportation bill when Congress pressed ahead with the Emergency Jobs Act of 1983. This bill was basically a grab bag of miscellaneous pork barrel projects that Congress slapped together in the name of job creation. Most of the projects funded just happened to be in the congressional districts of members of the House and Senate Appropriations Committees. Six months later, there was little evidence that the bill had created any jobs whatsoever. Almost a year later, there was still no evidence.[60]

A GAO study of the Emergency Jobs bill was highly critical. It noted that the legislation was not passed until 21 months after the beginning of the recession. As of June 1984, a year and a half after its enactment, only one third of the appropriated funds had been spent. And as late as June 1985, half of the funds had still not been spent. The peak number of jobs created came in June 1984 and constituted just one percent of the total private jobs created since passage of the bill. Only about a third of jobs went to the unemployed.[61]

LONG-TERM CONSEQUENCES

If these antirecession programs simply wasted money, it would be bad enough. But there is strong evidence that they may actually have been harmful to the economy, especially in the long run. Among the reasons economists have identified are these:

- As builders and suppliers for public works become accustomed to the government enacting countercyclical programs, they tend to underinvest during upturns, thus adding to inflation and the cost of public works.[62]
- Even very small lags in the implementation of countercyclical programs are highly destabilizing, and the larger the lag, the greater the destabilization. In short, the effort to moderate recessions may increase the depth and frequency of recessions.[63]
- Public works programs may artificially stimulate demand for particular goods and services, thus delaying the readjustment process that ultimately ends recessions.[64]
- Countercyclical policies add to inflationary pressures during upturns, thus setting the stage for future recessions. Because of the inability to correctly forecast cyclical turning points, and thereby to target fiscal stimulus properly, and because of the consequent lags in implementation, the stimulus comes during economic upturns.[65]
- Countercyclical programs may slow growth because they lead to higher taxes or deficits. Higher taxes reduce incentives and consumer spending, while deficits may create crowding-out in financial markets by preempting private borrowers and raising interest rates.[66]

While few economists would say that governments should never take action against recessions, especially deep ones, it is clear that the fundamental barriers to effective implementation of countercyclical programs are the lag in perceiving a downturn and getting programs executed in a timely manner. Such lags result partially from forecast errors—the failure of economists to accurately predict cyclical turning points is overwhelming. They also result from the slow pace of Congress in enacting antirecession legislation.[67] In the words of a 1997 *New York Times* editorial, "Congress is always slow to recognize downturns and never nimble enough to react in time."[68] (Appendix I illustrates this problem graphically.)

Most importantly, it simply takes a long time, often years, to design, plan, contract for, and actually begin building major public works projects. This was true even during the Roosevelt administration, which was frequently praised for using public works to reduce unemployment. As a result, public works spending throughout the postwar era has consistently been procyclical—worsening rather than moderating business cycles.[69]

Another fundamental problem is that the federal government must necessarily funnel public works expenditures through state and local governments. In the short run, virtually 100 percent of such outlays simply enable state and local governments to build up budget surpluses.[70] Funds not spent, of course, cannot be stimulative in the Keynesian model. An even more serious problem, however, is the substitution effect between federal and state and local expenditures: federal aid tends to displace state and local spending that would otherwise have occurred. Thus, the effectiveness of federal spending in increasing the aggregate amount of public works spending and jobs is seriously compromised.

Numerous studies have been done on the substitution effect of federal public works and jobs programs. They typically find long-term substitution rates of 60 percent to 100 percent.[71] The latter figure means that no net jobs at all are created. Moreover, federal aid seldom reduces unemployment in areas where public works projects are located because contractors bidding on such projects may not be from the local area and will bring their own workers with them. Only about 30 percent of all jobs created by a public works project will be generated in the local area where it is located.[72]

Even Keynes himself recognized the limitations of counter-cyclical policy. Toward the end of his life he said, "Organized public works...may be the right cure for a chronic tendency to a deficiency of effective demand. But they are not capable of sufficiently rapid organization (and above all cannot be reversed or undone at a later date), to be the most serviceable instrument for the prevention of the trade cycle."[73] The postwar U.S. experience is ample confirmation of this conclusion.

THE 2009 STIMULUS BILL

As Congress debated the Obama administration's stimulus bill in early 2009, it was clear that it had many of the same problems that previous countercyclical programs had suffered from: state and local government cutbacks in anticipation of federal funds, the timeliness of projects, the lag time created by procedures, and the effectiveness of funds in creating jobs in localities hit hard with high unemployment.

- There was evidence that state and local governments cut back on their own public works projects as soon as it appeared that the federal government might fund them. As the *New York Times* reported in December: "California and other states are clearly holding out hope that President-elect Barack Obama will pump some federal money into the stalled infrastructure projects, and some may even be delaying work until they have a chance to make the case for federal spending." In the state of New York alone, $42 billion worth of state construction projects were put on hold as localities bid for $4 billion in federal aid.[74]
- Questions were raised about whether stimulus spending could come online quickly enough to make a meaningful difference in moderating the downturn or whether it would impact well after the economy had recovered on its own. According to the CBO, only 21 percent of the

stimulus bill's spending would be effective in 2009, with much coming online as late as 2013.[75]

- Although many public works projects were said to be "shovel ready," needing only a government check to begin construction, in fact this was not the case. It took considerable time to advertise for contracts, collect bids, choose a contractor, and get work underway. Typically, it takes at least three months from the day that funds are received to the start of simple projects such as road paving; more complex projects take much longer. The CBO estimates that only 27 percent of highway funds are normally spent in the year in which they are received. And pushing forward projects hastily virtually ensured that there would be more than the usual amount of waste.[76]

- There was little evidence that stimulus funds flowed to where unemployment was the highest. According to an analysis by Propublica, an investigative journalism group, the top three states in terms of receiving infrastructure funds per unemployed worker were Wyoming, North Dakota, and South Dakota—each having an unemployment rate just over 3 percent.[77] The national unemployment rate was almost three times higher.

The Obama administration estimated that 3.7 million jobs would be created by its stimulus by 2010. Yet even those supporting the stimulus plan expressed doubt that the impact would be so large. The CBO concluded that the administration's estimates could only be achieved under its most optimistic scenario.[78]

CHAPTER 4

THE CONSERVATIVE COUNTERREVOLUTION

Keynesian economics reached the pinnacle of its influence on policy in the early 1960s, when John F. Kennedy appointed prominent Keynesians such as Walter Heller and James Tobin as his economic advisers and promoted a big tax cut in 1963 on Keynesian grounds. On December 31, 1965, John Maynard Keynes appeared on the cover of *Time* magazine even though he had been dead for more than 20 years.

But a counterrevolution was already underway. Centered at the University of Chicago, its leaders were Milton Friedman and Robert Mundell, both of whom would receive the Nobel Prize in economics. Their work complemented each other's. Friedman was mainly interested in domestic monetary policy and microeconomics; Mundell was primarily concerned with international economics and fiscal policy. Between the two of them they pretty well covered the economic waterfront.

One weakness of Keynesian theory in the 1960s was that its adherents had forgotten that fiscal policy was a means to an end—the end being the injection of additional liquidity into the economy to counter a deflation. But 30 years after Keynes put forward his theory, his followers had come to believe that an expansive fiscal policy was sufficient to stimulate growth on its own. The essential connection to monetary policy was largely lost among the Keynesians. The popularity of the Phillips curve as an explanation for inflation reinforced the de-emphasis of monetary policy.

To Keynesians, the key economic variable was the federal budget deficit. It didn't really matter very much whether a deficit arose due to lower revenues or higher spending, they thought. A deficit resulting from a tax cut was just as good as a deficit caused by an increase in spending. Another consequence of this exclusive focus on the deficit was that economists paid little attention to the structure of taxation or spending. As noted in the previous chapter, spending on national defense was just as stimulative as spending on social welfare in the Keynesian model.

But when inflation and unemployment began rising simultaneously in the 1970s, the Keynesians had little to offer except wage and price controls, which failed drastically when instituted by Richard Nixon in 1971. It took a refocus on monetary policy, which Friedman was highly successful in doing, to get at the root of the inflation problem. But monetarism had little to say about growth. That component was added by Mundell, who argued for tax rate reductions to accompany tight money. By increasing the incentive to produce, lower rates would simultaneously reduce unemployment and inflation.

By the late 1970s Republican politicians fully endorsed the idea of tight money to combat inflation and tax cuts to raise growth and reduce unemployment, which came to be called supply-side economics. Still under the influence of Keynesian economics, Democrats strenuously resisted both prongs of this emerging economic program. They saw tight money as ineffective against inflation and highly detrimental to growth because it would raise interest rates, while tax rate reductions would aggravate inflation and be only modestly stimulative to growth. Having tight money and tax cuts at the same time was like putting one's foot on a car's brake and gas pedal at the same time, most

Keynesians thought. As economist William Nordhaus of Yale put it in 1981, "I know of no economic theory that says you can suppress money growth to fight inflation and simultaneously use fiscal policy to spur growth."[1]

But lacking a coherent cure for the twin problems of slow growth and inflation, dubbed "stagflation," the Keynesians lost the argument by default. The monetarists and supply-siders slowly gained influence and a powerful advocate in Ronald Reagan. Upon taking office in 1981, he encouraged the Federal Reserve to maintain a tight money policy even in the face of the severe recession that began late that year.[2] Reagan was also able to overcome powerful resistance to an across-the-board tax rate reduction and got it enacted into law in August 1981.

Although many analysts continue to insist that an alternative policy mix might have worked better, the rapid decline of inflation and unemployment in the 1980s was widely viewed as vindication of conservative economics, just as the end of the Great Depression during World War II was taken as confirmation of Keynesian economics.

MONETARISM

The pinnacle of Keynesian economics—the moment when it reached its highest point of influence before beginning a precipitous fall—can be dated precisely. It came on January 6, 1971. On that day Richard Nixon was taping an interview with Howard K. Smith of ABC News. In an offhand comment after the end of the interview, Nixon mentioned in passing that he was "now a Keynesian in economics." Smith was struck by the statement because Republicans had historically been unrelentingly hostile to Keynesian economics and deficit spending. To Smith, Nixon's conversion to Keynesianism was equivalent to a Christian saying, "All things considered, I think [Islam founder] Mohammad was right."[3]

Ironically, just one week before Nixon's interview, economist Harry Johnson had given the prestigious Richard T. Ely Lecture to the American Economic Association in which he warned that the Keynesians' inability to deal with the growing problem of inflation was making it vulnerable to a counterrevolution from monetarism.[4] The monetarists, led principally by Friedman, argued that inflation was almost purely a monetary problem having little, if anything, to do with budget deficits, unemployment, or economic rigidities, as the Keynesians supposed.

In his memoirs, Friedman says he was a conventional Keynesian until after World War II. It's not clear at what point monetary policy became his central interest, but certainly there was a long tradition of emphasis on that subject at the University of Chicago dating back at least to the work of J. Laurence Laughlin, who had been deeply involved in creation of the Federal Reserve System. Being somewhat isolated from the hotbeds of Keynesian thinking in Cambridge, Massachusetts, and Washington, D.C., undoubtedly made it easier to chart a different path. But at the same time, there was less resistance to some of the basic concepts of Keynesian economics in Chicago than is generally believed.[5]

After publication of Friedman's 1962 book, *Capitalism and Freedom,* he became closely aligned with the Republican Party and was an adviser to Barry Goldwater's campaign in 1964.[6] Friedman soon became the dominant figure in developing the Republican Party's economic policy for the next three decades. Publication of his *Monetary History of the United States* in 1963 cemented Friedman's reputation as the leading monetary economist in the country. He was often called upon to testify before congressional committees on the subject and Friedman was frequently quoted in the national media.

Like Keynes, to whom he is often compared, Friedman was no ivory tower academic. After publication of the *Monetary History,* his work increasingly turned away from scientific pursuits to more popular venues, including a column in *Newsweek* magazine and an extremely popular television series called "Free to Choose" in 1980.

The core of Friedman's technical work in the late 1960s and early 1970s was refutation of the Phillips curve as neither an adequate explanation for inflation nor an effective policy response to it. Inflation, he argued, had almost nothing to do with unemployment or anything other than excessive money growth by the Federal Reserve. To the extent that there was any trade-off between inflation and unemployment, it was purely temporary. Over time inflation actually raised unemployment by creating malinvestment and economic misallocations.[7]

It's probably fair to say that the manifest failure of the Keynesians to deal with the growing problem of inflation had more to do with Friedman's ultimate success than the power of his ideas. In a sense, he won by default. The last gasp of the Keynesians was enactment of a surtax in 1968 to sop up excess purchasing power. Monetarists like Friedman argued that this wouldn't work because it didn't get at the monetary roots of inflation. Indeed, because monetary policy remained loose, they predicted that inflation would worsen. When it did, Friedman gained enormous credibility.[8]

Ironically, Nixon's embrace of Keynesian economics seems to have been a factor causing some liberal economists to reexamine their support for it. In 1973 economist Melville J. Ulmer was forced to admit that "the economic strategy of the Nixon administration is more or less pure Keynesian...the same as that endorsed by the Democratic Party." Therefore, the failure of Keynesian economics to achieve full employment without inflation could not be blamed on an unwillingness of politicians to fully implement it. This must mean that Keynesian economics was inherently flawed, Ulmer concluded.[9]

By 1976 Friedman's ideas were so well accepted that he was awarded the Nobel Prize in economics. In his presidential address to the American Economic Association that year, economist Franco Modigliani, a prominent Keynesian who would win the Nobel Prize in 1985, waved the white flag of surrender. "We are all monetarists," he declared.[10]

SUPPLY-SIDE ECONOMICS

Although monetarism explained inflation, it didn't have much to say about stimulating growth. Adding a growth component to monetarism was the principal contribution of Mundell. He believed that inflation reduced growth mainly through its interaction with the tax system. Workers receiving pay increases were pushed up into higher tax brackets, even though they might not have received any real increase in purchasing power; corporations found that depreciation allowances based on historical cost were inadequate to replace old equipment while taxes were assessed on illusory inventory profits; and investors found that much of their capital gains simply represented inflation but were taxed as if they were real.[11] For example, in 1977 investors paid taxes on $5.7 billion of nominal gains on sales of corporate stock, but when adjusted for inflation this gain was actually a $3.5 billion loss.[12]

A two-pronged strategy was therefore needed to end stagflation, Mundell said. First, money growth needed to be sharply tightened, preferably by targeting the price of gold—when the price of gold rose, it would be a signal to the Fed to tighten. Thus, Mundell's views on monetary policy dovetailed with Friedman's, although Friedman thought that any linkage to gold was archaic and inefficient.[13] Second, tax rates needed to be cut in order to restore incentives and increase the demand for money. Although Friedman had no problem with cutting taxes, this was never a focus of his academic research. Mundell first spelled out this tight-money-and-tax-cuts policy mix in a 1971 paper published by Princeton's International Finance Section:

> Monetary expansion stimulates nominal *money* demand for goods, but, without rigidities or illusions to bite on, it does not lead to real expansion. But growth of *real* output raises real money demand and thus abets the absorption of real monetary expansion into the economy without inflation. Tax reduction increases employment and growth and this raises the demand for money and hence enables the Federal Reserve to supply additional real money balances to the economy without causing sagging interest rates associated with conditions of loose money. Monetary acceleration is inflationary, but tax reduction is expansionary when there is unemployment.[14]

At this time, Arthur Laffer was teaching at the University of Chicago business school, where he came to know Mundell's work.

Their mutual interest in international monetary issues brought them together and Laffer absorbed Mundell's ideas. In 1974 Laffer organized a conference sponsored by the American Enterprise Institute on the problem of worldwide inflation.[15] This was the first opportunity many Washington policymakers had to hear about what came to be called supply-side economics.

Although most of the AEI conference dealt with monetary issues, Mundell reiterated the point made in his 1971 paper about the vital role of tax cuts in the fight against inflation. This was important because of the widespread view that budget deficits caused inflation. Indeed, few now recall that when Representative Jack Kemp first began pushing for big tax cuts in the late 1970s, the principal attack against him was such a policy would be massively inflationary because it would increase the deficit.[16]

Jude Wanniski, then an editorial writer for the *Wall Street Journal,* attended the AEI conference and was fascinated by the discussion. He immediately wrote an article for the *Journal* explaining the Laffer-Mundell world view. This article is probably what led to Mundell's invitation to a White House conference on December 19, 1974, at which he argued for a tight monetary policy to fight inflation and a big tax cut to stimulate growth.[17]

That same month, Wanniski set up a meeting with Donald Rumsfeld, White House chief of staff, and his deputy, Dick Cheney, at which Laffer drew on a napkin his famous curve for the first time. Unfortunately, Gerald Ford and his economic advisers rejected a tax rate reduction, opting instead for a one-shot tax rebate.[18]

Wanniski expanded his Mundell-Laffer analysis in a 1975 article for *The Public Interest,* a quasi-academic journal edited by Irving Kristol. Interestingly, Wanniski's discussion of the tax side of their work appeared only in a footnote. This was the first published statement of Laffer's famous curve, which shows that tax rate cuts could theoretically increase government revenue. As Wanniski wrote:

> Taxes should be cut and government spending maintained through
> deficit financing only when a special condition exists, a condition

Mundell and Laffer say exists now. "There are always two tax rates that produce the same dollar revenues," says Laffer. "For example, when taxes are zero, revenues are zero. When taxes are 100 percent, there is no production, and revenues are also zero. In between these extremes there is one rate that maximizes government revenues." Any higher tax rate reduces total output and the tax base, and becomes counterproductive even for producing revenues. U.S. marginal tax rates are now, they argue, in this unproductive range and the economy is being "choked, asphyxiated by taxes," says Mundell. Tax rates have been put up inadvertently by the impact of inflation on all the progressivity of the tax structure. If the tax rate were below the rate that maximizes revenues, tax cuts would reduce tax revenues at full employment. But a multiplier effect operates if the economy is at less than full employment, and the tax cut then raises output and the tax base, besides making the economy more efficient. Even if a bigger deficit emerges, sufficient tax revenues will be recovered to pay the interest on the government bonds issued to finance the deficit. Thus, future taxes would not have to be raised and there would be no subtraction from future output. Tax cuts, therefore, actually can provide a means for servicing the public debt.[19]

Wanniski later wrote the first book about supply-side economics, *The Way the World Works* (1978). He also wrote many unsigned editorials for the *Wall Street Journal* spelling out various aspects of supply-side theory and helped supply-siders such as Laffer and Paul Craig Roberts get published in the *Journal,* thereby raising their visibility and stature as economic commentators.[20] Indeed, when Wanniski left the *Journal* in 1978 to found a private consulting firm called Polyconomics, where I later went to work, Roberts was hired by the *Journal* to replace him on the editorial page staff.

Wanniski was responsible for converting Kristol and Bob Bartley, editorial page editor of the *Wall Street Journal,* to supply-side economics. By his own admission, Kristol knew almost nothing about economics at the time. But he saw the political potential of supply-side economics to refocus the Republican Party's economic thinking away from stability and toward growth. Upon his retirement, Bartley cited his support for supply-side economics as among his greatest accomplishments.[21]

THE DEATH OF KEYNESIAN ECONOMICS

By the mid-1970s, inflation had created an economic crisis throughout the West. Even those on the political left were forced to admit that Keynesian economics offered no way out from the twin problems of rising prices and slow growth. Whatever was done to cure one problem would only make the other worse. The idea that inflation caused unemployment, rather than curing it as the Phillips curve posited, became widespread both among economists and policymakers. In July 1976 Johannes Witteveen, managing director of the International Monetary Fund, spoke for many when he said, "There seems to have developed of late such an unusual sensitivity to inflation that an acceleration in the rate of price increase in all likelihood would have significant adverse effects on demand, production and employment."[22]

Soon after, British Prime Minister James Callaghan of the Labor Party eloquently expressed his frustration with the lack of options presented by Keynesian economic thinking. In a September 28, 1976, speech to a party conference, Callahan said:

> We used to think that you could just spend your way out of a recession and increase employment by cutting taxes and raising government spending. I tell you, in all candor, that that option no longer exists and that it only worked on each occasion since the war by injecting bigger doses of inflation into the economy, followed by higher levels of unemployment as the next step.[23]

A few months later, German Chancellor Helmut Schmidt of the Social Democratic Party declared that "the time for Keynesian ideas is past because the problem of the world today is inflation." By the end of 1977, the popular media had proclaimed the death of Keynes.[24]

Increasingly, academic economists followed suit. A 1978 article in the *Journal of Economic Literature,* a publication of the American

Economic Association that tries to reflect the consensus view of the profession, said, "There appears to be no long-run trade-off between inflation and unemployment."[25] This marked the death of the Phillips curve among professional economists.

It also marked the death of Keynesian economics. "By about 1980, it was hard to find an American academic macroeconomist under the age of 40 who professed to be a Keynesian," economist Alan Blinder of Princeton later wrote.[26]

Writing in *The Public Interest* in 1981, Martin Feldstein of Harvard said that while Keynesian ideas may have worked in the 1930s, "it has become very clear that those ideas were not appropriate for the U.S. economy of the 1960s and 1970s when they achieved their greatest acceptance and influence."[27]

Speaking to the annual meeting of the American Economic Association that same year, Edmund Phelps of Columbia, winner of the Nobel Prize in 2006, said that while Keynesian economics might one day be reborn, "for now, the old Keynesian notion of fiscal stimulus is so beset by doubts that fiscal policy, if not truly incapacitated, is in a deactivated state."[28]

CAPITAL GAINS AND REVENUE ESTIMATING

In the midst of these developments, an important legislative fight took place that highlighted both the weakness of the Keynesian approach to fiscal policy and the failure of standard revenue-estimating methods to account for the supply-side effects of tax changes. It involved a cut in the long-term capital gains tax rate.

The roots of the capital gains controversy dated back to 1969, when the maximum long-term tax rate on capital gains was increased to 35 percent from 25 percent. On April 13, 1978, Representative William Steiger, Republican of Wisconsin, introduced legislation to return the top rate to 25 percent. The ensuing debate was extremely important to the development of supply-side economics for two reasons. First, a number of highly respected economists such as Feldstein argued vigorously that a cut in the capital gains tax rate would almost immediately recoup the static revenue loss through a combination of unlocking and increased investment. Second, the obvious expansionary potential of a capital gains tax cut clearly illustrated the supply-side argument that tax rate cuts could be stimulative by increasing incentives without any Keynesian impact on disposable income. Thus the 1978 capital gains debate was seminal in the development and acceptance of supply-side theories by mainstream economists.[29]

Of course, the idea that cutting the capital gains tax might not reduce federal revenue was not a new one. It had been long recognized that capital gains are a unique form of income because taxpayers have the freedom to decide when and whether to realize gains for tax purposes. When rates are high they encourage a lock-in effect that reduces revenues as investors hold on to potentially taxable gains. Therefore, a rate reduction might result in a rapid unlocking of past gains that could cause revenue to rise quickly.[30]

Feldstein was outspoken in his conviction that the Steiger bill would increase federal revenue almost immediately and testified before Congress to that effect. The basis for his testimony was a National Bureau of Economic Research paper that circulated on Capitol Hill in June 1978. Other prominent economists forecasting higher revenues from the Steiger bill included Gary Ciminero of Merrill Lynch Economics and Michael Evans of Chase Econometrics. Although the Steiger bill was officially scored as a revenue-loser, after it was enacted into law in 1978 the Joint Committee on Taxation (JCT) conceded that the bill would probably raise revenue, which was confirmed by subsequent research.[31]

The capital gains proposal set off a fierce debate over how to estimate the revenue effects of changes in tax policy that was critical to advancing supply-side economics and undermining Keynesian economics. The focus of the debate was on the mathematical models used by economists to forecast the economy. These models were often used to evaluate public policies and almost universally had Keynesian underpinnings. This tended to bias public policy in favor of Keynesian policies long after they were generally discredited.[32]

This was especially a problem after enactment of the Budget Act of 1974 because no tax bill could even be considered in Congress unless there was provision for it in the annual budget resolution. This meant that Congress needed to know in advance the precise revenue loss expected from a tax cut before it could be voted upon. Although revenue estimates had been done for many years previously, they had never been an essential requirement for consideration of tax legislation.

Revenue estimates for Congress are done by the JCT, although Treasury estimates were often sufficient for its needs.[33] These estimates were usually made by accountants for one or two years out. But by the 1970s, economists had replaced the accountants and computers started to be used in lieu of adding machines. Moreover, the budget act generally required five-year revenue estimates, which increased the need for economic forecasts on which to base the estimates.

These forecasts were prepared by the Congressional Budget Office and generally did not incorporate any macroeconomic effects from tax changes. The JCT revenue estimate was largely a function of the CBO baseline forecast. Nor did the JCT incorporate behavioral effects in its revenue estimates. The effect of holding economic variables constant regardless of the magnitude of a proposed tax change sometimes led to absurd results. For example, Senator Bob Packwood, Republican of Oregon and former chairman of the Senate Finance Committee, once asked the JCT how much revenue would be raised by a 100 percent tax rate on all incomes over $200,000. The JCT reported that it would raise $204 billion in 1990, $232 billion in 1991, $263 billion in 1992, and $299 billion in 1993.[34] Of course, the true revenue yield would have been zero since no one would have realized any taxable income over $200,000 if they couldn't keep any of it.

Supply-siders argued that if a tax cut raised GDP, then the base of taxation would be larger, thus recouping some of the revenue lost from the rate cut. Conversely, a tax increase might reduce GDP, thereby reducing the revenue potential. In other words, a 10 percent tax rate cut might only reduce revenues by 6 or 7 percent, and a 10 percent tax rate increase might only raise revenues by 6 or 7 percent.

CBO's forecasts relied on commercial econometric models, such as those of Data Resources, Inc. (DRI), Wharton Econometric Forecasting Associates (WEFA), and Chase Econometrics. Largely based on Keynesian assumptions, these models tended to make the budgetary cost of tax cuts high relative to equivalent government spending programs and thereby biased the legislative process in favor of temporary tax cuts designed to stimulate consumption and against supply-side tax cuts such as marginal tax rate reductions.

An example of how this worked in practice can be seen in one of the CBO's earliest studies, which looked at various fiscal options for reducing unemployment. Because of the Keynesian underpinnings used to evaluate the alternatives—spending drives growth in the Keynesian model while saving is a drag on it—increased government spending appeared preferable to tax cuts. Direct spending created more jobs per $1 billion increase in the deficit than tax cuts because all of the former was assumed to be spent while some of the latter was saved. In political terms, therefore, supply-side tax cuts were at a disadvantage compared with Keynesian-style public service jobs programs. Permanent tax rate reductions were also deemed more costly and less effective than temporary tax rebates.[35]

BUDGET PROCESS OPPORTUNITY

Paul Craig Roberts was the first supply-sider to recognize that the breakdown of the Keynesian system and institution of the new congressional budget process created an opportunity to promote the supply-side approach to fiscal policy.[36] Given the constraints of the econometric models and the budget process, it suddenly became very important to be able to show that certain types of tax cuts did not increase the deficit as much as direct spending programs.

Traditional tax-writers, such as Senator Russell Long, Democrat of Louisiana and Senate Finance Committee chairman, now found themselves at a disadvantage relative to the appropriators. The CBO gave spending programs the benefit of a Keynesian multiplier in calculating their economic effects. But tax cuts were calculated by the JCT on a static basis, as if they had no economic impact on growth or incentives.

Long was no supply-sider, but he had been around a long time and seen a lot of tax changes and their effects at close hand. His experience told him that there was something to the supply-side argument that tax cuts would not lose as much revenue as static forecasts said they would. During a 1977 hearing, Long had this to say:

> Revenue estimates have a way of being very, very far off base because of the failure to anticipate everything that happens. . . . Now, when we put the Investment Tax Credit on, we estimated that we were going to lose about $5 billion. . . . Instead of losing money, revenues went up in corporate income tax collections. Then we thought it was overheating the economy. We repealed it. We thought that the government would take in more money. But instead of making $5 billion, we lost $5 billion. Then, after a while, we thought we made a mistake, so we put it back on again. Instead of losing us money, it made us money. Then, after a while, we repealed it again and it did just exactly the opposite from what it was estimated to do again by about the same amount. It seems to me, if we take all factors into account, we wind up with the conclusion that taking the Investment Tax Credit alone and looking at it by itself, it is not costing us any money. Because the impression I gain from it is that it stimulates the economy to the extent, and brings about additional investment to the extent, that it makes us money rather than loses us money.[37]

Long commissioned Michael Evans, an experienced econometric modeler, to build a supply-side model for the Senate Finance Committee. By the time Evans finished his work, however, control of the committee had shifted to the Republicans and Senator Bob Dole of Kansas became its chairman. Bob Lighthizer, the new chief of staff of the Finance Committee, told me personally that he had no interest in the project because it originated on the Democrats' watch. When I asked Evans himself what happened to the model, he wrote me to say that he made one copy, sent it to the Finance Committee in fulfillment of his contract, and had no other copies.[38]

Economists associated with the rational expectations school played a part as well in undermining the foundations of Keynesian economics. From the point of view of supply-siders, a key element of their critique related to econometric models. They argued that people learn from policy changes and thus change their behavior accordingly. People may react to a policy one way the first time and differently the second time. Interestingly, Keynes basically agreed with this idea.[39]

SUPPLY-SIDE ECONOMICS IN CONGRESS

It was in this atmosphere that Kemp and Senator William Roth, Republican of Delaware, introduced the legislation that defined supply-side economics. It grew out of Kemp's desire to duplicate the Kennedy tax cut by having a pure, across-the-board individual income tax rate reduction, without the many corporate provisions that had been the central features of his earlier tax efforts.

Kemp was already drawing parallels to his early tax proposals—such as the business-oriented Jobs Creation Act—with John F. Kennedy's legislation when I joined his staff in 1976. Norman Ture was a Kemp adviser and an important link to the Kennedy experience because he had worked for Wilbur Mills, who chaired the House Ways and Means Committee during the time of the Kennedy tax cut.

In August 1976 Kemp received data from the Congressional Research Service on the estimated revenue loss from the Kennedy tax cut.[40] By comparing these revenue loss figures with actual revenue collections from the 1960s, Kemp concluded that the Kennedy tax cut increased federal revenue. His point was more of an assertion than hard evidence since he had no data on what aggregate revenues were expected to be in the absence of the Kennedy tax cut. Interestingly, however, Walter Heller, who chaired Kennedy's Council of Economic Advisers, soon made the case for him. In testimony before the Joint Economic Committee on February 7, 1977, he was asked by Senator Jacob Javits, Republican of New York, to comment on Kemp's analysis of the CRS memo. I was in the hearing room when Heller responded:

> What happened to the tax cut in 1965 is difficult to pin down, but insofar as we are able to isolate it, it did seem to have a tremendously stimulative effect, a multiplied effect on the economy. It was the major factor that led to our running a $3 billion surplus by the middle of 1965, before escalation in Vietnam struck us. It was a $12 billion tax cut, which would be about $33 or $34 billion in today's terms. And within one year the revenues into the Federal Treasury were already above what they had been before the tax cut.... Did it pay for itself in increased revenues? I think the evidence is very strong that it did.[41]

Heller was later embarrassed to have provided the supply-siders with the proof they lacked and tried to take it back.[42] But as a witness to the event, I had no reason to think he was not stating a sincere belief. Indeed, a review of statements by Kennedy, his advisers and his supporters at the time clearly indicates they expected the tax cut would in fact raise federal revenue. As Kennedy said in his Economic Club of New York speech on December 14, 1962, "It is a paradoxical truth that tax rates are too high today and revenues are too low, and the soundest way to raise the revenues in the long run is to cut the rates now."

During floor debate on September 24, 1963, Wilbur Mills, manager of the Kennedy tax cut in the House of Representatives, said, "There is no doubt in my mind that this tax reduction bill, in and of itself, can bring about an increase in the gross national product of approximately $50 billion in the next few years [$350 billion today]. If it does, these lower rates of taxation will bring in at least $12 billion in additional revenue [$84 billion today]."[43]

Contemporary analyses by the CEA and economists Arthur Okun and Lawrence Klein show that Mills was definitely in the ballpark with his estimate.[44] Once the impact of the Kennedy tax cut became a political issue in the late 1970s, further analyses were undertaken. DRI and WEFA were contracted to study the impact of the

Kennedy tax cut.[45] After reviewing these studies, the CBO drew the following conclusion:

> The effect of the 1964 tax cut on the federal deficit has been a matter of controversy.... The direct effect of the tax cut was to reduce revenues by some $12 billion (annual rate) after the initial buildup. The increase in output and later in prices produced by the tax cut, according to the models, recaptured $3 to $9 billion of this revenue at the end of two years. The result was a net increase in the federal deficit of only about 25 to 75 percent of the full $12 billion.[46]

Thus, while the Kennedy tax cut may not have paid for itself immediately, there is overwhelming evidence that the federal government did not lose nearly as much revenue as expected, owing to the expansionary effect of the tax cut on the economy.[47]

The real importance of the feedback argument had to do with how much additional federal borrowing was necessitated by tax cuts. If they led to higher interest rates, it would be plausible to argue that this could offset much of the beneficial impact of tax cuts on incentives. In this respect, it is also important to know whether a tax cut increased private saving. If saving expands, it is reasonable to include this in revenue feedback estimates.

In a 1981 study for the Federal Reserve Bank of San Francisco, economist Paul Evans concluded that the Kennedy tax cut actually raised saving by more than the total amount of the tax cut. That is, households saved more than 100 percent of the tax cut. Therefore, the Kennedy tax cut could not put upward pressure on interest rates due to an increase in the federal budget deficit. Supply-siders often made this point with regard to the Reagan tax cut when questions were raised about its impact on federal borrowing and interest rates.[48] Thus Ronald Reagan was really not too far off when he asserted in his October 1981 news conference that the Kennedy tax cut paid for itself.

ORIGINS OF KEMP-ROTH

Work on the legislation began in early 1977. It was my job to figure out exactly what it meant to "duplicate" the Kennedy tax cut, given that the rate structure had changed dramatically in the years since 1964, when the Kennedy tax cut was rammed through Congress by Lyndon Johnson. Working together with Bruce Thompson from Roth's office, Pete Davis of the JCT, Norman Ture, and others, we eventually decided to reduce the top statutory rate from 70 percent to 50 percent and the bottom rate from 14 percent to 10 percent. We felt that this was roughly comparable to Kennedy's reduction in the top rate from 91 percent to 70 percent and the bottom rate from 20 percent to 14 percent.

It took about a year before the Kemp-Roth proposal began to get attention. Interestingly, the idea that it would stimulate growth enough to pay back some of the static revenue loss was not especially controversial at first. Indeed, Bert Lance, Jimmy Carter's Office of Management and Budget director, had testified shortly before Kemp-Roth was introduced to that effect:

> My personal observation is that as you go through the process of permanent tax reduction, that there is an awfully good argument to be made for the fact that the revenues of the government actually increase at a given time. I think it has been proven in previous circumstances. I have no problem in following that sort of thing.[49]

Treasury Secretary Michael Blumenthal was also sympathetic to the idea that lowering tax rates would raise revenue: "The simpleminded notion underlying all of this is that if it works I would hope there would be a bigger pie and higher levels of activity producing more revenue."[50]

When the CBO reviewed the Kemp-Roth bill, it estimated that feedback effects would recoup between 14 percent and 19 percent of the static revenue loss the first year, rising to between 26 percent and 38 percent in the fourth. This is consistent with what the supply-siders themselves thought would happen. Contrary to popular belief—including Ronald Reagan's—they never thought there would be no revenue loss at all. Clearly, there would be large revenue losses in the short-run. But the supply-siders thought the net revenue loss would be much less than the static estimates predicted.[51]

Although supply-siders certainly thought there would be increases in economic growth, investment, and labor supply from marginal tax rate cuts, this was not by any means the only way they expected revenues to be recouped. They anticipated many changes in behavior that would have the effect of increasing taxable income. Among the most important areas where expansion of the tax base was anticipated was from shrinkage of the so-called underground economy. I vividly remember reading economist Peter Gutmann's path-breaking 1977 article, which estimated the underground economy equaled about 10 percent of recorded gross national product. Although not motivated solely by tax evasion, high tax rates unquestionably contributed heavily to its growth. Hence, tax rate reduction would cause some underground economic activity to move above ground, so to speak, and become taxable.[52]

Supply-siders further anticipated that workers would alter their compensation so as to increase the taxable portion of their wages. In particular, tax-free fringe benefits would be less attractive relative to cash wages. There is considerable evidence that rising tax rates in the 1970s were behind much of the growth in fringe benefits such as health insurance.[53]

Investors were also expected to alter their portfolios in ways that would raise taxable income. For example, with lower rates, the value of tax losses and other deductions, such as for Individual Retirement Accounts, would no longer be as valuable. Home ownership, with its many tax advantages, would no longer be as appealing relative to renting. And taxable dividends and interest would become more attractive compared with more lightly taxed capital gains and tax-free municipal bonds. All of these factors were expected to have a powerful effect on raising taxable income even in the absence of any growth effects from lower tax rates.[54]

ARTHUR LAFFER'S VIEW

Supply-siders believed that spending would fall automatically to some extent if expansionary tax cuts were enacted. They saw much government spending for such things as unemployment compensation and welfare as costs of slow growth that would become much smaller as employment rose.[55] Hence, the supply-siders believed that the impact on the deficit from something like Kemp-Roth should account for both the revenue reflows and the automatic reduction in spending for cyclical spending programs. That is why Laffer always emphasized the impact of Kemp-Roth on the deficit and not just on revenues. In his first formal statement on the legislation in 1978, he said, "Kemp-Roth would partially redress the counterproductive structure of current tax rates leading to a substantial increase in output, and may well, in the course of a very few years, reduce the size of total government deficits from what they otherwise would have been."[56]

Laffer also frequently talked about the effect of revenue reflows on all levels of government.[57] Because state and local governments tended to run budget surpluses in the aggregate, higher revenues in that sector would add to national saving. In 1978 congressional testimony Laffer observed:

> As I look at the Roth-Kemp bill, it cuts tax rates across the board over three years by approximately 30 percent.... On the federal level, there is quite a reasonable chance that within a very short period of time, a year or two or three, that not only will the cut in taxes cause more work output and employment, but the incomes, profits, and taxes, because of the expansion of the tax base, would actually increase. It is very clear to me that a cut in these tax rates, along the lines you suggested...would increase state and local revenues substantially. There is no ambiguity there. Any increase in incomes, productivity and production will increase state and local revenues substantially. If you take the government as a whole, it is likely that more revenues will increase.[58]

Laffer pulled all these points together in a 1979 academic paper in which he included higher federal revenues, higher state and local government revenues, lower government spending, and higher private saving in the reflows expected from a tax rate reduction. "The relevant question," he wrote,

is not whether revenues actually rise or not but whether a change in tax rates is "self-financing." Therefore, one should focus not only on the specific receipts for which the rates have been changed but also on other receipts, on spending, and on savings. Other receipts must rise if a rate is reduced. The expansion of activity will elicit a greater base upon which all other unchanged rates will obtain greater revenue. Government spending at all levels will fall because of lowered unemployment, reduced poverty, and thus less welfare. Likewise, government employees will require less in real wages because with lower tax rates the same real wages will yield greater after-tax wages, and so on. Finally, a cut in tax rates will yield greater savings in order to finance any deficit. Using a broader interpretation these tax rates and revenue positions should refer basically to the self-financing nature of tax rate changes.[59]

Laffer never made a precise estimate of the economic or revenue impact of the Kemp-Roth bill or the Reagan tax cut in 1981. The closest he ever came to saying that the Reagan tax cut would pay for itself was in a 1981 academic paper:

It is reasonable to conclude that each of the proposed 10 percent reductions in tax rates would, in terms of overall revenues, be self-financing in less than two years. Thereafter, each installment would provide a positive contribution to overall tax receipts. By the third year of the tax reduction program, it is likely that net revenue gains from the plan's first installment would offset completely the revenue reductions attributable to the final 10 percent tax rate cut. It should be noted that a significant portion of these revenues would accrue to state and local governments, relieving much if not all of the fiscal stress evident in these governmental units as well.[60]

These vague statements about relatively fast reflows from across-the-board tax rate reductions, however, contrast with more detailed estimates by Norman Ture and Michael Evans that explicitly included supply-side effects. Ture's estimate of Kemp-Roth in 1978 saw substantial revenues losses, net of feedback, even 10 years after enactment, when revenues would still be $53 billion (in 1977 dollars) below baseline.[61] Evans's figures were very similar, showing a current dollar increase in the deficit in 1987 of $61 billion.[62]

DAVID STOCKMAN

Among the strongest supporters of Kemp-Roth in Congress was Representative David Stockman, Republican of Michigan, who became Reagan's OMB director in 1981 and, famously, broke with him over the problem of deficits.[63] Stockman would often speak on the House floor and in committee in favor of passing an across-the-board tax rate reduction and against tax increases for the purpose of reducing budget deficits. For example, on March 1, 1978, he said,

> A tax increase to achieve budget balance would be even less appropriate. Such a move would "crowd-out" output just as surely as more pump priming will "crowd-out" investment. Mr. Speaker, these considerations make clear that the time is ripe for implementing the only new fiscal policy idea that has been proposed in decades: A deliberate across-the-board reduction in marginal tax rates for the purpose of reducing the burden of government on the productive sectors of the economy.[64]

In testimony before the Senate Finance Committee on July 14, 1978, Stockman explicitly refuted charges that Kemp-Roth would lead to larger deficits and inflation:

> These charges are based on a total misunderstanding of what Kemp-Roth is all about. We are not merely advocating a simple tax cut, an election-year gimmick. Instead, we view this measure as just one policy step in a whole, new fiscal policy program based on the supply side of the economy; based on the idea of getting more labor, capital, innovation, risk-taking and productivity into the economy by removing government barriers and deterrents, the most important of which, I would suggest to the committee today, is the rapidly rising marginal tax rates that Congressman Kemp has just discussed. . . . I would like to suggest to the committee that if this proposal that we are making

is properly looked at, that these scare stories about these horrendous fiscal results, the deficits, cannot be validated at all. If you understand that we are substituting tax cuts and an incentive, supply-side approach for pump priming and demand stimulus, it can clearly be done with a large surplus produced within less than four years.[65]

There were many other occasions as well when Stockman defended unilateral tax cuts.[66] Having worked with him closely at the time, I never heard the slightest concern from him that the basic supply-side message was not sound. And this was long before there was even the remotest prospect of Reagan being elected or of Stockman becoming OMB director. Remember also that Stockman supported former Texas governor John Connally during the primaries, endorsing Reagan only after Connally dropped out of the presidential race. So I conclude that he was not merely posturing about tax cuts in hopes of getting a cabinet appointment, but expressing a sincere belief.

In 1980 Reagan essentially adopted the Kemp-Roth bill as his principal campaign economic issue. After taking office, one of his first actions was to send a proposal to Congress on February 17, 1981, requesting passage of a tax cut closely modeled on Kemp-Roth. It showed a loss in revenue of $53.9 billion the first year, rising to $221.7 billion by 1986. No revenue feedback was assumed.[67]

Interestingly, old-time Keynesian economists were more optimistic about the potential revenue reflows of the Reagan tax cut than was the White House. For example, Richard Musgrave of Harvard, dean of America's public finance economists, testified before the Joint Economic Committee in early 1981 that the Reagan plan would likely recoup 18 percent of the static revenue loss through increased demand and another 30 percent to 35 percent through increased supply.[68] Gardner Ackley, the CEA's chairman under Lyndon Johnson, compared Reagan's plan favorably to Kennedy's, saying,

> I think the response to the proposed Reagan tax cuts would be similar to that of the Kennedy tax cuts. I think, yes, in a general way, taking the tax cut part by itself, independently of everything else. I think we would find a response of aggregate demand very substantially to a tax

cut, and this would tend, as it did following 1963, to stimulate additional production and employment and investment. It would do so
again today. The results of that would be beneficial.[69]

Laffer testified that it would take ten years before the Reagan tax
cut paid for itself, a view he said was consistent with what he had said
about Kemp-Roth.[70] Joseph A. Pechman of the liberal Brookings
Institution was largely in agreement with Laffer's assessment. Speaking
at the same congressional hearing, Pechman said he was pleased

> to hear that Arthur Laffer did not exaggerate some of the things that
> have been attributed to the supply-side economists. What he told us
> was that, if you reduce taxes or increase the net return to saving and
> to labor, there will be an increase in the incentives to work and to
> save. I think every economist, regardless of his persuasion, would
> agree with that.[71]

Again, Stockman spoke forcefully about the need for tax rate
reduction to accompany budget control. Because of bracket creep
and still-high inflation rates, future revenue projections always tended
to show budget balance within reach a few years out. But spending
always increased by a greater amount. Hence, tax reduction was
essential to holding down the growth of spending, which was the
Reagan administration's goal, not budget balance. As Stockman told
the Senate Finance Committee at his confirmation hearing as OMB
director:

> It is my very strongly held belief that if we fail to cut taxes then we
> have no hope, over the next 3 or 4 years of bringing the budget into
> balance, and of closing this enormous deficit that we face again this
> year. Of course, there are those who will show you a paper projection,
> a computer run, and will try to demonstrate that if we can keep the
> rate of inflation high and allow the tax rates on businesses and indi-
> viduals to continue to creep up, we will then automatically, by fiscal
> year 1983 or 1984, have a balanced budget. But that is pure mythol-
> ogy. That is only a computer projection. That is only a paper exercise
> that would never come true in the real world. We have had those fore-
> casts made every year for the last 4 or 5, but as we have moved down

the path toward the target year, these balanced budgets have seemed to disappear like the morning haze. There are reasons for that. The primary reason is that the tax burden today is so debilitating that it prevents the economy from growing, and without a growing economy we simply cannot hope to achieve a balanced budget.[72]

Eventually, Stockman broke with Reagan over the problem of budget deficits. But he always conceded that the tax cut was not really the cause of them because all it did was offset tax increases that would have resulted automatically from inflation. In his 1986 book, *The Triumph of Politics,* Stockman wrote:

> The Carter revenue estimates assumed the greatest sustained period of income tax bracket creep in U.S. history. But when you started with an inflation- and bracket-creep-swollen revenue level and trotted it out four or five years into the future, fiscal miracles were easy.... With high inflation, the Reagan program amounted to little more than indexing the fiscal status quo; the Kemp-Roth tax cut simply offset bracket creep.[73]

A number of analysts pointed out that the Reagan tax cut was not even big enough to fully offset bracket-creep, including the *New York Times,* which attacked it for this very reason. Subsequent analyses confirmed that the Reagan tax cut did little more than effectively index the tax system, keeping aggregate revenues from rising as a share of GDP.[74] Indeed, federal revenues as a share of GDP were actually higher in the decade of the 1980s than they had been in the 1970s and only slightly less than in the 1990s. Revenues averaged 17.93 percent of GDP in the 1970s, 18.25 percent in the 1980s, and 18.56 percent in the 1990s, according to CBO data.

REAGAN'S DEFICITS

With the emergence of large budget deficits after passage of the Reagan tax cut in 1981, the issue of its supply-side effects was answered in the minds of many. The simple cause-and-effect relationship seemed obvious: tax cut enacted, deficits emerged, therefore tax cuts caused deficits.[75]

Economist Lawrence Lindsey was the first to look at the effect of the Reagan tax cut on revenues after the fact, taking into account the economy's actual performance as opposed to projections based on forecasts and assumptions. In his initial effort, he concluded that on net the tax cut induced reflows of about 25 percent of the static revenue loss through behavioral effects. An estimate by some CBO economists came to a similar conclusion.[76] Lindsey's final calculation was that reflows paid for about a third of the direct cost of the tax cut, including both Keynesian demand-side effects and supply-side effects. "So who was right about the effect of tax changes on the economy," asked Lindsey, "the Keynesians or the supply-siders?"

> The answer is both, at least in part. The Keynesians were right in claiming that such a substantial reduction in rates would powerfully boost demand, a point the supply-siders never denied but perhaps underestimated. The demand-side revenue feedbacks and the combined behavioral feedbacks (supply-side and pecuniary) turned out to be roughly equal. On the other hand, the revenue results vindicate the supply-siders' most important claim: The tax cut produced quite large changes in taxpayer behavior. That claim, strongly confirmed by results, ran directly counter to Keynesian theory and most Keynesian predictions. The combined supply-side and pecuniary effects recouped well over one-third of ERTA's estimated direct cost, a very powerful response.[77]

So if the tax cut was too small to fully offset bracket creep and feedback effects recouped a third of the static revenue loss, then where did the huge budget deficits come from? Obviously, much came from higher spending on defense and other programs, as well a deep recession in 1981 and 1982. But Paul Craig Roberts argues that most of it came, ironically, from the enormously greater success against inflation than anyone thought was possible.[78]

Remember, the conventional wisdom said that even without additional demand stimulus in the form of a tax cut, it would take many years to get inflation down from its double-digit level in 1980 to the low single digits. Indeed, a simple Okun's Law calculation would have suggested the need for something like another Great Depression to bring inflation down to tolerable levels.[79]

Since taxes are assessed on nominal incomes, not real incomes, the fall of inflation from 12.5 percent in 1980 to about 4 percent in 1982 and throughout the 1980s simply collapsed the expected tax base. Ironically, the Reagan administration was counting on inflation coming down fairly slowly—even though it was frequently attacked for being far too optimistic on this score—which would increase revenues from bracket creep even as tax rates were cut. The Reagan administration anticipated an increase in the GNP deflator of 36 percent between 1981 and 1986. It actually came in at 21 percent.[80] When inflation came down far faster than anyone inside or outside the administration thought possible, revenues inevitably came in far lower than expected as well.

To put this effect into perspective, the Carter administration's last budget forecast 12.6 percent inflation in 1981 and 9.6 percent in 1982. It further estimated that each one percentage point decline of inflation below forecast would reduce revenues by $11 billion.[81] With actual inflation coming in at 8.9 percent in 1981 and 3.8 percent in 1982, this suggests that lower-than-expected inflation alone increased the deficit by about 50 percent, adding $41 billion to the deficit in 1981 ($180 billion in today's dollars) and $64 billion in 1982 ($270 billion today).

It has been argued that budget deficits offset all of the stimulative effect of the 1981 tax cut.[82] This extreme view, however, isn't shared by most economists. Even many of Reagan's political opponents concede that bringing down inflation so rapidly at far less economic cost than was previously imaginable was a remarkable accomplishment. Moreover, the rebound of growth and productivity in the 1980s, after the malaise of the 1970s, was at least in part due to the stimulative effect of the tax cut.

In 1989 Nobel Prize–winning economist Paul Samuelson of MIT admitted, "The latter half of the 1980s, historians will recognize, has been an economic success story." Even Bill Clinton's CEA conceded that the 1981 tax cut had been a major factor in stimulating growth. "It is undeniable that the sharp reduction in taxes in the early 1980s was a strong impetus to economic growth," it said in the 1994 *Economic Report of the President*.[83]

CHAPTER 5

THE RISE AND FALL OF SUPPLY-SIDE ECONOMICS

To critics of supply-side economics, the whole thing was never anything except hokum cooked up to justify big tax cuts for the rich. Some critics even suggest that the supply-siders were put up to devising their theories at the behest of those that would benefit from the tax cuts.[1]

In reality, the supply-siders got their theories from perfectly respectable sources. I know because I was there. As the previous chapter notes, respected economists like Robert Mundell sowed the seeds of supply-side economics in theoretical work published in obscure academic journals. But they also got their ideas from history. While the Kennedy tax cut was their most important historical influence, they were also aware of other tax cutting episodes, such as those in the 1920s.

Although it is often asserted that supply-side economics was a failure due to the deficits of the 1980s, its basic propositions have, in fact, been thoroughly incorporated into mainstream economic thinking. Economists today are much more sensitive to the incentive effects of taxation than they were before supply-side economics came along. But as with Keynesian economics, the supply-side model became overused and misapplied. This was clearly evident during the administration of George W. Bush. He and other high ranking officials of that administration frequently asserted that *all* tax cuts raise revenue, something the original supply-siders never believed. They thought that some very special tax cuts might pay for themselves right away, and that others wouldn't lose as much revenue as static estimates assumed, but they also knew that a lot of tax cuts had no growth or behavioral effects at all and were pure revenue losers. By the end of the George W. Bush administration, supply-side economics had become a caricature of itself, largely disconnected from its original principles.

INTELLECTUAL ORIGINS OF SUPPLY-SIDE ECONOMICS

It will come as a surprise to many people that the intellectual origins of supply-side economics can be traced to a fourteenth-century Muslim philosopher named Ibn Khaldun. In his masterwork, *The Muqaddimah,* he argued that high taxes were often a factor in causing empires to collapse, with the result that lower revenue was collected from high rates. "It should be known that at the beginning of the dynasty, taxation yields a large revenue from small assessments. At the end of the dynasty, taxation yields a small revenue from large assessments," Khaldun wrote.[2]

It may seem implausible that this ancient philosopher could have exercised any direct influence on 1970s American policymakers. However, there is a paper trail. In 1971 the *Journal of Political Economy* published an article about Khaldun by economist Jean David Boulakia, which quoted the passage above. Mundell had been editor of that journal until just before this article appeared, and he was responsible for accepting it for publication.[3] On September 29, 1978, the *Wall Street Journal* published a long passage from *The Muqaddimah.*

It was probably this excerpt that caught Ronald Reagan's eye. He referred to Khaldun by name during an October 1, 1981, press conference.

Another unlikely influence was Jonathan Swift, the famous satirist and author of *Gulliver's Travels*. In a 1728 article he noted the negative effect of high tariff rates on government revenue. His catchy phrase, "in the business of heavy impositions, two and two never make more than one," influenced many eighteenth-century thinkers regarding the deleterious effect of tax rates on revenue, including David Hume, Adam Smith, and Alexander Hamilton.[4]

These eighteenth-century thinkers unquestionably were influential in the development of supply-side economics. Supply-siders often drew parallels between their views on tax cutting and those of the Founding Fathers.[5] Adam Smith's work in particular was well known to the Founding Fathers as well as to all supply-siders, who would find the following quote from *The Wealth of Nations* (1776) especially apt: "High taxes, sometimes by diminishing the consumption of the taxed commodities, and sometimes by encouraging smuggling, frequently afford a smaller revenue to the government than what might be drawn from more moderate taxes."[6]

The Founding Fathers also found inspiration in the work of political philosopher Baron de Montesquieu, who wrote in *The Spirit of the Laws* (1748): "Liberty produces excessive taxes; the effect of excessive taxes is slavery; and slavery produces a diminution of tribute."[7]

Another influence on supply-siders was nineteenth-century economist Jean-Baptiste Say. I began the first chapter of my 1981 book, *Reaganomics*, with this observation: "In many respects, supply-side economics is nothing more than ... Say's law of markets rediscovered."[8] By this I meant that Say had placed supply above demand in importance to the economy. Aggregate demand can be stimulated easily by printing money; calling forth additional work and production is much harder. Hence, economic policy should be more concerned with the production of goods and services than with the stimulation of demand. As Say put it, "The encouragement of mere

consumption is no benefit to commerce; for the difficulty lies in sup-
plying the means, not in stimulating the desire of consumption.... It
is the aim of good government to stimulate production, of bad government to encourage consumption."[9]

John Stuart Mill made much the same point. In addition to
quoting Say and Mill in my book, I was aware of my contemporar-
ies in twentieth-century economics, such as Thomas Sowell and
W. H. Hutt, who were rehabilitating Say's Law.[10] Say's concern
with incentives for production led him easily into the idea that high
taxes can reduce revenue by stifling output. "Taxation pushed to the
extreme," he wrote,

> has the lamentable effect of impoverishing the individual, without
> enriching the state.... The diminution of demand must be followed
> by diminution of the supply of production; and, consequently, of the
> articles liable to taxation. Thus, the taxpayer is abridged of his enjoy-
> ments, the producer of his profits, and the public exchequer of its
> receipts.... This is the reason why a tax is not productive to the pub-
> lic exchequer, in proportion to its ratio; and why it has become a sort
> of apophthegm, that two and two do not make four in the arithmetic of
> finance. Excessive taxation... extinguishes both production and con-
> sumption, and the taxpayer into the bargain.[11]

The idea that high rates can reduce revenue was also known to
nineteenth-century trade theorists, who noted that high tariff rates
often reduced tariff revenue. The American statesman John C. Calhoun
made one of the clearest statements of this. While serving in the U.S.
Senate in 1842, he made this observation about the revenue effects
of tariffs:

> On all articles on which duties can be imposed, there is a point in the
> rate of duties which may be called the maximum point of revenue—
> that is, a point at which the greatest amount of revenue would be
> raised. If it be elevated above that, the importation of the article
> would fall off more rapidly than the duty would be raised; and, if
> depressed below it, the reverse effect would follow: that is, the duty
> would decrease more rapidly than the importation would increase. If

the duty be raised above that point, it is manifest that all the intermediate space between the maximum point and that to which it may be raised, would be purely protective, and not at all for revenue.... [A]ny given amount of duty, other than the maximum, may be collected on any article, by two distinct rates of duty—the one above the maximum point, and the other below it.[12]

So widespread was this view that in 1861 the *New York Times* said it was "a well known principle of political economy that duties which are too high are as unproductive of revenue as those which are too low." Indeed, in the 1880s, trade protectionists explicitly supported tariff rates so high that they were intended to lose revenue by reducing imports.[13] Advocates of cigarette tax increases often make the same point today. Their goal, they say, is not so much to raise revenue as to reduce smoking. In the words of New York Mayor Michael Bloomberg, "If it were totally up to me, I would raise the cigarette tax so high the revenues from it would go to zero."[14]

In the twentieth century a number of economists wrote about the limits of taxation from the point of view of revenues. An early contribution was by economist Edwin Cannan, who posited a version of the Laffer curve by pointing out that a 100 percent tax rate would raise zero revenue. During World War II there was much discussion of the limits of taxation, focusing mainly on labor supply. In the postwar era, economist Colin Clark argued that excessive taxes become inflationary above 25 percent of the gross national product. John Maynard Keynes agreed with Clark that "25 percent taxation is about the limit of what is easily borne." Keynes had previously noted, "Aggressive taxation may defeat its own ends by diminishing the income to be taxed."[15]

In *Human Action,* Austrian economist Ludwig von Mises added his voice to the debate in 1949, writing, "The true crux of the taxation issue is to be seen in the paradox that the more taxes increase, the more they undermine the market economy and concomitantly the system of taxation itself.... Every specific tax, as well as a nation's whole tax system, becomes self-defeating above a certain height of rates."[16]

Political scientist C. Northcote Parkinson, famous for his law about work expanding to fill the time for its completion, put forth a second law about expenditures rising to meet income. In *The Law and the Profits* (1960), he suggested that there were diminishing returns once taxes reached 20 percent of national income. And in a 1973 article economist Richard B. McKenzie found that "it is distinctly possible on theoretical grounds that statutory rate increases may result in lower tax collections for some groups (i.e., lower effective rates)."[17]

In short, the ground was well plowed long before the first supply-sider showed up making the case that excessive tax rates can reduce government revenue and that, conversely, lower rates can, under certain conditions, raise revenue.

HISTORICAL EPISODES

It was not just theoretical discussions about lower tax rates raising revenues that influenced supply-side thinking. They were also aware of actual experience, most especially in the United States during the 1920s and 1960s. Herb Stein's *Fiscal Revolution in America* (1969) was an invaluable resource on the history of these episodes. Indeed, Jude Wanniski told me that Stein's discussion regarding the belief by politicians in the 1920s that lower tax rates might raise revenue was the first he ever heard of the idea.[18]

The federal income tax came into being permanently in 1913 with a top statutory rate of just seven percent. Due to the extraordinary revenue demands of World War I, however, tax rates were sharply increased; by war's end, the top rate had risen to 77 percent. Although Republican presidents of the 1920s got most of the credit for reducing wartime tax rates, the initiative actually began in Woodrow Wilson's administration.[19] Indeed, in his 1919 State of the Union address, Wilson used supply-side arguments to urge tax rate reduction:

> The Congress might well consider whether the higher rates of income and profits taxes can in peace times be effectively productive of

revenue, and whether they may not, on the contrary, be destructive of business activity and productive of waste and inefficiency. There is a point at which in peace times high rates of income and profits taxes discourage energy, remove the incentive to new enterprise, encourage extravagant expenditures and produce industrial stagnation with consequent unemployment and other attendant evils.

Treasury Secretary Andrew Mellon, who served continuously through the administrations of Warren G. Harding, Calvin Coolidge, and most of Herbert Hoover, spearheaded the tax reduction effort. By 1929, he managed to get the top statutory rate down to just 24 percent. In his book, *Taxation: The People's Business* (1924), Mellon made plain his belief that high tax rates on the wealthy lowered government revenue and that lower rates would raise revenue. As he put it:

> The history of taxation shows that taxes which are inherently excessive are not paid. The high rates inevitably put pressure upon the taxpayer to withdraw his capital from productive business and invest it in tax-exempt securities or to find other lawful methods of avoiding the realization of taxable income. The result is that the sources of taxation are drying up; wealth is failing to carry its share of the tax burden; and capital is being diverted into channels which yield neither revenue to the government nor profit to the people.[20]

The evidence strongly indicates that the tax cuts of the 1920s did indeed raise revenue among those most affected by the rate reductions. Historian Benjamin Rader concluded, "Despite sharply reduced tax rates for upper income groups...the wealthy paid a larger share of the federal tax burden at the end of the decade than at the beginning."[21] Economists Gene Smiley and Richard H. Keehn confirm this conclusion:

> Though the marginal tax rates were cut much more for the highest income taxpayers, the effective burden of taxation shifted away from the lower-income taxpayers toward the higher-income taxpayers. The resulting decline in tax avoidance, in conjunction with economic growth, led to some increase in personal income tax receipts despite the huge tax cuts from 1921 through 1926. Thus, the tax rate cuts

worked much as Mellon and other early "supply-side" supporters had argued that they would.[22]

Supply-siders were also aware of examples at the state and local level where relatively easy opportunities for moving to other jurisdictions magnified the economic impact of tax changes. Economist Ron Grieson, for example, concluded in 1980 that Philadelphia's income tax was so high that it was reducing city revenues below what lower rates would have brought in.[23]

THE JEC JOINS THE SUPPLY-SIDE

Adding important institutional support to the growth of supply-side economics in the late 1970s was the congressional Joint Economic Committee under the leadership of its chairman, Senator Lloyd Bentsen, Democrat of Texas. In the 1950s and 1960s the JEC had been a hotbed of Keynesian economics, so the intellectual collapse of that school hit the committee hard, leading to much soul-searching on the part of both its members and staff.[24] By 1979, the JEC started to make a break. In a number of hearings and staff studies, the committee began placing increasing emphasis on the role of supply in the economy, concluding that inadequate incentives for saving and investment lay behind the national economic malaise.

By 1980 the JEC was a full-blown advocate of supply-side economics, despite having a majority of liberal Democrats, such as Senators Edward Kennedy of Massachusetts and George McGovern of South Dakota. Its annual report that year was titled, "Plugging in the Supply Side." Bentsen summarized the committee's new view in his introduction:

> The 1980 annual report signals the start of a new era of economic thinking. The past has been dominated by economists who focused almost exclusively on the demand side of the economy and who, as a result, were trapped into believing that there is an inevitable trade-off between unemployment and inflation.... The Committee's 1980

report says that steady economic growth, created by productivity gains and accompanied by a stable fiscal policy and a gradual reduction in the growth of the money supply over a period of years, can reduce inflation significantly during the 1980's without increasing unemployment. To achieve this goal, the Committee recommends a comprehensive set of policies designed to enhance the productive side, the supply side of the economy.[25]

The JEC also injected itself into the debate over econometric modeling. A 1980 hearing strongly supported the idea that existing models were too heavily based on Keynesian assumptions and gave short shrift to the economy's supply side. Partly as a consequence of the JEC's prodding, the commercial econometric firm Data Resources, Inc. changed its model to incorporate more supply-side features.[26]

The JEC's conversion to supply-side economics was extremely important in adding respectability and bipartisanship to the idea. For example, it led Leonard Silk, economics columnist for the *New York Times*, to write sympathetically about the new philosophy: "A major change is on the way in economic theory and policy; that change will involve a deeper integration of supply-side and demand-side economics, and an integration of thinking about both the long and short run. The change is long overdue."[27]

Even after Ronald Reagan had taken office and liberal Representative Henry Reuss, Democrat of Wisconsin, replaced the more conservative Bentsen as chairman of the JEC, it remained skeptical of old-fashioned Keynesianism. Said Reuss in 1981, "We have learned from our mistakes in the past. We've given up blind pursuit of Keynesian demand acceleration." Supply-side economics was important in depriving demand-side economics of "an undeserved primacy," he added.[28]

THE TRIUMPH OF SUPPLY-SIDE ECONOMICS

Less was heard about supply-side economics after the 1980s because so much of what the original supply-siders were trying to accomplish had been achieved. That is, many supply-side propositions that were highly controversial when first made in the 1970s are now accepted as conventional wisdom among professional economists.

- A vast number of studies now show that taxes and the size of government are critical determinants of economic growth and most demonstrate that higher taxes and bigger government reduce growth.[29]
  - Although the tax/GDP ratio has risen in every major country, the tax structure in most countries has changed dramatically in a supply-side direction. Marginal tax rates are significantly lower on both individuals and corporations, the burden of taxation has shifted away from capital and toward consumption, and tax systems are much more sensitive to their effects on entrepreneurship, risk-taking, and innovation than they were in the 1970s.[30]
  - The World Bank, International Monetary Fund, and Organization for Economic Cooperation and Development now routinely advise countries to reform their tax systems in ways consistent with supply-side principles.[31]
- The welfare or deadweight cost of the U.S. tax system—the burden of taxation over and above the revenue collected due to reduced output—is now generally considered to be very high.[32] In the 1960s, this cost was not considered a problem by economists; a common estimate of the welfare burden of the income tax was just 2.5 percent of revenue.[33]
  - A 1999 study by economist Martin Feldstein found that the deadweight cost of the tax system was 32 percent of revenue collected, but could be as high as $2.06 on each additional tax dollar raised.[34]
  - A 2002 study by economist Ian Parry found that economic distortions caused by deductions in the income tax system discouraged 30 cents to 50 cents of output for every $1 raised. However, the output loss may be as high as $2 for every $1 raised.[35]
  - A 2005 survey by the GAO found that the efficiency cost of the federal tax system was between 2 percent and 5 percent of GDP in the mid-1990s.[36]
- The economic cost of tax progressivity and capital taxation is now considered to be far higher than previously thought and there is growing support among reputable tax experts for a flat rate tax on a consumption base and total elimination of taxes on capital.[37]
  - Brookings Institution economist Joseph A. Pechman virtually defined the mainstream on the economics of taxation for a generation. In

innumerable books and papers, he argued forcefully for a highly progressive tax system on a comprehensive income base. So it is revealing that Pechman made this observation in his presidential address to the American Economic Association in 1989:

> The federal income tax has been under attack by the economics profession for more than a decade. The attack comes from two directions: supply-siders who believe that progressive income taxation impairs economic incentives, and more traditional economists who would substitute a progressive expenditure tax for the income tax.... Today, it is fair to say that many, if not most, economists favor the expenditure tax or a flat rate income tax.[38]

○ Almost every significant tax reform proposal of the last 30 years produced by the Treasury Department, presidential and congressional commissions, and private organizations has endorsed supply-side principles: urging lower tax rates, elimination of special tax provisions that bias investment decisions, a reduction in taxes on capital, and increased taxation of consumption.[39]

• The Laffer curve is a generally accepted analytical device that represents the inverse relationship of tax rates to government revenues and is a widely discussed subject in respected academic journals.[40] Despite a reduction in the top marginal income tax rate from 70 percent in 1980 to half that since 2003, the share of total income taxes and the effective rate of taxation by taxpayers with high incomes has risen sharply—exactly as the supply-siders predicted.[41] Indeed, the IMF has found considerable evidence of Laffer curve effects in foreign countries.

○ A 1997 study concluded, "The simulation results...point to the presence of 'self financing,' whereby reductions in various tax rates lead to lower budget deficits in the long run, as the result of an expanding tax base and lower unemployment insurance outlays."[42]

○ According to the summary of a 1999 IMF seminar, "A number of countries maintain tariff rates that exceed revenue maximizing levels. These countries could liberalize, at least initially, without significantly adverse consequences for revenues from trade taxes."[43]

○ A 2000 study estimated that the elasticity of taxable income is sufficiently high that a tax rate reduction could increase net revenue.[44]

○ A 2005 study of Russia's tax reform found that replacement of the income tax with a 13 percent flat rate caused revenues to rise by 26 percent.[45]

○ A 2008 study found that high tax rates produce so much evasion that tax rate reductions can raise net revenue just through increased compliance, quite apart from any growth effects.[46]

• The conventional wisdom among economists used to be that labor supply and saving rates were insensitive to changes in tax rates.[47] Today, it is generally recognized that they are much more responsive than previously believed.[48]

○ Since the 1970s, hours worked have declined in almost every major country while taxes have risen. Economist Edward Prescott, winner of the Nobel Prize in economics in 2004, believes that almost all of the decline in hours can be attributed to higher taxes.[49]

○ Supply-siders were among the first to call attention to the high implicit tax rates on the poor resulting from means-tested welfare programs—as incomes rise and benefits are withdrawn, the impact on welfare recipients is the same as if tax rates were increased.[50] Today, this problem is commonly acknowledged and the impact on labor supply is significant.[51]

○ The labor supply of entrepreneurs and small businessmen is now viewed as far more sensitive to taxes than was previously believed.[52]

• It is now estimated that a tax rate reduction would recoup 30 percent to 50 percent of the static revenue loss through macroeconomic and behavioral effects.[53] Conversely, tax rate increases may only raise half the revenue predicted by static forecasts that do not account for changes in taxpayer behavior.[54] A 2004 CBO study suggested that there was now a consensus among economists that the elasticity of income with respect to tax changes is about 40 percent.[55] Even critics of supply-side economics concede that tax and tariff cuts may produce substantial revenue reflows, lowering their net cost, and that tax increases may produce negative reflows, increasing their net cost.

○ Paul Krugman, *New York Times* columnist and winner of the 2008 Nobel Prize in economics: "The basic idea of dynamic scoring is reasonable."[56]

○ Lawrence Chimerine, former chief economist for both Chase Econometrics and the Wharton Econometric Forecasting group: "Credible evidence overwhelmingly indicates that revenue feedback from tax cuts is 35 cents per dollar."[57]

○ Former House Minority Leader Richard Gephardt, Democrat of Missouri: "The purpose of tax cuts is not just to have a tax cut for a particular time. It is to get the economy to grow. If you can get the economy to grow, you will start having more money coming into the government. It's a synergistic process that moves both the budget forward and the economy forward."[58]

○ Although the Clinton administration was generally critical of incorporating supply-side factors in its tax revenue estimates, it nevertheless argued that tariff cuts resulting from the Uruguay Round of trade negotiations would raise federal revenues. Said U.S. Trade Representative Mickey Kantor at a congressional hearing in 1994: "I think everyone here would agree, certainly economists agree, that because of the tariff cuts and because of the increase in exports, because of the growing jobs here, the Federal Treasury would gain many, many more dollars than it will lose in terms of the tariff cuts."[59]

Perhaps the best evidence that supply-side economics has entered the mainstream is Robert Mundell's Nobel Prize in 1999. Although his citation does not mention any of his relevant work in this area, it would be naive to think that the Nobel committee was unaware of it, since Mundell was often referred to as a supply-side "guru" in the popular press.[60] It is also well known that the committee thoroughly researches all aspects of a candidate's life and work before making an award. Therefore, it is reasonable to assume that the committee was well aware that in giving Mundell the Nobel Prize for his work in international macroeconomics and monetary theory would be seen as recognition of his work in supply-side economics as well.[61]

Supply-siders can also claim a piece of 1995 Nobel Prize–winner Robert Lucas. In a neglected 1990 article, he declared himself to be a born-again supply-sider:

I have called this paper an analytical review of "supply-side economics," a term associated in the United States with extravagant claims about the effects of changes in the tax structure on capital accumulation. In a sense, the analysis I have reviewed here supports these claims: Under what I view as conservative assumptions, I estimated that eliminating capital income taxation would increase capital stock by about 35 percent.... The supply-side economists, if that is the right term for those whose research I have been discussing, have delivered the largest genuinely free lunch I have seen in 25 years in this business, and I believe we would have a better society if we followed their advice.[62]

By 1996 even the Clinton administration said that it was practicing supply-side economics. "Our growth policies are supply side," claimed Council of Economic Advisers Chairman Joseph Stiglitz.[63]

Of course, supply-side economics still has its critics. In 2001, Gerard Baker, economics columnist for London's *Financial Times,* referred to "quack theories about supply-side tax cuts."[64] However Floyd Norris, a columnist for the *New York Times,* was more sympathetic:

Two decades ago, the supply-siders performed a valuable service. They persuaded a popular new president, who had been elected as a fiscal conservative, to slash taxes and claim that no budget deficit would result. Lower tax rates, they said, would miraculously bring higher tax revenues. That proved to be wrong. But it was a good idea nonetheless. The United States was going through painful economic times, and the tax cut provided real relief for the majority who were not to be victims of the cutbacks that were needed to make American businesses more competitive. The economic stimulus helped to end a severe recession.[65]

GEORGE W. BUSH, SUPPLY-SIDER?

Despite this success and George W. Bush's oft-stated support for supply-side economics, his administration proved to be its downfall. Policies with no meaningful connection to supply-side principles were proposed as being based on them. And even when the correct supply-side view was understood, Bush and his supporters were quick to cast it aside whenever political expediency demanded it. In the end, his administration represented a bastardized version of supply-side economics that had more in common with the caricature of it depicted by its opponents than anything approximating its core principles.

The abandonment of supply-side principles by George W. Bush occurred very early. Although he put forward a campaign tax plan that had been devised by supply-siders such as Lawrence Lindsey, Bush himself was responsible for watering down the supply-side elements. In particular, there was heavy emphasis on doubling the child credit as well as the creation of many other tax credits for charitable giving, education, health, and other purposes.[66] This was in keeping with Bush's desire to be seen as a "compassionate conservative."

Historically, supply-siders strenuously opposed tax credits because they generally don't affect incentives at the margin.[67] The preferred supply-side approach to tax-cutting involves reductions in tax rates or provisions that reduce taxable income because the tax saving is a function of one's marginal tax bracket. By contrast, tax credits are subtracted directly from one's tax liability and have no impact at the margin because all taxpayers are treated the same regardless of their income or tax bracket. This is precisely why tax credits are politically attractive—they are perceived as more fair. But once a tax credit has been created, pressure quickly builds to make it refundable so that even those with no tax liability will benefit. When this happens, there is no meaningful difference between a tax cut and an increase in government spending.[68]

The second abandonment of supply-side principles by George W. Bush came soon after he took office. Rather than reformulate his campaign tax proposal to reflect changing economic conditions, he decided to simply add a tax rebate on top. Although both theory and experience said that consumers were likely to save, rather than spend, any rebate, politicians of both parties were anxious to be seen as responding aggressively to the economic slow-down that was becoming increasingly apparent.

In a revealing episode reported by journalist Ron Suskind, Bush's chief economic adviser, CEA Chairman Glenn Hubbard, went to see him to explain that a vast amount of economic research showed that rebates are a very ineffective means of stimulating the economy.[69] Hubbard told Bush that the rebate was "bad policy." Rather astonishingly, Bush responded, "I don't ever want to hear you use those words in my presence again." What words, Hubbard asked? "Bad policy," Bush replied. "If I decide to do it, *by definition* it's good policy. I thought you got that."[70]

The tax rebate was signed into law on June 7, 2001. Taxpayers received an advance rebate on their 2001 taxes based on their 2000 taxes. They got back 10 percent of their 2000 tax payment up to $300 for a single person and $600 for a couple. Thus, anyone without a tax liability in 2000 was ineligible, which excluded many of those with incomes too low to pay any taxes. Presumably, these would also have been the people most likely to spend the rebate. By limiting the rebate to those with a positive tax liability, the legislation virtually ensured that rebates would go primarily to those with relatively high incomes who would probably save all of it.[71]

Retailers were underwhelmed by the response to the rebates. Sears, for example, decided not to even bother doing any advertising linked to them.[72] Numerous polls found that the vast bulk of those receiving rebates planned to save the money or use it to pay down debt, which amounts to the same thing for the economy. A July Gallup poll found that 47 percent of respondents would use the money to pay down debt, 32 percent planned to save it, and just 17 percent thought they would spend more. A Bloomberg poll in September found 42 percent paying off debts, 28 percent saving the rebate, and just 15 percent spending it. An October University of Michigan poll found 85 percent of respondents either saving the rebate or using it to pay down debt, with just 15 percent spending it.

According to the Commerce Department, disposable personal income increased by $215.2 billion in the third quarter of 2001 as the rebates were paid out. However, personal saving jumped to

$261.6 billion, up from just $88.7 billion in the second quarter. In short, 80 percent of the increase in disposable income was saved, meaning that there was very little stimulus to spending.

Although the 2001 tax rebate was probably the best-timed counter-cyclical program of the postwar era, subsequent analysis found its impact to be modest at best. Studies based on surveys found virtually no impact whatsoever.[73] The largest impact was found in a study of aggregate consumption, which estimated that it was 0.8 percent higher in the third quarter of 2001 and 0.6 percent higher in the fourth quarter than it would have been without the rebate. Since consumption represents about 70 percent of GDP, this suggests that GDP was higher by at most 0.56 percent in the third quarter and 0.4 percent higher in the fourth.[74]

Despite the failure of the 2001 rebate, the Bush administration responded to the growing economic crisis in 2008 by pushing through yet another rebate. I argued at the time that the money would have been better spent making a down payment on cleaning up the bad debts in the housing sector that were at the root of the problem, but to no avail.[75] As predicted, the new rebate was just as ineffective as the last one.[76] The economy moved into recession anyway.

Finally, even when Bush promoted tax cuts that had some semblance of genuine supply-side principles, he totally undermined their effectiveness by agreeing to have them phased-in and setting termination dates after which they would expire. Both factors considerably undermined their effectiveness. Supply-siders always argued that phase-ins are bad because people will put off behavioral changes until tax changes are effective and that only permanent tax changes would have meaningful economic effects.[77]

SUPPLY-SIDE ECONOMICS, R.I.P.

Much of George W. Bush's presidency always seemed to me like an effort to vindicate what he saw as his father's mistakes. George H. W. Bush stopped short of conquering Iraq in 1991, so his son felt compelled to finish the job in 2003. And it was George H. W. Bush who called supply-side economics "voodoo economic policy," so perhaps his son thought he needed to be more of a supply-sider than any of those who actually formulated it.[78] No serious supply-sider would have ever made the kinds of extravagant claims for Bush's tax cuts that he made for them.[79] Among his claims were these:

> "Make no mistake about it . . . the deficit would have been bigger without the tax relief package."[80]

> "These [tax] proposals will help stimulate investment and put more people back to work. . . . That growth will bring the added benefit of higher revenues for the government."[81]

> "One of the interesting things that I hope you realize when it comes to cutting taxes is this tax relief not only has helped our economy, but it's helped the federal budget . . . You cut taxes and the tax revenues increase."[82]

> "Supply-side economics yields additional revenues."[83]

Bush's CEA, however, was much more restrained in its analysis of the economic and revenue effects of his tax cuts. As it explained, "Although the economy grows in response to tax reductions . . . it is unlikely to grow so much that lost tax revenue is completely recovered by the higher level of economic activity."[84]

To be sure, some of Bush's tax cuts, such as the cut in the capital gains tax, did have supply-side effects and undoubtedly recouped much of the static revenue loss. But the vast bulk of Bush's tax cuts in dollar terms involved rebates and tax credits that had no supply-side effects whatsoever. Therefore, to claim, as Bush often did, that his tax policies as a whole had such strong supply-side effects that they paid for themselves is the grossest of exaggerations. The truth is that they increased growth a little, but at a very large cost in terms of federal revenue, and far less than would have been the case had the supply-side elements of Bush's tax cuts been made permanent and not been phased-in.

In my opinion, it is time for supply-side economics as a distinctive school of thought to go peacefully into the night. It is an idea that once had validity and made a real contribution to improving economic policy—but which became increasingly divorced from that contribution as time went by, and eventually found itself as a mere slogan without anything meaningful to say about current economic problems. The things that were right about supply-side economics have been fully incorporated into mainstream economics. To the extent that supply-side ideas have not been accepted, it is mainly because they are invalid.

To continue to maintain that there is a separate supply-side view of the economy or economic policy today creates unnecessary alienation between those who still call themselves supply-siders, on the one hand, and those who agree with most of what the original supply-siders were trying to accomplish on the other. These latter now see supply-side economics as either nothing more than an obsession for massively cutting taxes in response to every economic problem, an increasingly implausible justification for the failed policies of the George W. Bush administration, or an absurd belief that all tax cuts will pay for themselves.

Under these circumstances, I think it is time for supply-siders to declare victory and go home. The economic problems of today and those likely to arise in the future don't require a particular supply-side insight that is lacking in mainstream economics. To the extent that supply-siders continue to insist upon a separate identity, they only end up making enemies out of potential allies in the economics profession and the policymaking community.

CHAPTER 6

STARVING THE BEAST DIDN'T WORK

One weakness of the supply-side argument that became increasingly apparent over time was its lack of focus on the spending side of the budget. The problem is that in the long run revenues must equal the level of spending because all spending eventually has to be paid for. To a certain extent, this fact was glossed over by hopes that faster economic growth would recoup some of the revenues lost to a tax cut and simultaneously reduce the demand for spending on programs such as unemployment compensation. But there was also a belief among supply-siders that tax cuts would force cuts in spending.

The idea that tax cuts would channel concerns about budget deficits into political pressure to cut spending has come to be called starving the beast. Although there was good reason to believe that this strategy might work when it was first proposed—a period when high inflation and interest rates created strong opposition to deficit spending—the budgetary experience of recent years, in which large tax cuts have been accompanied by large increases in spending, has thoroughly destroyed its validity. Indeed, some economists now believe that the starve-the-beast theory may be perverse, leading to higher spending and deficits.

EARLIEST REFERENCES

The earliest reference to the term "starve the beast" that I have been able to locate appeared in a *Washington Post* article a little over 100 years ago. The author, Charles Edward Barnes, used it literally to refer to intentionally starving an animal.[1]

In Barnes's account, an Indian native had captured a tiger in a pit and needed to get it into a cage so that it could be transported and sold. The tiger had no desire to enter the cage and so the native simply starved it until it was forced to enter the cage to get some food that had been placed inside—a variation of the old carrot-and-stick idea.

The oldest expression I have been able to find of the notion that tax cuts will hold down government spending comes from liberal economist John Kenneth Galbraith. In the early 1960s he was on leave from teaching while serving as ambassador to India for President John F. Kennedy, whom he had tutored at Harvard. Despite being far from Washington, Galbraith remained keenly interested in economic policy debates in the United States, especially the debate swirling around the idea of a big tax cut to give the economy a Keynesian boost.

During a trip stateside in June 1962, Galbraith first heard about the administration's plans for a big tax cut and argued strenuously against it, even going so far as to tell Kennedy himself that it was a bad idea. In his diary, Galbraith said his main concern was that "lower tax revenues will become a ceiling on spending."[2] Being an administration appointee, however, he had to keep his reservations about the tax cut private. But by 1965 he was back at Harvard and free to speak his mind publicly. On February 24 of that year, Galbraith testified before the Joint Economic Committee of Congress:

> I was never as enthusiastic as many of my fellow economists over the tax reduction of last year. The case for it as an isolated action was undoubtedly good. But there was danger that conservatives, once introduced to the delights of tax reduction, would like it too much. Tax reduction would then become a substitute for increased outlays on urgent social needs. We would have a new and reactionary form of Keynesianism with which to contend.[3]

Soon after, Galbraith's concern was echoed by socialist Michael Harrington: "In the United States it is quite possible to envisage a conservative Keynesian policy which substitutes tax cuts for social investments, increases the maldistribution of income (the rich and the corporations gain more from tax cuts than the workers and the poor) *and* maintains a prosperity as that term would be defined by business."[4]

Galbraith and Harrington were prescient. At the time, most conservatives were adamantly in favor of a balanced budget under just about any and all circumstances. In Congress, Republicans largely opposed the Kennedy tax cut for this reason. In the House of Representatives, 126 of 155 Republicans voted against the Kennedy tax cut. Liberals even teased them by using Republican Treasury Secretary Andrew Mellon's arguments for it.[5] But as Galbraith anticipated, Republicans would eventually come to change their views.

The earliest reference I have been able to find to the precise term "starve the beast" as it relates to Reaganomics appeared in a *Wall Street Journal* news story in 1985. Reporter Paul Blustein quoted an unnamed White House official as lamenting that not enough had been done to cut spending during the Reagan administration. "We didn't starve the beast," the official said. "It's still eating quite well—by feeding off future generations."[6]

Lawrence Kudlow, an Office of Management and Budget official during that period and now a popular CNBC commentator, told me that he remembers first hearing the term "starve the beast" from Senator Daniel Patrick Moynihan at a hearing in early 1981. This makes sense if the term is indeed of Indian origin since Moynihan had served as U.S. ambassador to India from 1973 to 1975 and may have picked it up there. However, I cannot find him using that term in the record of any hearing in 1981.

BALANCED BUDGET ORTHODOXY

Republicans had enacted tax cuts in the 1920s. But in 1932 Herbert Hoover supported a large tax increase to shore up federal finances, which were ravaged by the onset of the Great Depression. Economists today generally view this as one of the worst economic policy mistakes in American history, one that did much to make a bad situation worse.[7]

Nevertheless, when the next Republican president, Dwight Eisenhower, took office in 1953, he strenuously resisted efforts by Republicans in Congress to cut taxes. He was quite insistent that balancing the budget had to take precedence, even though tax rates were at historically high levels due to the Korean War.[8] The top income tax rate was 92 percent on incomes over $200,000. It is not known exactly why Eisenhower was so adamant about balancing the budget, but he offered this explanation at a press conference on February 17, 1953:

> Whether we are ready to face the job this minute or any other time, the fact is there must be balanced budgets before we are again on a safe and sound system in our economy. That means, to my mind, that we cannot afford to reduce taxes, reduce income, until we have in sight a program of expenditures that shows that the factors of income and of outgo will be balanced. Now that is just to my mind sheer necessity.

Richard Nixon, who had served as Eisenhower's vice president, continued this policy of resisting tax cuts in favor of balancing the budget after his election to the White House in 1968. One of his earliest actions in 1969 was to ask Congress for extension of the 10 percent surtax despite having promised during the campaign to allow it to expire.[9] Lyndon Johnson had imposed the surtax on corporate and individual taxes through the end of fiscal year 1969, which ended on June 30 in those days. At Nixon's request, Congress extended it for another year.

Gerald Ford, who succeeded Nixon in 1974, similarly resisted political pressure to cut taxes permanently, supporting only a temporary tax rebate in 1975 while asking for higher taxes on individuals and corporations. In addition, he allowed inflation to raise taxes automatically as taxpayers were pushed into higher tax brackets and business depreciation allowances were eroded.[10]

In an influential article in early 1976, *Wall Street Journal* editorial writer Jude Wanniski blasted Ford for timidity in cutting taxes. He argued that the nation needed each political party to be a different type of Santa Claus—the Democrats being the spending Santa Claus and the Republicans being the tax cut Santa Claus. By refusing to play its proper role and instead being the party of the balanced budget, Republicans had hurt not only themselves, politically, but the nation as a whole. "The political tension in the marketplace of ideas," Wanniski wrote, "must be between tax reduction and spending increases, and as long as Republicans have insisted upon balanced budgets, their influence as a party has shriveled, and budgets have been unbalanced.[11]

Had Ford defeated Jimmy Carter in 1976, Republicans might have concluded that budget balancing was still good politics. But, combined with large losses in the 1974 congressional elections, they were in a desperate political situation by 1977. This made them receptive to ideas they had previously rejected, such as cutting taxes. The generally held Republican view had been that tax cuts could not be considered unless spending was cut by an equal amount simultaneously. In practice, this meant that Republicans were never for tax cuts.

But after Ford's defeat, Republicans in Congress and in the states became receptive to tax cuts as a way of reviving both the economy and their political fortunes. In 1977 Representative Jack Kemp, Republican of New York, and Senator Bill Roth, Republican of Delaware, introduced the Kemp-Roth tax bill, which proposed cutting statutory tax rates by about 30 percent across-the-board without corresponding spending cuts. This legislation eventually formed the basis of Ronald Reagan's 1981 tax cut.

Support for Kemp-Roth increased enormously after passage of Proposition 13 in California on June 6, 1978. This initiative cut and capped property tax rates and was enacted by voters over strong resistance from the entire political establishment. It led to further tax reduction efforts in other states and gave rise to a national tax revolt.[12]

CHANGING PERSPECTIVES

The political popularity of these two measures—Kemp-Roth and Proposition 13—encouraged a reconsideration of the balanced budget orthodoxy among conservative intellectuals, a revision that was eventually accepted by almost all Republican politicians. They found the starve-the-beast idea to be a way in which they could support tax cuts without abandoning a commitment to fiscal responsibility. At a hearing of the Senate Finance Committee on July 14, 1978, Alan Greenspan, who had lately chaired the Council of Economic Advisers under Ford, endorsed the Kemp-Roth bill, explaining: "Let us remember that the basic purpose of any tax cut program in today's environment is to reduce the momentum of expenditure growth by restraining the amount of revenues available and trust that there is a political limit to deficit spending."[13]

At same time, economist Milton Friedman addressed the question of deficits that might arise from a reduction in taxes without a concomitant cut in spending. He argued that the deficit is essentially meaningless, that what mattered is the size of government as measured by spending. Thus, a cut in taxes, even without accompanying spending cuts, was not a matter of concern for conservatives, to whom he issued this warning:

> By concentrating on the wrong thing, the deficit, instead of the right thing, total government spending, fiscal conservatives have been the unwitting handmaidens of the big spenders. The typical historical process is that the spenders put through laws which increase government spending. A deficit emerges. The fiscal conservatives scratch their heads and say, "My God, that's terrible; we have got to do something about that deficit." So they cooperate with the big spenders in getting taxes imposed. As soon as the new taxes are imposed and passed, the big spenders are off again, and there is another burst in government spending and another deficit.[14]

In a *Newsweek* column, Friedman made his point more succinctly: "I have concluded that the only effective way to restrain government spending is by limiting government's explicit tax revenue—just as a limited income is the only effective restraint on any individual's or family's spending."[15]

Writing on the *Wall Street Journal*'s editorial page, which often sets the Republican agenda on economic policy, columnist Irving Kristol made clear the political connection between tax cuts and government spending. Tax cuts, Kristol explained, are essential to shrinking the size of government. Republicans and conservatives, he said,

> have learned the lesson of Proposition 13, which is that tax cuts are a prerequisite for cuts in government spending. The politics of the budgetary process is such that a cut in any particular program will provoke intense opposition from a minority, and only indifference from the majority. In such a case, it is unreasonable to expect politicians to pay the high political costs involved. They can only cut when they are seen to have no alternative.[16]

At this point, the circle was largely squared. Instead of being viewed as the height of fiscal irresponsibility, cutting taxes without any corresponding effort to cut spending was now seen as the epitome of conservative fiscal policy. Trying to cut spending in isolation was both doomed to failure and counterproductive because focusing attention on the deficit was more likely to lead to tax increases than spending cuts, and to an expansion in the size of government. The only way off the treadmill of higher spending leading to higher taxes leading to still more spending was to refuse to play the game. Just cut taxes, the conservative intelligentsia now argued, and concern about deficits will be channeled into lower spending.

The political popularity of tax cuts would also help elect more members of Congress who yearned to shrink government. Republicans believed that the Democratic coalition, which had controlled Congress continuously since 1955, was vitally dependent on ever-increasing spending to gain the votes needed to keep it together. If spending could be cut or just kept from rising, Republicans thought, the Democratic coalition would break apart. Many Democrats agreed. As Representative

Tom Foley, Democrat of Washington who later became Speaker of the House, put it in a 1979 interview, "Tight budgets strain all the natural fault lines of the Democratic Party. The pressures will intensify as we approach the presidential election year and each group starts pressing its claims. You can see it happening already. Holding this team of wild horses together is a job for the most skilled congressional coachman."[17]

This changing view of what defined fiscal conservatism—smaller government via tax cuts replacing the balanced budget—became a topic of increasing theoretical discussion as well, especially among those belonging to the public choice school of economics, which integrates economics and political science and looks especially at the way institutions affect political and economic outcomes.

For many years, James Buchanan, who won the Nobel Prize in economics in 1986 for his work in developing public choice theory, had been the leading academic supporter of a balanced budget amendment to the Constitution. He thought that if politicians were forced to consider the cost of new government spending programs in terms of painful taxes instead of implicitly painless deficits, then there would be much less support for new spending. The deficit, in his view, allowed voters to feel that they were getting something for nothing: new spending at no cost in terms of taxation.

In 1977 Buchanan published an influential book that blamed John Maynard Keynes for destruction of an implicit balanced budget requirement imposed by the Founding Fathers. Until the 1930s, he argued, deficits had been universally viewed as evil—sometimes necessary, but evil nevertheless. Keynes's great error was in viewing them as good, Buchanan said. This destroyed the stigma attached to deficits and opened the floodgates to ever higher spending.[18]

The passage of Proposition 13 in California seems to have influenced Buchanan's thinking about other ways of constraining government besides a balanced budget requirement. In a series of papers culminating in his 1980 book, *The Power to Tax,* Buchanan endorsed Proposition 13–style tax cuts unaccompanied by spending cuts as an appropriate way of restraining the size of government.[19]

Subsequent research is mixed on whether tax limitation initiatives such as Proposition 13 were in the long run successful in holding down government spending.[20] It is important, however, that at a critical moment in the late 1970s an economist so well known for his commitment to a balanced budget rule would also endorse Proposition 13–style tax cuts as a way of forcing action to downsize government. It was a significant step in making starve-the-beast theory not just a populist slogan but an idea to be taken seriously.

In the 1980s public choice theory developed the idea that conservative governments might intentionally increase the national debt through tax cuts in order to bind the hands of a subsequent liberal government.[21] More of the budget would be dedicated to interest payments, thereby precluding a liberal government from spending as much on consumption as it might like.

RONALD REAGAN

During the 1980 presidential campaign, Ronald Reagan endorsed the Kemp-Roth tax cut but also insisted that he would sharply cut government spending. Upon taking office in 1981, he followed through on this promise and asked Congress for spending cuts as well as tax cuts.[22] But Reagan was unwilling to hold his tax cuts hostage to congressional inaction on spending. In explaining to the American people why tax cuts should precede spending cuts, he said that the former would pave the way for the latter, as starve-the-beast theory presupposed. In a national television address on February 5, 1981, Reagan put it this way:

> Over the past decades we've talked of curtailing government spending so that we can then lower the tax burden. Sometimes we've even taken a run at doing that. But there were always those who told us that taxes couldn't be cut until spending was reduced. Well, you know, we can lecture our children about extravagance until we run out of voice and breath. Or we can cure their extravagance by simply reducing their allowance.

Not everyone in the Reagan Administration agreed with this strategy. Murray Weidenbaum, Reagan's first CEA chairman, thought it was "wishful thinking" to believe that tax cuts would lead to cuts in spending. But Friedman endorsed the Reagan strategy. In particular, he supported his call for a permanent tax cut and argued against the idea of a temporary one just to deal with the economic slow-down. A one-year tax cut could too easily be offset with one-shot spending cuts, Friedman said. Hence one of the virtues of a permanent tax cut was that it would force permanent cuts in spending.[23]

Although Reagan was successful in getting his tax cut through Congress in 1981, he was much less successful in getting the kinds of permanent spending cuts he had hoped for. With an economic recession beginning in July of that year, projections of budget deficits began growing, leading to calls in Congress and the media for tax increases. Reagan addressed this issue directly in his January 1982 State of the Union address:

> The doubters would have us turn back the clock with tax increases that would offset the personal tax-rate reductions already passed by this Congress. Raise present taxes to cut future deficits, they tell us. Well, I don't believe we should buy that argument.... Higher taxes would not mean lower deficits. If they did, how would we explain that tax revenues more than doubled just since 1976; yet in that same six-year period we ran the largest series of deficits in our history.... Raising taxes won't balance the budget; it will encourage more government spending and less private investment.

Reagan promised not to ask for a tax increase in 1982, but this proved to be a promise he could not keep. Congressional demands for action against the deficit, which rose by 63 percent between 1981 and 1982, were too strong and there was no way of getting the votes to cut spending without also raising taxes. Later that year Reagan signed into law the Tax Equity and Fiscal Responsibility Act of 1982, the largest peacetime tax increase in American history.[24] This was the first of many tax increases that Reagan would ultimately acquiesce to, as shown in table 1. Because of continuing concern about the deficit, there were

Table 1   Legislated Tax Changes by Ronald Reagan as of 1988

Tax Cuts	Billions of Dollars
Economic Recovery Tax Act of 1981	−264.4
Interest and Dividends Tax Compliance Act of 1983	−1.8
Federal Employees' Retirement System Act of 1986	−0.2
Tax Reform Act of 1986	−8.9
Total cumulative tax cuts	−275.3

Tax Increases	Billions of Dollars
Tax Equity and Fiscal Responsibility Act of 1982	+57.3
Highway Revenue Act of 1982	+4.9
Social Security Amendments of 1983	+24.6
Railroad Retirement Revenue Act of 1983	+1.2
Deficit Reduction Act of 1984	+25.4
Consolidated Omnibus Budget Reconciliation Act of 1985	+2.9
Omnibus Budget Reconciliation Act of 1985	+2.4
Superfund Amendments and Reauthorization Act of 1986	+0.6
Continuing Resolution for 1987	+2.8
Omnibus Budget Reconciliation Act of 1987	+8.6
Continuing Resolution for 1988	+2.0
Total cumulative tax increases	+132.7

Source: Office of Management and Budget, *Budget of the United States Government, Fiscal Year 1990* (Washington: USGPO, 1989), 4–4.

almost annual budget crises throughout the 1980s that necessitated budget deals containing spending cuts and tax increases.

Although Republicans saw Reagan's support for tax increases as a setback, Democrats saw the accompanying spending cuts as culmination of the starve-the-beast philosophy. Pat Moynihan regularly blamed his former student, OMB Director David Stockman, for selling Congress a pig in a poke by promising that the 1981 tax cut would so expand the economy that revenues would not fall, while knowing all along that they would, thereby forcing massive cuts in social spending.[25]

Stockman's response to Moynihan was, basically, that no one in the Reagan administration was that smart. "In truth, not six of the six hundred players in the game of fiscal governance in the Spring and Summer of 1981 would have willed this outcome," he later wrote.[26]

In fact, no one was fooled about anything. The Reagan administration's budget forecasts used standard revenue-estimating methodologies and did not incorporate any supply-side effects—much to the displeasure of some supply-siders.[27] In any case, Congress has its own budgetary and tax-estimating organizations—the CBO and JCT—and was not solely reliant on administration estimates even if they were bogus. As table 2 demonstrates, OMB and CBO had almost identical estimates of federal revenues, including the effects of the Reagan tax cut.

Another liberal charge was that Reagan intentionally increased the deficit by cutting taxes in 1981 in order to trick Democrats into taking the lead in proposing politically unpopular tax increases. If so, Walter Mondale, the Democratic presidential nominee in 1984, fell right into

Table 2 OMB and CBO Deficit Estimates, March 1981 (fiscal years, billions of dollars)

	1981	1982	1983	1984
Revenues				
OMB	600	650	709	771
CBO	599	654	707	769
Actual	599	618	601	666
Outlays				
OMB	655	695	732	770
CBO	662	721	766	818
Actual	678	746	808	852
Deficit/Surplus				
OMB	−55	−45	−23	+1
CBO	−63	−67	−59	−49
Actual	−79	−128	−208	−185

Source: Congressional Budget Office, *Economic Policy and the Outlook for the Economy* (Washington: USGPO, 1981), 47. See also CBO, *An Analysis of Congressional Budget Estimates for Fiscal Years 1980–1982* (Washington: USGPO, 1984).

the trap by endorsing a big tax increase during the campaign. Said Mondale at the Democratic National Convention, "Mr. Reagan will raise taxes, and so will I. He won't tell you. I just did."[28]

DO TAXES FEED SPENDING?

Reagan's support for the 1982 tax increase, which took back much of the 1981 tax cut, led to considerable debate about whether tax increases were effective in reducing deficits. A number of economists argued that they led to higher spending—feeding the beast instead of starving it. This debate continued throughout the 1980s and constituted a variation of the starve-the-beast idea. If tax cuts forced spending cuts, then the flip side is that tax increases raised spending.

As early as 1971, economist Robert Eisner argued that one reason for the failure of the 1968 surtax to restrain inflation was because it caused spending to rise by more than the revenue raised by the tax.[29] The first to argue against tax increases on the grounds that they fed spending was a top Reagan administration economist, Beryl Sprinkel, undersecretary of the Treasury for monetary affairs. Writing in the *Wall Street Journal* in 1983, he rejected charges that the deficit resulted from inadequate revenues. Consequently, tax increases were an inappropriate response; the problem was too much spending and would only be cured by spending cuts. Said Sprinkel:

> Clearly, it is in the interest of the big spenders to blame the deficit on under-taxation, rather than on their own spending habits. The argument for tax increases is analogous to a compulsive shopper blaming his continued need to borrow on the boss, who will not finance that habit by granting continual salary increases that represent an ever-increasing share of the company's total budget.[30]

Academic economists quickly took up the challenge of determining whether tax increases fed the beast—leading ultimately to higher spending with no meaningful impact on the deficit—or whether they did in fact reduce deficits. The first academic paper to address this question was by economists George M. von Furstenberg, Jeffrey Green, and Jin-Ho Jeong. They concluded that the direction of causality was from spending to taxes. Higher taxes were, in effect, a late charge for excessive spending.[31]

In response, Michael Marlow, an economist in Reagan's Treasury Department, published several studies showing that tax cuts may not do much to hold down spending, but tax increases do nothing whatsoever to reduce deficits in the long run. In the first of these studies, he wrote:

> The most important conclusion to be drawn from these causality tests is that proposals that endorse tax increases to close the federal budget deficit do not necessarily offer permanent solutions to underlying fiscal problems. While our tests do not indicate final answers to the deficit issue, it is obvious that our results do *not* favor tax increases over spending reductions as a means of closing future deficit levels of the Federal government.... In general, a tax increase may not even offer a temporary solution to unacceptably large federal deficits.[32]

Subsequently, several published papers supported the view that higher taxes had no effect on stimulating spending but were the inevitable result of too much spending—the late charge argument.[33] Others concluded that higher taxes stimulated additional spending, leaving the deficit largely unaffected.[34] Finally, some studies found the causality running in one direction during some periods and circumstances but not during others.[35]

One explanation for these contradictory findings is the existence of a binding balanced budget requirement, either implicit or explicit. If, as discussed earlier, there was a hard implicit balanced budget rule at the federal level through the 1930s and a soft one through the mid-1970s, then it stands to reason that higher spending would tend to force tax increases during these periods. This would show up as well in causality studies based on state and local data, since governments at that level have always operated under a hard explicit balanced budget constraint. Since the Republican Party abandoned strong support for a balanced budget in the late 1970s, it is not surprising that the data since then fail to show causality, and this also influences studies utilizing more recent data.

POLITICAL DEVELOPMENTS

In many respects, ultimate empirical resolution of the starve-the-beast debate is irrelevant to its political implications. The data are sufficiently ambiguous that studies, especially of the informal sort that proliferate on Capitol Hill, can always be generated to support the political preferences or demands of the moment.

One such study was done by economists Richard Vedder, Lowell Gallaway, and Christopher Frenze in 1987. It concluded that higher taxes actually led to higher deficits, because each dollar of tax increase led to an increase in spending of $1.58. In other words, the deficit rose by 58 cents for each dollar of tax increase.[36] This study was significant because a version of it was cited by Ronald Reagan during his October 24, 1987 radio address:

> In 1982, for example, TEFRA, as it was called, the Tax Equity and Fiscal Responsibility Act, raised taxes by $131 billion over four years, with Congress pledging to slash spending by $3 for every dollar of increased revenue. Instead, four years later, taxes had gone up the expected $131 billion, but spending over this same period had risen by $244 billion. In fact, every dollar in increased revenue since 1980 had been matched by $1.25 of increased spending.

In his 1988 campaign, George H. W. Bush endorsed the modified starve-the-beast theory that tax increases feed spending and are ineffective in reducing the deficit. "Unless you can control Congress's spending, increased revenues will go to increased spending," he said.[37]

In Congress as well, the modified starve-the-beast theory made inroads even among moderates who had previously supported tax increases to reduce budget deficits. Apparently, after taking so much political heat, many members were dismayed to see that so little progress was made toward permanent resolution of the deficit problem.

One of these was Senator Bob Packwood, Republican of Oregon, who said this during floor debate on Bill Clinton's tax increase in 1993:

> The history of the U.S. Government is that when we increased taxes, we spent them; we did not apply it to the deficit. It does not matter that the President has stated, "Let us have a deficit reduction trust fund." We have never followed that; we instead spent it. I predict that if we raise these new taxes, we will spend them, also. We will not cut spending. We will spend it on new programs or expansion of existing programs.[38]

Ronald Reagan endorsed this soft version of the starve-the-beast theory in a *Wall Street Journal* op-ed article that same year. He essentially disowned all of the budget deals he had signed into law, saying he had been double-crossed into supporting tax increases in return for spending cuts that never emerged. Said Reagan:

> Despite the "assurances," "promises," "pledges" and "commitments" you are given, the spending cuts have a way of being forgotten or quietly lobbied out of future budgets. But the tax increases are as certain to come as, well, death and taxes.
>
> In 1982, Congress wanted to raise taxes. It promised it would cut federal spending by $3 for every $1 in new taxes. Being a new kid in town, I agreed to this. Unfortunately, although the new taxes went into effect, Congress never cut spending by even a penny.[39]

During the 2000 campaign, one of George W. Bush's major themes was the need for a tax cut to reduce the budget surplus that had been accumulated during the Clinton administration. Again echoing the starve-the-beast theory, Bush argued against the virtues of a surplus, saying that it would only fuel additional spending. Commenting on Federal Reserve Board chairman Alan Greenspan's suggestion that the surpluses be saved, Bush countered, "Mr. Greenspan believes that money around Washington, D.C. will be spent on a single item—debt reduction. I think it will be spent on greater government. He has got greater faith in the appropriators than I do."[40]

Bush's campaign budget adviser, economist John Cogan of Stanford's Hoover Institution, later put it this way, "It is wrong to allow surpluses because these surpluses invariably lead to higher spending."[41]

Once in office, Bush justified his proposal for a big tax cut in 2001 partly on the grounds that budget surpluses led to bigger government. Therefore, the prudent, fiscally conservative thing to do was get rid of the surplus by reducing taxes. As he put it at an August 24, 2001 press conference, the tax cut would put Congress into a "fiscal straitjacket." In one of his last interviews as president, Bush told the *Wall Street Journal* that one of the greatest accomplishments of his tax cuts was to hold down domestic discretionary spending.[42]

According to journalist Ron Suskind, influential Bush adviser Karl Rove invoked the starve-the-beast idea during tax debates within the White House. It also remained popular among Republicans in Congress. For example, in 2003, Senator Rick Santorum, Republican of Pennsylvania who formerly served in the House of Representatives, said, "I came to the House as a real deficit hawk, but I am no longer a deficit hawk. I'll tell you why. I had to spend the surpluses. Deficits make it easier to say no."[43]

That same year, James A. Baker, Reagan's chief of staff and Treasury secretary who was widely viewed as the driving force behind the many budget deals of the 1980s that resulted in higher taxes, decided that he had been wrong. Echoing the modified starve-the-beast theory, he concluded that the tax increases largely fueled additional spending.[44]

THE FUTURE

The *Wall Street Journal* editorial page continues to hold steadfastly to the view that tax cuts force spending cuts. As recently as June 2006 its principal economics editorial writer said, "For 25 years, virtually every bipartisan budget deal has meant higher taxes, higher spending and political carnage for the GOP."[45]

Thus, the starve-the-beast theory continues to be operationally important in terms of conservative political strategy. It is routinely invoked by conservatives as if it is self-evident.[46] However, the budgetary performance of recent years, which has seen substantial spending *increases* along with large tax cuts, has caused some conservatives to reassess their position. As columnist Steve Chapman of the *Chicago Tribune* put it:

> For years, conservatives have said [tax cuts] would yield a smaller government, through a process known as "starving the beast." Allow Congress less money to spend, they reasoned, and it would have to spend less.
>
> If that were the case, big government would be pretty emaciated by now. Instead, the beast looks more like a product of the obesity epidemic. Since the GOP won control of the House of Representatives in 1994, federal outlays have grown by nearly a third, after accounting for inflation.[47]

Bill Niskanen, chairman of the libertarian Cato Institute and a member of the CEA under Reagan, now argues that the starve-the-beast theory has actually been perverse. It led libertarians and conservatives to think that tax cuts are the *only* thing necessary to restrain the growth of government. Passage of large tax cuts during the George W. Bush administration led them to become "casual about the sustained political discipline necessary to control federal spending." Niskanen says it is a "fantasy" to think that tax cuts have any restraining influence on spending.[48]

To the extent that the "true" burden of government is measured by spending rather than taxes, as Milton Friedman long argued, the recent lack of budgetary discipline resulting from overreliance on the starve-the-beast theory could mean that taxes will be higher in the long run. As one study recently warned, "abandoning fiscal discipline on one side of the budget could induce . . . fiscal irresponsibility on both sides of the budget." This may explain why Niskanen now finds that tax cuts actually appear to cause spending to rise, a conclusion recently confirmed by economists Christina Romer and David Romer.[49]

Nevertheless, despite the lack of evidence during the George W. Bush administration that tax cuts even restrained spending, let alone causing spending to be cut, a number of leading conservative economists continue to maintain the basic validity of starve-the-beast theory, including Edward Lazear, who became chairman of the CEA under Bush in May 2006.[50]

One possibility is that the deficit just hasn't begun to really bite yet. When it does, somewhere down the road, perhaps the starve-the-beast theory will then lead to large cuts in basic entitlement programs. Joshua Bolten, Bush's OMB director who became White House chief of staff in 2006, suggested this when he observed that projected spending was now so great, it would be impossible to eliminate future deficits with taxes only. "In the longer run," he said, "no plausible amount of tax increases could possibly close the enormous gap that will be created by the unsustainable growth in entitlement programs. Our real fiscal danger can be solved only by reform of the entitlement programs themselves."[51]

This statement is just factually wrong. Practically every country in Europe has a tax/GDP ratio high enough to cover all of the projected increase in spending in the United States just through higher revenues. In 2006, the European members of the OECD had a tax/GDP ratio of 38 percent, compared with a U.S. ratio (total government) of 28 percent.[52] The difference between these figures would be more than enough to pay for all of the projected entitlement spending in the United States for many decades to come.

Nevertheless, many on the political left have long charged that the ultimate goal of the starve-the-beast advocates has been to create a deficit so massively large that entitlements would have to be cut when a fiscal crisis finally emerges. In the words of Peter Beinart, former editor of the *New Republic:*

> It's middle-class entitlements, however, such as Medicare and Social Security, which make the federal government so big (and so popular). And the GOP's only hope of undermining them is to create a fiscal crisis so huge that now-unpopular Republican solutions, such as privatizing Social Security and turning Medicare into a voucher program, become politically feasible. In roughly a decade, when multiple

Bush tax cuts and an enormous defense buildup run smack into the baby-boom retirement, they might just get their wish.[53]

Others on the left, such as economist Paul Krugman, have made a similar argument, just as Pat Moynihan did in the 1980s. It would have a lot more plausibility, however, if George W. Bush and a Republican Congress hadn't massively expanded Medicare spending in 2003 by adding a new, unfunded prescription drug benefit to the program costing trillions of dollars.[54]

Despite the apparent failure of the starve-the-beast theory to restrain spending in recent years, there is still a theoretical argument to be made on its behalf. One option would be to channel the desire for specific tax cuts into a mechanism that might reduce spending in some general way. This might possibly be done by reviving interest in a balanced budget amendment to the Constitution. Clearly, if tax cuts were achieved under a hard balanced budget rule, then spending would necessarily have to give way.[55]

If voters knew there was a hard balanced budget requirement, then presumably they would also know that their support for tax cuts would manifest itself in spending cuts as well. There is some support for this idea in the poll data. A poll by National Public Radio in April 2003 found that 44 percent of respondents favored higher taxes and more services; 48 percent favored lower taxes and reduced services. In September 2004 a Fox News/Opinion Dynamics poll asked likely voters if they would rather support a larger government that provided more services and required them to pay more taxes, or a smaller government that provided fewer services but allowed them to pay less taxes. The former position was supported by 38 percent and the latter by 45 percent. A September 2008 poll by Rasmussen found that 57 percent of voters would prefer fewer government services and lower taxes; only 31 percent favored more government spending and higher taxes.[56]

It appears that the starve-the-beast theory has undergone an evolution. In the beginning, it allowed fiscal conservatives traditionally wedded to a hard balanced budget requirement to rationalize their support for tax cuts unaccompanied by corresponding spending cuts. This proved extremely important to the modern evolution and success of conservatism in the political sphere. In the words of journalist Jonathan Rauch, "For modern conservatism and the country, the importance of Starve the Beast is impossible to overstate."[57]

Later, the starve-the-beast idea reappeared in opposition to tax increases to close budget deficits. As Newt Gingrich, former Republican Speaker of the House, often put it, this effort would just make fiscal conservatives tax collectors for the welfare state. Another version of this form of the starve-the-beast theory is that tax increases are futile in terms of reducing the deficit because they only fuel additional increases in spending, potentially making the deficit even worse.

Although starve-the-beast theory still has adherents among reputable economists, the growth of spending and deficits even in the face of large tax cuts has worn down at least a few of its former supporters. There is now a growing fear among such people that the ultimate result of reliance on starving the beast to support tax cuts may be to make future tax increases inevitable. Whether on balance taxpayers are better off at the end of the day than they would have been without the tax cuts remains to be seen. But there is at least a reasonable chance that they will be worse off.

There is still the possibility that a future fiscal crisis will provide political cover for massive cuts in entitlement programs that would be politically impossible except under such circumstances. Many analysts, including this writer, now think that the more likely result of such a crisis will be to implement massive tax increases that will move the tax/GDP ratio in the United States closer to that in Europe.

CHAPTER 7

DEALING WITH TOMORROW'S ECONOMIC CRISIS

As we have seen, economic theory has always evolved to deal with the particular crisis of the times. Keynesian economics came into being because classical economics was incapable of dealing with the Great Depression. It died when Keynesian economics was incapable of dealing with the stagflation of the 1970s, giving rise to monetarism and supply-side economics. Now they have run out of gas as well. A new approach must arise to deal with the economic problems we face today and going forward. What might that be?

It is clear from the reaction of policymakers to the financial crisis of 2008–2009 that they learned important lessons from the mistakes that led to the Great Depression. In particular, the Federal Reserve was determined to prevent the banking system from imploding and bringing on a massive deflation, which was at the root of the Great Depression. The nation was fortunate to have Ben Bernanke chairing the Fed at such a critical moment, because much of his career as an economist at Princeton University had been devoted to studying the origins of the Great Depression.[1] He summarized his views on the subject at a 2002 event honoring economist Milton Friedman, whose work had shown that the Fed was largely responsible for the depression. Said Bernanke, "You're right, we did it. We're very sorry. But thanks to you, we won't do it again."[2]

Unfortunately, the financial crisis also led to an enormous expansion of government spending. On top of the $150 billion for an economically worthless rebate early in 2008, another $700 billion was voted for a bailout of failing banks and other financial institutions in September. In February 2009 Congress enacted a $787 billion stimulus package that many members thought was too small. Yet, added to the fall-off in tax revenues resulting from the economic slow-down, the result was a doubling of the national debt. In September 2008 the Congressional Budget Office had estimated a national debt of $8 trillion in 2018; by March 2009 its estimate had risen to $16 trillion.

The financial crisis also exposed a problem that economists had seen coming for years, but had been ignored by policymakers and papered-over to a large extent by strong gains in the stock and housing markets. Those gains increased the wealth of many Americans in retirement and nearing retirement, making both them and policymakers complacent about the growing problem of an aging population and the enormous strains that will place on the economy and society. According to the Census Bureau, by 2030 the percentage of the population over age 65 will rise from 12.7 percent in 2008 to 19.3 percent.

The United States was facing a budget crisis of historic proportion, long before the recession caused spending to hemorrhage and revenues to collapse, due to the aging of the baby boom generation. The first member of that giant generation turned 62 and qualified for early Social Security benefits in 2008. The first baby boomer will turn 65 in 2011 and become eligible for Medicare. This will soon require a vast increase in spending for Social Security and Medicare.[3]

Unfortunately, the best chance to reform Social Security was lost when the budget surpluses of the 1990s were squandered without any of the money being used to implement fundamental reform of either the tax system or entitlement programs. In the end, liberals lost as much as conservatives from the failure to deal with entitlements. If the surpluses had been dedicated to entitlement reform they wouldn't have been available to finance George W. Bush's tax cuts in 2001.

In a larger sense, the problem going forward is one of debt. American families live beyond their means, borrow to finance current consumption, and fail to save adequately for retirement; corporations borrow to pay dividends or to buy other companies rather than investing in their core business; the federal government borrows to finance "stimulus" that doesn't stimulate; and the United States as a whole borrows from foreigners to maintain a standard of living that is unsustainable.

In the future, Americans must save more and consume less. This is the opposite of Keynesian economics, which says that spending is the *sine qua non* of growth. In many ways it is also the opposite of supply-side economics, which has come to mean that there is no economic problem that huge tax cuts can't fix. In my opinion, we are past the point where tax cuts can fix what ails us. Large tax increases will be necessary to pay for all the promises that have been made. Instead of opposing them entirely, supply-siders should use their insights to design a new tax system better able to raise higher revenues at the least possible cost in terms of economic growth and political freedom.

THE IMPENDING DEBT EXPLOSION

The burden of the federal debt, which is the cumulative total of past budget deficits less surpluses, is best viewed as a percentage of gross domestic product. By this measure, the gross debt peaked at 122 percent of GDP in 1946 after the enormous outlays associated with World War II and fell almost continuously for the next three and a half decades, bottoming out at 32.6 percent of GDP in 1981. This improvement had less to do with budgetary restraint than steady growth in the economy and inflation, which eroded the real value of the debt. The large budget surpluses of the late 1990s reduced the debt from 67 percent of GDP to only 57 percent in 2001, but the large budget deficits of the George W. Bush years completely reversed this progress. By the end of fiscal year 2008 the debt was back up to 67 percent of GDP.

The national debt, however, measures only a small portion of the federal government's total indebtedness. The greatest portion does not consist of Treasury securities sold to the public, but of promises made for retirement programs, especially Social Security and Medicare. These promises run into the trillions of dollars for benefits owed to those living today and trillions more for future generations. Although people pay taxes for these benefits, their cost greatly exceeds what most people pay for them. In any case, neither system is prefunded and both are essentially financed out of current tax revenues. The so-called trust funds for Social Security and Medicare are economically meaningless. As the federal budget notes, "From the standpoint of overall government finances, the trust funds do not reduce the future burden of financing Social Security or Medicare benefits."[4] In the case of Medicare, revenues have been insufficient to pay current beneficiaries for many years. In coming years this will be true of Social Security as well.

The unfunded portion of Social Security and Medicare constitutes a debt that will have to be paid by future taxpayers. This debt is calculated yearly by the actuaries for these programs and can be found in their annual reports, usually published in the spring. At the end of each fiscal year, the Treasury Department puts all of the federal government's debts, including those for veterans benefits and many other programs, together in a balance sheet called the Financial Report of the United States Government. It is usually published in December and posted on the website of the Financial Management Service, a Treasury bureau.[5]

As with corporate balance sheets, the really interesting stuff is in the footnotes. According to the 2008 financial report, the federal government had assets of $2 trillion and liabilities of $12.2 trillion, for a net debt of $10.2 trillion. But this is just the beginning. In another table, the financial report lists the unfunded future cost of retirement programs. At the end of 2008, Social Security was in the hole to the tune of $17.2 trillion and Medicare would need $31.8 trillion to cover expected costs over and above revenues. Thus, Uncle Sam had additional debt of $49 trillion on top of the national debt.

But even this calculation understates the problem because the financial report calculates the cost of retirement programs for only 75 years out. Since these programs are a permanent part of the law and very difficult to change, one really needs to know what their cost will be in perpetuity with some adjustment for the fact that future dollars are worth less than those today, something economists call discounting. The discounted present value of entitlement programs in effect measures how much money would have to be in a bank somewhere earning interest to pay promised benefits over and above future revenues. By this measure, Social Security had a debt of $15.7 trillion at the end of 2007 and Medicare had a debt of $74.4 trillion, for a total of $90 trillion for just these two programs.[6]

Of course, there will be future economic growth and higher incomes out of which to pay these debts.[7] What really matters to people is how much taxes will have to rise to pay future Social Security and Medicare benefits. According to Social Security's actuaries, the payroll tax rate would have to rise by 3.2 percentage points, from 12.9 percent to 16.1 percent, to pay all the benefits that have been promised to current and future beneficiaries. This tax increase would equal 1.1 percent of GDP.[8]

Medicare's problems are far worse. According to that program's actuaries, Part A, which covers hospital visits, has an unfunded liability of $34.4 trillion. The payroll tax rate would have to rise by 6.1 percentage points, from 2.9 percent to 9 percent, or 2.6 percent of GDP, to pay all the promised benefits just for this part of Medicare. But Medicare also has two additional programs with large unfunded costs. Part B, which pays for doctors visits, has an unfunded liability of $34 trillion or 2.6 percent of GDP in perpetuity. Part D covers prescription drugs and was enacted by the Bush administration and a Republican Congress in 2003. It has an unfunded liability of

$17.2 trillion in perpetuity or 1.3 percent of GDP. The actuaries don't calculate these liabilities in terms of payroll tax rates, because by law the portion of these programs not covered by premiums is already funded by general revenues.[9]

Thus, the combined Social Security and Medicare payroll tax rate, which now stands at 15.3 percent, would have to rise to at least 24.6 percent to keep paying all the benefits that have been promised to every retiree in perpetuity, not counting the costs of Medicare Parts B and D. Altogether, taxes would need to rise by 7.6 percent of GDP immediately and forever to keep Social Security and Medicare operating as they do now and pay all the benefits that have been promised to current and future beneficiaries. This is equivalent to raising the individual income tax by 90 percent—virtually doubling taxes for every taxpayer.

Finally, both the CBO and GAO annually make long-term projections of federal spending. According to the latest CBO report, spending on Social Security is expected to rise from 4.3 percent of GDP to 6.1 percent by the year 2030. Medicare spending will rise from 2.7 percent of GDP to 5.9 percent, and the cost of Medicaid will increase from 1.4 percent to 2.5 percent.[10] All other spending except interest on the debt is expected to remain roughly constant as a share of GDP.

We were looking at a 6.1 percentage point rise in federal spending as a share of GDP over just the next 21 years—and that was before the recent economic downturn. All federal taxes would have to rise by one third over this period to avoid a rise in the debt that would cause spending on interest to rise from 1.7 percent of GDP to 4.8 percent. If no action were taken and all the growth in spending was financed entirely by deficits, the annual budget deficit would rise to more than 10 percent of GDP by 2030 and the national debt would be well over 100 percent of GDP. GAO's numbers are roughly the same.[11]

IS THE U.S. GOVERNMENT BANKRUPT?

Insofar as the federal government has insufficient assets to cover its debts, it would be reasonable to say that it is bankrupt. Both Moody's and Standard & Poor's, the major credit rating agencies, have warned that the Treasury's triple-A credit rating is threatened by exploding debt.[12] This could cause investors to demand higher interest rates on Treasury bonds in the future to cover the risk of default.

Of course, it is not entirely appropriate to use the same criteria to evaluate sovereign debt as to measure corporate debt. Private businesses cannot compel people to buy their products, and therefore have no guaranteed revenue stream from which to pay their debts. But the federal government has taxing power that in principle is unconstrained; that is to say, there is no constitutional prohibition on any level of taxation that Congress chooses to impose. In the words of Justice Lewis F. Powell, "Congress' power to tax is virtually unlimited."[13] Whether it would be practical or even feasible to collect taxes above a certain level is another matter.

Obviously, at some point there would be political resistance to higher taxes as well as a severe decline in the tax base due to reduced incentives and tax evasion. But such limitations vary over time and from place to place. For example, during wartime people will bear tax burdens that they would strenuously resist in peacetime. They will also willingly bear a much heavier burden if they believe that they are getting value for their money in the form of government services, such as good schools for their children or health care. This is why people don't automatically move to countries or states and localities with the lowest taxes.[14] And over time, as incomes rise, people have long shown a willingness to accept higher taxes, a phenomenon called Wagner's law after Adolf Wagner, the economist who first observed it. One might think of government as a superior good (one that people consume more of as their incomes rise), rather than an inferior good (one that they consume less of as their incomes rise).

The larger question remains—when will rising spending and deficits really bite? In other words, when will the trends described earlier have such a profound effect on the economy and public opinion that action must be taken? And when such action is taken, what form will it take?

It is my view that budget deficits have significant political consequences only when they are viewed as having an impact on inflation
and/or interest rates; that is to say, when they are perceived as impact-
ing directly on peoples' lives in some meaningful way. As long as
deficits are abstractions, people may tell pollsters they are concerned
about them, but they will not pressure their elected representatives
to reduce them unless they believe they will benefit immediately and
materially in the form of lower inflation or interest rates.

This was not always the case. In years past, deficits were viewed
as immoral by many people and they voted on this basis. But in recent
years, opposition to deficit spending has mostly taken the form of lip-
service or opposition to trivialities such as earmarks in the budget that
collectively add up to about one half of one percent of spending.[15]
There has been no significant concern for deficits shown by voters
since Ross Perot's unsuccessful third party run in 1992, and no real
legislative action to reduce them since Bill Clinton's effort in 1993,
which was opposed by every Republican in Congress.

Looking at the trends discussed earlier, when can we expect rising deficits to begin raising inflation and interest rates? This is a hard
question to answer. Inflation is primarily a monetary phenomenon. As
long as the Federal Reserve keeps the money supply under control,
deficits have no inherent impact on inflation except temporarily. This
is where the monetarists were right and the Keynesians were wrong.
But the true relationship between deficits and inflation is more complex, because the Fed is a political institution with a legal mandate to
maintain high growth and low unemployment, not price stability.[16]

Historically, when deficits have forced a rise in interest rates, the
Fed has been pressured to moderate them by easing monetary policy. In effect, it buys the Treasury's bonds and pays for them with
money created out of thin air. Up to a point this works. But eventually the excess money creation causes prices to be bid up. Once inflation becomes widespread, it raises interest rates by itself as investors
demand higher yields to cover their lost purchasing power. At this
point, markets become keenly focused on the Fed, which is no longer

able to reduce interest rates except by reducing inflationary expectations by sharply reducing money growth. This is what happened between 1979 and 1981, but the result was extraordinarily high interest rates while tight money coexisted with high inflation. In 1981 the federal funds rate, the rate at which banks borrow from each other, reached 20 percent and prime rate reached 21.5 percent.

Looking at the impact of deficits on interest rates in isolation from monetary policy shows less of an impact than most people probably imagine. Much depends on what the deficits are used for. When the government increases purchases of goods and services this has a bigger effect on interest rates than increased spending on interest payments, which is just a transfer among bond holders. It also depends on whether market participants think an increase in the deficit is transitory or permanent. And it depends on the willingness of foreigners to buy Treasury securities, among other things. A 2003 study by a Federal Reserve economist estimated that a one percent increase in the debt/GDP ratio raised long-term rates by 25 basis points (0.25 percent). But a 2005 study by a former chairman of the CEA found that increasing the national debt by one percent of GDP would raise real interest rates by only 2 or 3 basis points.[17]

It almost doesn't matter what the truth is. When inflation and interest rates reach levels where they are politically unpalatable, one can be certain that the reaction of policymakers will be to reduce the deficit. It will be the one action that they can all agree upon that plausibly will help the situation and at least won't make it worse.

THE SHAPE OF DEFICIT REDUCTION TO COME

It would be highly desirable to reduce projected deficits well before an economic crisis makes it imperative. It would be better to cut entitlements in some sensible way, such as slowly raising the age to qualify for Social Security and Medicare. Life expectancy at birth has increased by 8 years since 1970 and by 3.5 years for those who reach age 65. It is estimated that life expectancy rises by 0.15 years annually. Thus, we would need to raise the retirement age by almost two months per year forever just to keep the work/retirement ratio—the percentage of one's life spent working versus the percentage spent in retirement—from falling more than it already has.[18]

As a practical matter, it is almost impossible to cut spending for these programs except by phasing in reductions over many years—if only because the political power of current beneficiaries is too great. It's a fact that the elderly vote in much higher percentages than the young—something routinely ignored by those who think it is possible to massively cut benefits for current retirees to keep the cost of entitlement programs in check. In 2004, 73.3 percent of those age 65 to 74 voted while just 46.7 percent of those age 18 to 24 did so. In congressional elections, the political power of the elderly and near-elderly is even greater. In 2006, almost two-thirds of voters were at least 45 years old; just 5.8 percent were under 24. It is simply unrealistic to think that a majority of voters are going to vote to cut their own benefits. They may support cuts in benefits for future retirees, but it will have to be for those in the far distant future if there is any real hope of gaining political support for such an effort.[19]

People also need time to adjust their affairs in response to changes in retirement programs. If they are going to have to work longer, they need to know decades in advance.

Unfortunately, it is very unlikely that politicians will act in advance of a crisis. It's not in their nature to impose pain on anyone unless they have no choice. And often it is only in a crisis atmosphere that there is sufficient political support to cut spending or raise taxes significantly. But if policymakers have a gun to their heads, they are less likely to make the best decisions about how to reduce deficits. Too much emphasis will necessarily be put on getting savings quickly, which tends to put entitlement programs off limits. Discretionary programs will necessarily bear the brunt of spending cuts even when everyone recognizes that this is both unfair and inefficient.

But cutting discretionary spending can never yield enough savings to make a sufficient impact on the deficit. Moreover, it is politically impossible to have a big deficit reduction package that only cuts spending. As Fed chairman Bernanke notes, even if we cut discretionary spending by 80 percent by 2030, we would still need to raise nonpayroll taxes by 35 percent to eliminate the deficit projected by CBO.[20] Furthermore, the biggest component of discretionary spending is national defense. And completely abolishing every domestic discretionary program would not have been enough to eliminate the deficit in 2008.

In practice, the only way Congress can cut the deficit quickly and meaningfully is by raising taxes. Historically, deficit reduction packages have always relied heavily on higher taxes. Indeed, in many cases the only real deficit reduction came from higher taxes because virtually all the spending cuts were in the form of promises to cut future appropriations without any means of enforcing those promises.[21]

This is not by any means to suggest that raising taxes is the best way to achieve deficit reduction—or even a good way. The experience of other countries clearly shows that the most successful long-term deficit reductions have come primarily from spending cuts, especially on entitlements.[22] But it is also true that higher revenues played an important role, although in many cases they did not take the form of legislated tax increases but rather were passive increases resulting from failure to fully index the tax system for inflation and real growth.[23] In any tax system with progressive rates, higher incomes resulting from either inflation or real growth will raise the tax burden as taxpayers are pushed up into higher brackets.

It is a pipe dream to think that our nation's looming fiscal problem can be dealt with solely on the spending side of the budget. As discussed in the previous chapter, the idea that depriving the government of revenue will somehow starve the beast is an idea that once seemed plausible but has been shown to be completely wrong in practice. Every serious budget expert who has looked at the American situation has long concluded that eventually revenues are going to need to rise substantially to pay the costs of an aging society.[24] Unlike private corporations, national governments cannot declare bankruptcy and wipe clean their burden of debt, at least not without using inflation to accomplish the task—a cure worse than the disease.

An important factor changing the dynamics of American indebtedness is the growing foreign ownership of Treasury securities. Once upon a time economists dismissed the national debt as a problem because we owed it to ourselves. That is no longer true. As of December 2008, foreigners owned 53 percent of the privately held national debt. As of early 2008, China and Japan together owned more than $1 trillion in Treasury securities.[25]

Although occasional threats by foreigners to stop buying Treasury securities have not been carried out, it remains a danger that could trigger the sort of financial crisis that would force serious action to reduce the deficit. In early 2009 the Chinese prime minister became so alarmed by the United States's exploding debt, he asked for special guarantees for the Treasury bonds his country holds. Sovereign wealth funds in the Middle East also expressed concern and 40 percent of Japanese investors said they feared a U.S. default on its debt.[26]

Even without a crisis from other countries' reducing their holdings of Treasury securities, it's unwise for the United States to be so dependent on foreign savings. For one thing, the returns accrue to other nations, which means that over time Americans will be less wealthy than if they had financed investment from domestic saving. Furthermore, many economists believe that the trade deficit is related to the budget deficit, that the trade deficit results primarily from a lack of domestic saving to finance domestic investment. When foreign saving is imported to finance investment, it shows up in the national accounts as a trade deficit. Insofar as the budget deficit represents negative saving, it soaks up resources that would otherwise be available to finance domestic investment, thus requiring the importation of foreign saving, which raises the trade deficit.[27]

So obvious is the necessity of higher revenues to maintain a semblance of fiscal integrity that even some hard-core supply-siders have given up on the idea that deficits will lead to spending cuts by starving the beast. Like it or not, they recognize that higher taxes are coming.

Just before the 2008 election Arthur Laffer was asked about Barack Obama's and John McCain's tax policies; he responded, "When the net debt goes from 35 percent of GDP to 50 percent in seven years and you add on these [bailout] programs, I don't see how they avoid massive tax increases."[28]

Laffer correctly noted that the real question isn't how to avoid any tax increase whatsoever, but rather how to ensure that when taxes are raised they don't impact on growth and incentives any more than absolutely necessary. The real danger is that politicians will think they can get the revenue that is needed just by soaking the rich or imposing punitive taxes on politically vulnerable industries such as oil. But there isn't nearly enough potential revenue from these sources to fill the fiscal hole that now exists even at confiscatory rates. Better, Laffer says, that taxes be raised with low rates on a broader base. He has also suggested that a carbon tax might be a viable option.[29]

HOW SHOULD TAXES BE RAISED?

Economists and philosophers have long known that the best way to raise revenue is by taxing consumption. There are two reasons. First, taxing consumption impacts on the economy less than taxes on income because no tax falls on saving, which is the wellspring of growth. Second, consumption taxes are less burdensome because people can usually choose to reduce their consumption to avoid the tax. As philosopher David Hume put it in 1754, "The best taxes are such as are levied on consumptions [*sic*]...because such taxes are...in some measure, voluntary; since a man may choose how far he will use the commodity which is taxed."[30] This view was strongly endorsed by Alexander Hamilton in Federalist 21:

> It is a signal advantage of taxes on articles of consumption that they contain in their own nature a security against excess. They prescribe their own limit, which cannot be exceeded without defeating the end proposed—that is, an extension of the revenue. When applied to this object, the saying is as just as it is witty, that, "in political arithmetic,

two and two do not always make four." If duties are too high, they lessen the consumption; the collection is eluded; and the product to the treasury is not so great as when they are confined within proper and moderate bounds. This forms a complete barrier against any material oppression of the citizens by taxes of this class, and is itself a natural limitation of the power of imposing them.

Yet although consumption-based tax systems have long been recognized for their efficiency, they suffered from two flaws. First was a view that they are unfair; because people generally consume less as their incomes rise, the rich would necessarily pay less of a consumption tax as a share of their income than the poor who consumed all of their income.[31] Second, was a belief that a consumption-based tax system was impractical; good in theory perhaps, but not viable in practice. As John Maynard Keynes put it, "An expenditure tax, though perhaps theoretically sound is practically impossible."[32]

Of course, the states have long had sales taxes. But these only work at relatively low rates. At rates of above 10 percent, tax evasion becomes a serious problem.[33] Manufacturers' excise taxes suffer from the problem of cascading—taxes being applied to taxes—which inhibits trade and encourages businesses to vertically integrate in order to reduce the tax. Another problem with consumption taxation is that it runs counter to the Keynesian idea that spending drives growth and saving is a drag on growth. These problems killed a serious effort by the Treasury Department to enact a "spendings" tax during World War II.[34]

Two developments gradually changed economists' views of consumption taxes. First, they came to recognize that it was not necessary to tax consumption or sales directly, as states and localities do, in order to have a consumption-based tax system; it just required elimination of taxes on saving. Since saving or spending are the only two things that can be done with income, elimination of taxation on saving necessarily means that the burden of taxation falls entirely on consumption.[35] Viewed in this light, a consumed-income tax is much easier to implement and economically equivalent to a sales tax. It also allows for progressive rates on consumption, something very hard to achieve with a sales tax.

The second development was invention of the value-added tax. This is a form of sales tax levied on producers rather than retail sales. The VAT avoids the problem of cascading by giving businesses a credit for previous taxes paid along the production-distribution chain. This also makes it self-enforcing to a large extent, thus improving compliance over an equivalent retail sales tax.

Here is the way a VAT typically works.[36] A farmer grows wheat and sells it to the miller. A tax is paid by the farmer on the sale price of the wheat and is included in the price. When the miller sells the flour made from the wheat, a tax is assessed on that sale as well. But the miller subtracts the tax he paid when he bought the wheat. When the baker buys the flour he pays the tax included by the miller, which also includes the tax paid by the farmer. When the baker sells bread made from the flour, the tax is assessed once again. But as in earlier cases, the baker gets credit for all the previous taxes paid. In the end, the full burden of the tax falls on the final purchaser, the consumer.

In each case, an invoice trail shows the taxes paid at each step. Those at each stage of production and distribution have an incentive to pay the tax so that they will get credit for the taxes they paid when they purchased goods from other businesses. Thus the tax is assessed only on value-added—the difference between what a producer paid for inputs and what he was able to sell what was made from those inputs.[37]

In the 1960s Europe began the process of full economic and political integration. One problem that quickly developed was how to prevent domestic sales taxes from creating a cascading effect—that is, goods could be much more heavily taxed depending only on how many countries they passed through. This was considered a serious barrier to free trade. At this point, the VAT's system of having an invoice trail was very attractive because it meant that the tax could be rebated on exports at the border. Consequently, goods would bear only the tax imposed in the country of final sale.[38] Eventually, all members of the European Union were required to use the VAT if they had a sales tax.

In the 1970s there was some talk of a VAT for the United States. Richard Nixon was sympathetic to the idea.[39] But in the end, conservatives decided that the VAT's greatest virtue—its efficiency; i.e., its ability to raise revenue at a very low deadweight cost (the cost over and above the revenue collected)—was actually a fatal defect. The fear was that a VAT would raise too much revenue, too easily, and would be a money machine.[40] Better to raise taxes as painfully and inefficiently as possible, many conservatives concluded, in order to limit the government's tax take. At a February 21, 1985, press conference, Ronald Reagan opposed a VAT for this reason.[41]

I myself long opposed the VAT on money-machine grounds.[42] I changed my mind when I realized that there was no longer any hope of controlling entitlement spending before the deluge hits when the baby boomers retire; therefore, the United States now needs a money machine.[43]

Also in the 1970s, there was renewed interest in the idea of a consumed-income tax, which had largely been forgotten since the 1940s. This resulted primarily from the work of legal scholar William D. Andrews of Harvard and economist David Bradford of Princeton. The main impact of their work seems to have been on convincing tax experts that such a system was workable.[44]

In the 1980s, most of the interest in a consumed-income tax was directed toward the idea of a flat-rate tax system. Popular discussion of this proposal seldom noted that its principal virtue was not the flat rate, but the fact that it would be imposed on a pure consumption base with all saving exempted from tax.[45] In the 1990s, there were several efforts to devise a tax system that would exempt saving and thus fall exclusively on consumption. The best developed was the USA Tax sponsored by Senators Sam Nunn, Democrat of Georgia, and Pete Domenici, Republican of New Mexico.[46] But in the 2000s there has been almost no serious discussion of tax reform. The report of a commission appointed by George W. Bush in 2005 was ignored.[47]

Although some liberals have periodically been attracted by the VAT's revenue potential, none have made a serious effort to enact one since House Ways and Means Committee Chairman Al Ullman, Democrat of Oregon, floated the idea in 1979 and was defeated the following year, a loss that was widely attributed to his support for a VAT. Ever after, Ullman's name has been invoked as proof that a VAT is politically suicidal. In the words of Congressman (later Senator) Byron Dorgan, Democrat of North Dakota, "The last guy to push a VAT isn't working here any more."[48]

Politicians are also aware that leaders imposing VATs in foreign countries often suffered electoral defeat as a consequence. After enacting a VAT in Japan in 1986, Prime Minister Yasuhiro Nakasone was defeated a few months later largely because of it. Prime Minister Brian Mulroney imposed a VAT in Canada in 1991 and it was considered the major factor in his 1993 defeat. Although Prime Minister John Howard survived enactment of a VAT in Australia in 1998, his party suffered major losses as a consequence.[49]

THE CASE FOR A VAT

Sadly, we are long past the point where it is even remotely realistic to think that our nation's fiscal problems can be solved entirely on the spending side. It's clear that simply denying revenue to the government—starving the beast—does not work. Eliminating earmarks—virtually the sole focus of budget resolve in recent years—would have only a trivial effect on spending. Indeed, complete elimination of all domestic discretionary spending would not be enough to balance the budget. The best opportunity to reform entitlements was lost in the distraction of the Monica Lewinsky scandal in 1998—Clinton and congressional Republicans were close to a deal on Social Security before it was torpedoed by the drive for impeachment.[50] And the last chance to do so before the fiscal storm hits went down the drain when George W. Bush massively expanded Medicare spending in 2003 and then put forward an ill-conceived Social Security privatization proposal that went nowhere in 2005.

By making Medicare's fiscal condition worse by far more than could be saved by adopting his Social Security reform, Bush deprived himself of the best argument for acting on Social Security. He could not argue that it was necessary to save money and prevent a future tax increase because he had no credibility. Bush also erred by not putting forward a Social Security plan right after his Social Security Commission issued its report in 2001.[51] Instead, the plan was shelved. When he revived Social Security reform in 2005, Bush refused to put a legislative proposal on the table in order to deprive his opponents of specific details that could be attacked. But he also deprived his supporters of a plan they could rally around. As a result, those favoring Social Security reform all ended up with their own plans, making it impossible for any one of them to gain traction.

Even if the political will to seriously cut entitlement spending is miraculously found in the near future, it will take many years for it to have an impact on spending given the necessity of phasing in such cuts. Therefore, it is inevitable—not desirable by any means, but inevitable—that taxes will rise to keep our nation's finances from deteriorating so badly that financial markets will force action. At some point, the bond and foreign exchange traders will make the politicians act because a collapsing dollar, inflation, and/or high interest rates will be such a problem that their concerns will have to be addressed.[52] It's impossible to know when or how a political or economic crisis will emerge that will put such overwhelming pressure on Congress and the White House that really significant deficit reduction measures must be enacted. I only know, given the undeniable fiscal trends, that it will happen in the near future.

When that day comes, it is a certainty that the Republican Party will steadfastly oppose even the tiniest tax increase, despite its own major responsibility for the fiscal mess that necessitated it. It was Republicans who dissipated the budget surpluses of the Clinton administration, and it was on their watch that the second worst financial crisis in

American history emerged, causing the budget to hemorrhage from an already serious deficit position. And it was Republicans that enacted a massive, unfunded expansion of Medicare just at the moment that program's costs were set to explode with the retirement of the baby boom generation.

Perhaps some Republicans will genuinely believe that any tax increase, no matter how small, will be highly detrimental to the economy. But they made this same argument in 1993 when Bill Clinton proposed a modest tax increase.[53] Yet the economy not only suffered no ill effects, it went on to grow at a historically fast rate. Real GDP grew 2.7 percent in 1993, 4 percent in 1994, 2.5 percent in 1995, 3.7 percent in 1996, 4.5 percent in 1997, and 4.2 percent in 1998. And it's obvious that many European countries have tax/GDP ratios far higher than here without suffering particularly ill effects. They may not be growing as fast as they would if taxes and spending were lower, but neither are their standards of living significantly below those of the United States. Even strenuous efforts to show that Europeans are poorer than Americans show that the differences are merely trivial.[54]

Nor have we observed the sort of creeping totalitarianism that F. A. Hayek predicted in *The Road to Serfdom* as a result of the growth of government. Annual reports from Freedom House show no correlation between political and social freedom, on the one hand, and the size of government, on the other. Many of the world's most oppressive states, especially in Africa, have very small governments based on taxes and spending as a share of GDP. In practice, democratic socialism is not the contradiction in terms that most conservatives believe it to be.

There are two reasons why the growth of government in Europe has been less detrimental to the economy and society than conservatives expected. The first is that governments are providing benefits for almost everyone, so to a large extent people are giving with one hand and receiving with the other.[55] This transfer is not costless, but it does substantially mitigate the impact of high taxes. Further, government spending in Europe tends to be more growth-enhancing than spending in the United States.[56] In America, people tend to think of their federal taxes as money down a rat hole and react accordingly.[57] But in Europe, the people are more apt to feel they are simply paying for services with their taxes that Americans have to pay out of pocket.

This fact is best illustrated by health care. Most Americans get health insurance through their employers. The cost reduced their cash wages by 7.9 percent on average in 2008 according to the Bureau of Labor Statistics. If we had national health insurance and employers were entirely relieved of this expense, they could afford to pay their workers 7.9 percent more and be no worse off.[58] If the payroll tax rate went up by 7.9 percent to pay for health insurance, it would all be a wash, but both taxes and government spending would be higher. To a large extent, this is exactly the situation in Europe. It also explains why the Social Security tax has little in the way of disincentive effects. Because it funds a specific cash benefit that workers know they will get in the future, they tend to view it the same way they think about deductions from their wages for health insurance or pensions—as part of their compensation rather than a reduction of it.[59]

The second reason why taxes have less of an impact on incentives in Europe than one might expect is because European countries raise much more of their revenue from consumption taxes than the United States does. Every European country has a VAT that raises a significant share of the central government's revenue, as well as excise taxes on such things as tobacco and gasoline that are substantially higher than those here. Taxes on goods and services average 32 percent of revenue in Europe (total government) versus 16.8 percent in the United States (including state and local governments). European countries also generally tax capital more lightly than the United States does.[60]

A number of commentators have suggested a VAT for the United States to pay for national health insurance or long-term care for the elderly.[61] This would have the advantage of relieving the perceived regressivity of the tax by tying it to a benefit that would significantly accrue to those with low incomes.[62] It would also eliminate an important burden on U.S. manufacturing companies as well as state and local governments, which are more likely than other sectors of the economy to provide health insurance to current and retired workers.[63] And if the slate of existing health insurance programs, including Medicare, were subsumed into a new comprehensive health insurance system, it might be possible to institute reforms to Medicare that would lower its costs. The political dynamics might make it possible to overcome resistance from the unions and the elderly that would be impossible to surmount if such reforms were attempted piecemeal.

It should be emphasized that higher taxes alone cannot solve Medicare's financial problems. Spending will also have to be reined in because the cost per beneficiary is rising along with the number of beneficiaries, which is due both to demographics and to increasing longevity. It is estimated that total health care spending, public and private, will rise from about 15 percent of GDP today to 29 percent in 2040.[64]

DEAL OF THE CENTURY?

There is an oft-repeated saying about the VAT made by economist Larry Summers back in 1988. The reason the United States doesn't have one, he said, is because conservatives view it as a money machine and liberals see it as a tax on the poor. We will have a VAT, Summers predicted, when liberals figure out that it is a money machine and conservatives see that it is a tax on the poor.[65]

Interestingly, in January 2009, Summers, who was appointed director of the White House's National Economic Council by Barack Obama, suggested that globalization may require implementation of a VAT. Capital now flows so feely across national borders that it is increasingly hard for governments to tax income. They will therefore be forced by necessity to shift more toward consumption taxes, Summers said.[66]

I believe that down the road not too many years in the future, the United States is going to need a new revenue source just to pay for all the government spending that is in the pipeline. It is clear that it will never be cut enough to prevent a vast rise in entitlement spending. It is equally clear that we cannot raise enough money by increasing corporate or individual income tax rates. Those sources of revenue are already breaking down under strain and are desperately in need of fundamental reform just to keep their yield from eroding through evasion and legal tax avoidance. Attempting to double tax rates—which would be needed over the next generation to pay for Social Security and Medicare—is not remotely feasible. The supply-siders are right about that. The impact on incentives would be too severe.

It is essential, then, that policymakers find a new source of revenue capable of raising the funds that will be needed and in such a way that the economy isn't crushed under the burden. Both theory and history tell us that some sort of flat-rate consumption tax is the best way to raise revenue in a way that is least damaging to incentives. According to recent OECD studies, taxes on consumption and real property are the least damaging to growth and income taxes are the most damaging.[67]

It goes without saying that all taxes have disincentive effects. But clearly, some taxes are more burdensome than others. As economist Henry George once explained, "The mode of taxation is, in fact, quite as important as the amount. As a small burden badly placed may distress a horse that could carry with ease a much larger one properly adjusted, so a people may be impoverished and their power of producing wealth destroyed by taxation, which, if levied in another way, could be borne with ease."[68]

Based on the experiences of other countries, an American VAT could raise about $50 billion per percentage point as an add-on tax. According to the IMF, the VAT base in other advanced economies varies between 35 percent and 38 percent of GDP.[69] However, I don't think the United States would initially be able to tax as much of the economy as countries with decades of experience with a VAT. I think one third of GDP would be a reasonable goal. Therefore, with GDP at about $15 trillion the tax base would be $5 trillion, which would yield $50 billion per percentage point. VAT rates in OECD countries averaged 17.7 percent in 2007 and ranged between 5 percent in Japan and 25 percent in Sweden and Denmark.[70] Recent research suggests that VATs don't have serious problems with evasion and avoidance at rates below 20 percent.[71]

Initially, a VAT could pay for essential fixes to the tax code such as permanently indexing or abolishing the Alternative Minimum Tax and maybe leave a bit for deficit reduction. Once in place, the VAT could be raised gradually to pay for the baby boomers' retirement. It would also be a way of getting them to pay for some of it themselves.

As noted earlier, Republicans will undoubtedly oppose any proposed tax increase and certainly fight a VAT with all the resources at their disposal. But their hand may be weaker than they think, because they themselves inserted expiration dates into all of the tax cuts of the George W. Bush years. Therefore, a major tax increase will take place at the end of 2010 if Congress simply does nothing. At some point, Republicans may accept that it is better to have a VAT than to allow marginal income tax rates to rise sharply.

Democrats will certainly have their own reservations about a VAT, especially its impact on the poor. But if the poor get health insurance as part of the deal that may be viewed as a reasonable trade-off. A VAT rate of 3 percent would be enough to pay for the proposal Obama put forward during the 2008 campaign. Another option would be to use VAT revenue initially to completely eliminate federal income taxes on all but the very well to do.[72] Parties of the left in Europe decided decades ago that if they wanted to expand the welfare state, it had to be financed conservatively.[73]

Institution of a major new tax will certainly be difficult and costly. But the IRS, GAO, JCT, and CBO have been studying the issue for years and know what to do.[74] Furthermore, the IMF, OECD, and World Bank are filled with experts on the operation and implementation of a VAT because virtually every other country has one. The United States is the only member of the OECD that doesn't.

Of course, no one is going to raise taxes as long as the economy is in the doldrums. But the debate over fundamental tax reform will take years, and many more to actually begin collecting revenue from a VAT. The sooner the process starts, the sooner we will be ready for the impending fiscal storm.

REPUBLICANS AND THE WELFARE STATE

Even without the election of Obama and Democratic gains in Congress in 2008, Republicans were going to have to reassess much of their philosophy on the key issues of taxing and spending. The financial crisis led to a vast expansion of spending, so the deficit would have gotten much worse even if John McCain had won the election. And the aging of the baby boom generation means there will be increasing demands for Social Security, Medicare, and other programs for the elderly in coming years.

Moreover, Americans' zeal for tax cutting—the Republicans' best issue for the past 30 years—has clearly waned. A *Wall Street Journal/ NBC News* poll shows Americans now favoring the Democrats on taxes, and polls by Gallup, Rasmussen, and Harris show an increased willingness to tax the rich and redistribute income.

Given this reality, Republicans must adapt. If they continue to insist upon rolling back the welfare state by using tax cuts to starve the beast or trying to privatize Social Security and Medicare, they will fail. There is simply no appetite for big spending cuts or for the radical restructuring of programs that benefit a huge percentage of Americans, especially after the severe downturn in the stock market that has wiped out trillions of dollars in retirement savings.

Historically, Republicans have come back from electoral losses by accepting the fact that Americans mostly like government spending. Rather than make a futile effort to take away something most voters want, Republicans have instead worked to make the welfare state function efficiently, targeting benefits to those that play by society's rules, and financing those benefits without additional debt.

When Dwight Eisenhower won the presidency in 1952 with solid Republican majorities in both the House and Senate, he explicitly rejected any attempt to repeal the New Deal. Instead, he pushed for efficiency and economy in government and emphasized that its bills needed to be paid. Balancing the budget was Eisenhower's main concern.

Similarly, Richard Nixon made no effort to roll back the Great Society after he was elected in 1968. Like Eisenhower, he emphasized proper management of government programs and the necessity of financing them even if it meant raising taxes.

Even Ronald Reagan accepted the permanence of the welfare state and the need to pay for what has been promised to our senior citizens. This is most apparent with the Social Security rescue in 1983, which left benefits virtually untouched but raised taxes sharply to keep the system solvent.

But Reagan had a critical insight. He understood that the burden of government is more easily borne if economic growth is high. This required keeping tax rates as low as possible—especially on our nation's most productive citizens—maintaining price stability, and minimizing government regulation of private industry. Reagan's idea was that government could continue to grow, but if the economy grew faster there would be a relative decline in spending as a share of the gross domestic product. The ultimate guarantor of America's financial commitments, he believed, was not a balanced budget, as Eisenhower and Nixon thought, but a strong economy.

Reagan also knew that to the extent it was possible to trim domestic programs, this could only be done in times of prosperity. In a troubled economy, people are too dependent on them. Proof of this proposition is that welfare reform only happened in 1996 because economic growth was unusually rapid at the time.

To his credit, George W. Bush made Social Security reform a major issue. He argued that it was possible to improve retirement security, reduce the burden of this program, and put it on a sounder financial footing without higher taxes. But despite a booming economy and stock market, support for Bush's initiative was virtually nonexistent. Any future president attempting Social Security reform will certainly confront a political climate that is even less hospitable to privatization.

I think Republicans would do better to spend their diminished political capital figuring out how to finance the welfare state at the least cost to the economy and individual liberty, rather than fighting a losing battle to slash popular spending programs. But this will require them to accept the necessity of higher revenues. It is simply unrealistic to think that tax cuts will continue to be a viable political strategy when the budget deficit exceeds $1 trillion. Nor is it realistic to think that taxes can be kept at 19 percent of GDP when spending is projected to grow by about 10 percent of GDP over the next generation, according to both the CBO and the GAO. And that was before the recent economic crisis caused spending to skyrocket.

If Republicans refuse to participate in the debate over how revenues will be raised, then Democrats will do it on their own, which will likely give us much higher tax rates and a tax system that is more harmful to growth than necessary to fund the government. Instead of opposing any tax hike, I think it makes more sense for Republicans to figure out how best to raise the additional revenue that will be raised in any event.

In the end, the welfare state is not going away, and it will be paid for one way or another. The sooner Republicans accept that fact, the sooner they will regain political power.

Appendices

APPENDIX I

Dates of Postwar Recessions and Antirecession Programs

Beginning	End	Antirecessionary Legislation Enacted
November 1948	October 1949	October 1949[1]
August 1957	April 1958	April 1958[2]
		July 1958[3]
April 1960	February 1961	May 1961[4]
		September 1962[5]
December 1969	November 1970	August 1971[6]
November 1973	March 1975	March 1975[7]
		July 1976[8]
		May 1977[9]
July 1981	November 1982	January 1983[10]
		March 1983[11]
July 1990	March 1991	December 1991[12]
		April 1993[13]
March 2001	November 2001	June 2001[14]
December 2007	n/a	February 2008[15]
		February 2009[16]

Source: National Bureau of Economic Research and author's research[17]

Notes:

1. Advance Planning for Public Works Act, P.L. 81-352, Oct. 13, 1949.
2. Federal Aid Highway Act of 1958, P.L. 85-381, April 16, 1958.
3. River and Harbor Act of 1958, Flood Control Act of 1958, and Water Supply Act of 1958, P.L. 85-100, July 3, 1958.
4. Area Redevelopment Act, P.L. 87-27, May 1, 1961.
5. Public Works Acceleration Act, P.L. 87-658, Sept. 14, 1962.
6. Public Works and Economic Development Act Amendments, P.L. 92-65, Aug. 5, 1971.

7. Tax Reduction Act of 1975, P.L. 94-12, March 29, 1975.
8. Public Works Employment Act of 1976, P.L. 94-369, July 22, 1976.
9. Local Public Works Capital Development and Investment Act of 1976, P.L. 95-28, May 13, 1977.
10. Surface Transportation Assistance Act of 1982, P.L. 97-424, Jan. 6, 1983.
11. Emergency Jobs Appropriations Act of 1983, P.L. 98-8, March 24, 1983.
12. Intermodal Surface Transportation Efficiency Act of 1991, P.L. 102-240, Dec. 18, 1991.
13. Emergency Supplemental Appropriations Act of 1993, P.L. 103-24, April 23, 1993.
14. Economic Growth and Tax Relief Reconciliation Act of 2001, P.L. 107-16, June 7, 2001.
15. Economic Stimulus Act of 2008, P.L. 110-185, Feb. 13, 2008.
16. American Recovery and Reinvestment Act of 2009, P.L. 111-5, Feb. 17, 2009.
17. www.nber.org/cycles.html. I relied heavily on various issues of *Congressional Quarterly* to determine what legislation was particularly oriented toward counteracting recessions.

APPENDIX II

Taxes and Hours Worked

	Total Taxes as a Share of GDP			Average Hours Worked Per Year		
	1975	2006	Increase	1979	2006	Change
Australia	25.8	30.6	18.6%	1,823	1,714	−6.0%
Canada	32.0	33.3	4.1%	1,832	1,738	−4.6%
Denmark	38.4	49.1	27.9%	1,624	1,577	−2.9%
Finland	36.5	43.5	19.2%	1,869	1,721	−7.9%
France	35.4	44.2	24.8%	1,855	1,564	−15.7%
Germany	34.3	35.6	3.8%	1,770	1,421	−19.7%
Italy	25.4	42.1	65.7%	1,949	1,800	−7.6%
Japan	20.9	27.9	33.5%	2,126	1,784	−16.0%
Norway	39.2	43.9	12.0%	1,580	1,407	−10.9%
Spain	18.4	36.6	98.9%	2,022	1,764	−12.7%
Sweden	41.2	49.1	19.2%	1,530	1,583	+3.5%
U.K.	35.2	37.1	5.4%	1,818	1,669	−8.2%
U.S.	25.6	28.0	9.4%	1,834	1,804	−1.6%

Source: Organization for Economic Cooperation and Development

APPENDIX III

United States: Tax and Income Shares of Wealthy Taxpayers (in percent)

Year	Top Income Tax Rate	Tax Share		Income Share	
		Top 1%	Top 10%	Top 1%	Top 10%
1980	70	19.3	49.5	8.5	32.1
1981	70	17.9	48.2	8.3	32.0
1982	50	19.3	48.8	8.9	32.3
1983	50	20.7	50.1	9.3	32.8
1984	50	21.8	51.1	9.7	33.3
1985	50	22.3	51.9	10.0	33.8
1986	50	25.8	54.7	11.3	35.1
1987	38.5	24.8	55.6	12.3	36.9
1988	28	27.6	57.3	15.2	39.5
1989	28	25.2	55.8	14.2	39.0
1990	28	25.1	55.4	14.0	38.8
1991	31	24.8	55.8	13.0	38.2
1992	31	27.5	58.0	14.2	39.2
1993	39.6	29.0	59.2	13.8	39.0
1994	39.6	28.9	59.5	13.8	39.2
1995	39.6	30.3	60.8	14.6	40.2
1996	39.6	32.3	62.5	16.0	41.6
1997	39.6	33.2	63.2	17.4	42.8
1998	39.6	34.8	65.0	18.5	43.8
1999	39.6	36.2	66.5	19.5	44.9
2000	39.6	37.4	67.3	20.8	46.0
2001	39.1	33.9	64.9	17.5	43.1
2002	38.6	33.7	65.7	16.1	41.8
2003	35	34.3	65.8	17.8	42.4
2004	35	36.9	68.2	19.0	44.4
2005	35	39.4	70.3	21.2	46.4
2006	35	39.9	70.8	22.1	47.3

Source: Internal Revenue Service; Tax Foundation

APPENDIX IV

United Kingdom: Tax and Income Shares of Wealthy Taxpayers (in percent)

Year	Top Income Tax Rate	Tax Share		Income Share	
		Top 1%	Top 10%	Top 1%	Top 10%
1978	83	11.2	35.0	n/a	n/a
1979	60	10.4	n/a	↓	↓
1980	60	10.9	n/a		
1981	60	11.3	35.0		
1982	60	11.7	n/a		
1983	60	11.1	n/a		
1984	60	11.8	n/a		
1985	60	12.0	n/a		
1986	60	14.0	39.0		
1987	60	n/a	n/a		
1988	40	n/a	n/a		
1989	40	n/a	n/a		
1990	40	15.0	42.0		
1991	40	16.0	43.0		
1992	40	16.0	44.0		
1993	40	16.0	44.0		
1994	40	17.0	45.0		
1995	40	17.0	45.0		
1996	40	20.0	48.0		
1997	40	20.0	48.0		
1998	40	21.0	49.0		
1999	40	21.3	50.3	11.0	32.9
2000	40	22.2	51.5	11.5	33.7
2001	40	21.8	51.9	11.1	33.4
2002	40	21.0	51.5	10.8	33.1
2003	40	20.8	50.9	11.0	33.3
2004	40	21.4	51.4	11.3	33.6
2005	40	22.7	52.9	12.2	34.8
2006	40	22.7	52.8	12.2	34.8
2007	40	22.7	52.9	12.2	34.9
2008	40	23.0	53.1	12.1	34.5

Source: Her Majesty's Revenue & Customs; Institute for Fiscal Studies

APPENDIX V

Capital Gains Taxes and Realizations
(in percent)

Year	Maximum Tax Rate[1]	Realizations/GDP
1967	25	3.30
1968	26.9	3.91
1969	27.5	3.19
1970	32.21	2.01
1971	34.25	2.51
1972	35.5	2.89
1973	36.5	2.58
1974	36.5	2.01
1975	36.5	1.89
1976	39.875	2.17
1977	39.875	2.23
1978[2]	39.875/33.85	2.20
1979	28	2.86
1980	28	2.65
1981[2]	28/20	2.58
1982	20	2.77
1983	20	3.47
1984	20	3.57
1985	20	4.08
1986	20	7.36
1987	28	3.13
1988	28	3.18
1989	28	2.81
1990	28	2.13
1991	28.93	1.86
1992	28.93	2.00
1993	29.19	2.29
1994	29.19	2.17
1995	29.19	2.43
1996	29.19	3.34
1997[2]	29.19/21.19	4.39
1998	21.19	5.18
1999	21.19	5.96
2000	21.19	6.56
2001	21.17	3.45
2002	21.16	2.57
2003[2]	21.05/16.05	2.95
2004	16.05	4.27

Continued

Appendix V Continued

Year	Maximum Tax Rate[1]	Realizations/GDP
2005	16.05	5.56
2006	15.7	6.06

Source: Office of Tax Analysis, U.S. Treasury Department, Nov. 3, 2008

Notes:
1. Maximum effective rate can exceed the maximum statutory rate because of interactions with the Alternative Minimum Tax and other tax provisions.
2. Rate changed in midyear.

APPENDIX VI

Marginal Federal Income Tax Rate on a Four-Person Family, 1958–1988 (in percent)

Year	One-Half Median Income	Median Income	Twice Median Income
1958	0	20	22
1959	0	20	22
1960	20	20	22
1961	20	20	22
1962	20	20	26
1963	20	20	26
1964	16	18	23.5
1965	14	17	22
1966	14	19	22
1967	15	19	22
1968	15	20.42[2]	26.88[2]
1969	15	20.90[2]	27.50[2]
1970	15	19.48[2]	25.62[2]
1971	15	19	28
1972	15	19	28
1973	16	19	28
1974	16	22	33[3]
1975	27[1]	22	32
1976	17	22	32
1977	17	22	36
1978	19	25	39
1979	16	24	37
1980	18	24	43

Continued

Appendix VI Continued

Year	One-Half Median Income	Median Income	Twice Median Income
1981	18	24	42.46
1982	16	25	39
1983	15	23	35
1984	14	22	38
1985	14	22	38
1986	14	22	38
1987	15	15	35
1988	15	15	28

Sources: Office of Tax Analysis, U.S. Treasury Department, unpublished data

Notes: Marginal rate refers to the tax on each additional dollar earned.
1. Unusually high rate results from phase-out of the earned income tax credit.
2. Surtax in effect.
3. Includes phase-out of tax rebate.

APPENDIX VII

Deflation, 1929–1933

Category	1929	1933	Percent Decline
Consumer Price Index	51.3	38.8	24.4
Food	48.3	30.6	36.6
Rent	76.0	54.1	28.8
Clothing	48.5	36.9	23.9
Wholesale Price Index	61.9	42.8	30.8
Crude materials	57.9	33.6	42.0
Finished goods	64.1	47.8	25.4
Wheat	$1.18	$0.72	39.0
Flour	$5.79	$4.63	20.0
Sugar	$0.05	$0.04	20.0
Cotton	$0.19	$0.09	53.0
Wool	$0.99	$0.66	33.3
Coal	$12.89	$10.06	21.9
Steel rails	$43.00	$39.33	8.5
Copper	$0.18	$0.07	61.1
Turpentine	$0.55	$0.46	16.4

Sources: Bureau of Labor Statistics; Census Bureau

List of Abbreviations

AAAPSS	*Annals of the American Academy of Political and Social Science*
ACIR	Advisory Commission on Intergovernmental Relations
AEI	American Enterprise Institute
AER	*American Economic Review*
BHR	*Business History Review*
BPEA	*Brookings Papers on Economic Activity*
CBO	Congressional Budget Office
CEA	Council of Economic Advisers
CRS	Congressional Research Service
CUP	Cambridge University Press
EI	*Economic Inquiry*
EJ	*Economic Journal*
ERP	*Economic Report of the President*
ERTA	Economic Recovery Tax Act, formal name for 1981 tax cut
FRBAER	*Federal Reserve Bank of Atlanta Economic Review*
FRBMQR	*Federal Reserve Bank of Minneapolis Quarterly Review*
FRBPBR	*Federal Reserve Bank of Philadelphia Business Review*
FRBRER	*Federal Reserve Bank of Richmond Economic Review*
FRBSLR	*Federal Reserve Bank of St. Louis Review*
FT	*Financial Times*
GAO	Government Accountability Office/General Accounting Office
GATT	General Agreement on Tariffs and Trade
GDP	gross domestic product
HOPE	*History of Political Economy*
HUP	Harvard University Press
IER	*International Economic Review*
IMF	International Monetary Fund
JAH	*Journal of American History*
JASA	*Journal of the American Statistical Association*

List of Abbreviations

JCT	Joint Committee on Taxation
JEC	Joint Economic Committee of Congress
JEH	*Journal of Economic History*
JEL	*Journal of Economic Literature*
JEP	*Journal of Economic Perspectives*
JF	*Journal of Finance*
JLE	*Journal of Law and Economics*
JMCB	*Journal of Money, Credit and Banking*
JME	*Journal of Monetary Economics*
JPE	*Journal of Political Economy*
LAT	*Los Angeles Times*
NBER	National Bureau of Economic Research
NTAP	*National Tax Association Proceedings*
NTJ	*National Tax Journal*
NYT	*New York Times*
NYTM	*New York Times Magazine*
OECD	Organization for Economic Cooperation and Development
OEP	*Oxford Economic Papers*
OMB	Office of Management and Budget
OUP	Oxford University Press
PC	*Public Choice*
PFQ	*Public Finance Quarterly*
PSQ	*Presidential Studies Quarterly*
PUP	Princeton University Press
QJE	*Quarterly Journal of Economics*
RES	*Review of Economics and Statistics*
RIW	*Review of Income and Wealth*
SEJ	*Southern Economic Journal*
TNR	*The New Republic*
TPI	*The Public Interest*
UCP	University of Chicago Press
USGPO	U.S. Government Printing Office
VAT	value-added tax
WP	*Washington Post*
WSJ	*Wall Street Journal*

Notes

NOTE ON SOURCES

I've mostly limited quotations from John Maynard Keynes to the 30-volume set of his collected works, edited by economist Donald Moggridge and published by Macmillan and the Cambridge University Press between 1971 and 1989, with references made to volume and page number. I did this to make access by researchers easier and because the edited volumes also include corrections and explanatory material that would be absent from the original sources. Moreover, many of these sources are extremely obscure and do not exist in published form outside Keynes's collected writings.

When referring to White House statements, I have relied exclusively on the online collection of presidential documents compiled by the American Presidency Project at the University of California, Santa Barbara. This collection is very complete and easily accessible—one only needs the title and date of a document to find it quickly. For this reason I have not cited published sources for presidential statements. The Internet address for the project is www.presidency.ucsb.edu.

An extremely valuable research source regarding topics discussed in this book is the Federal Reserve Bank of St. Louis. It has put an enormous amount of historical material relating to the economy and the history of the Federal Reserve in its Federal Reserve Archival System for Economic Research, online at http://fraser.stlouisfed. org. These include many of the papers of William McChesney Martin, chairman of the Federal Reserve Board from 1951 to 1970, as well as every Economic Report of the President, among many other things. There is also an invaluable companion to Allan Meltzer's definitive history of the Federal Reserve System, published by the University of Chicago Press. Footnotes in that study are directly linked to original online sources, including congressional hearings, statistical sources, and Federal Reserve publications. It is essential to examine these original documents in order to understand what information was available to policymakers in real time.

Congressional Research Service reports are generally not available to the public, but many are online at www.opencrs.com.

In converting dollar figures from the past to those of the present, I did more than adjust for inflation, because that would understate the magnitude of the economic change by leaving out real growth. Therefore, I have made conversions based on changes in GDP using the online calculator here: www.measuringworth.com.

INTRODUCTION

1. For details, see Richard W. Stevenson, "In Sign of Conservative Split, a Commentator Is Dismissed," *NYT*, Oct. 18, 2005; David Brooks, "The Savior of the Right," *NYT*, Oct. 23, 2005; Elisabeth Bumiller, "An Outspoken Conservative Loses His Place at the Table," *NYT*, Feb. 13, 2006.
2. Jeffrey Sachs, "The Roots of Crisis," *The Guardian*, March 21, 2008. See also John B. Taylor, *Getting Off Track* (Stanford: Hoover Institution Press, 2009). Greenspan has angrily denied any responsibility for the housing bubble or its collapse: Alan Greenspan, "The Fed Didn't Cause the Housing Bubble," *WSJ*, March 11, 2009.
3. CBO, *Housing Wealth and Consumer Spending*, Jan. 2007.
4. Jane Gravelle, Thomas Hungerford, and Marc Labonte, "Economic Stimulus: Issues and Policies," CRS Report for Congress no. R40104, Jan. 23, 2009.
5. Vikas Bajaj and Michael M. Grynbaum, "Investors Buy Federal Debt at Zero Yield," *NYT*, Dec. 10, 2008.
6. Hal Varian, "Boost Private Investment to Boost the Economy," *WSJ*, Jan. 7, 2009.

CHAPTER 1   THE GREAT DEPRESSION

1. Steven Mufson, "For Insight on Stimulus Battle, Look to the '30s," *WP*, Feb. 12, 2009.
2. *Financial Chronicle*, March 9, 1929, 1444.
3. "Fisher Denies Crash Is Due" and "Babson Predicts 'Crash' in Stocks," *NYT*, Sept. 6, 1929; "Fisher Sees Stocks Permanently High," *NYT*, Oct. 16, 1929; "Says Stock Slump Is Only Temporary," *NYT*, Oct. 24, 1929.
4. Gerald Sirkin, "The Stock Market of 1929 Revisited: A Note," *BHR*, Summer 1975, 223-31; Charles P. Kindleberger, *The World in Depression, 1929-1939* (Berkeley: University of California Press, 1986), 96; Ellen R. McGrattan and Edward C. Prescott, "The 1929 Stock Market: Irving Fisher Was Right," *IER*, Nov. 2004, 1003.

5. "If Tariff Fight Shakes the Stock Exchange, Let Exchange Go, Borah Says to Banker Critic," *NYT*, Nov. 13, 1929.

6. The standard political history of Smoot-Hawley is E.E. Schattschneider, *Politics, Pressures and the Tariff* (New York: Prentice-Hall, 1935).

7. "Kent to Be Called in Lobby Inquiry," *NYT*, and "Kent's Statement to Be Investigated," *WP*, both, Nov. 17, 1929; "New York Bankers Face Lobby Inquiry," *NYT*, Nov. 19, 1929; "Kent and Senators Clash As He Lays Market Upset to the Tariff Coalition," *NYT*, and "Kent Challenged on Senate Attack," *WP*, both, Nov. 23, 1929.

8. Roger W. Babson, "Babson Flays Congress for Business Ills," *WP*, Nov. 20, 1929.

9. Alan Reynolds, "What Do We Know About the Great Crash?" *National Review*, Nov. 9, 1979, 1416–21; Benjamin M. Anderson, *Economics and the Public Welfare* (Princeton: Van Nostrand, 1949), 224–25.

10. Barry Eichengreen, "The Political Economy of the Smoot-Hawley Tariff," *Research in Economic History*, v. 12 (1989), 1–43; F. W. Taussig, *The Tariff History of the United States* (New York: Putnam, 1931), 519; Robert B. Archibald *et al.*, "Effective Rates of Protection and the Fordney-McCumber and Smoot-Hawley Tariff Acts: Comment and Revised Estimates," *Applied Economics*, July 2000, 1223–26; Douglas A. Irwin, "The Smoot-Hawley Tariff: A Quantitative Assessment," *RES*, May 1998, 326–34; Sumner H. Slichter, "Is the Tariff a Cause of Depression?" *Current History*, Jan. 1932, 519–24; Robert B. Archibald and David H. Feldman, "Investment During the Great Depression: Uncertainty and the Role of the Smoot-Hawley Tariff," *SEJ*, April 1998, 857–79; Mario J. Crucini and James Kahn, "Tariffs and Aggregate Economic Activity: Lessons from the Great Depression," *JME*, Dec. 1996, 427–67; Jacob B. Madsen "Trade Barriers and the Collapse of World Trade During the Great Depression," *SEJ*, April 2001, 848–68; Judith A. McDonald, Anthony P. O'Brien, and Colleen M. Callahan, "Trade Wars: Canada's Reaction to the Smoot-Hawley Tariff," *JEH*, Dec. 1997, 802–26.

11. Robert J. Shiller, *Irrational Exuberance* (Princeton: PUP, 2000), 223.

12. Lester V. Chandler, *Benjamin Strong: Central Banker* (Washington: Brookings, 1958), 427.

13. Lester V. Chandler, *American Monetary Policy, 1928–1941* (New York: Harper & Row, 1971), 37–53.

14. Chandler, *Benjamin Strong*, 465; Milton Friedman and Anna J. Schwartz, *A Monetary History of the United States, 1867–1960* (Princeton: PUP, 1963), 413–19; "Reserve Board Warning Sends Stocks Tumbling; London Raises Bank Rate," *NYT*, Feb. 8, 1929; Eugene N. White, "The Stock Market Boom and Crash of 1929 Revisited," *JEP*, Spring 1990, 67–83.

15. "Fed Reserve Fisher Target," *WSJ*, Dec. 30, 1929; Irving Fisher, "The Stock Market in 1929," *JASA*, March 1930, 96. For a recent exposition of this theory, see Barry Eichengreen and Kris J. Mitchener, "The Great Depression as a Credit Boom Gone Wrong," *Research in Economic History*, v. 22 (2004), 183–237.

16. H. Parker Willis, "Who Caused the Panic of 1929?" *North American Review*, Feb. 1930, 174–83. The inherent contradiction of the Fed running an inflationary monetary policy to offset the inflationary effect of gold inflows was criticized in C. Reinold Noyes, "The Gold Inflation in the United States, 1921–1929," *AER*, June 1930, 181–98.

17. J. Laurence Laughlin, "The Gold-Exchange Standard," *QJE*, Aug. 1927, 644–63; Michael D. Bordo, Ehsan U. Choudhri, and Anna J. Schwartz, "Was Expansionary Monetary Policy Feasible During the Great Contraction? An Examination of the Gold Standard Constraint," *Explorations in Economic History*, Jan. 2002, 1–28.

18. Barry L. Anderson and James L. Butkiewicz, "Money, Spending, and the Great Depression," *SEJ*, Oct. 1980, 388–403; Friedman and Schwartz, *Monetary History*, 352. The closure of so many banks also eliminated a key means of financial intermediation, so even if the Fed had tried to expand the money supply, the mechanism for injecting it into the economy was severely disabled. See Ben S. Bernanke, "Nonmonetary Effects of the Financial Crisis in the Propagation of the Great Depression," *AER*, June 1983, 257–76; James D. Hamilton, "Monetary Factors in the Great Depression," *JME*, March 1987, 145–69.

19. Irving Fisher, *Booms and Depressions: First Principles* (New York: Adelphi, 1932), 140; Friedman and Schwartz, *Monetary History*, 307; Michael W. Keran, "Velocity and Inflation Expectations: 1922–1983," *Federal Reserve Bank of San Francisco Economic Review*, Summer 1984, 47–48; E. W. Kemmerer, "Controlled Inflation," *AER*, March 1934, 90–100; Richard T. Selden, "Monetary Velocity in the United States," in Milton Friedman, ed., *Studies in the Quantity Theory of Money* (Chicago: UCP, 1956), 179–257.

20. "Commodity Prices Down 1⅜ Per Cent," *NYT*, Dec. 3, 1930.

21. "Urges Bond Buying By Reserve Board," *NYT*, Sept. 25, 1930.

22. Elmus R. Wicker, *Federal Reserve Monetary Policy, 1917–1933* (New York: Random House, 1966), 172–96.

23. Thomas F. Cargill, "Irving Fisher Comments on Benjamin Strong and the Federal Reserve in the 1930s," *JPE*, Dec. 1992, 1275–76.

24. "Fiat Money Urged to Inflate Prices," *NYT*, Sept. 17, 1931.

25. Louis Stark, "Say Reserve Banks Can Bring Recovery," *NYT*, Dec. 31, 1931; "Urges Quick Action to Check Deflation," *NYT*, Jan. 10, 1932; "Economists Advise Credit 'Expansion,'" *NYT*, Jan. 16, 1932; Louis Stark, "Say Reserve

Notes

Banks Can Bring Recovery," *NYT*, Dec. 31, 1931; "Urges Quick Action to Check Deflation," *NYT*, Jan. 10, 1932; "Economists Advise Credit 'Expansion,'" *NYT*, Jan. 16, 1932; Quincy Wright, ed., *Gold and Monetary Stabilization* (Chicago: UCP, 1932), 161–63; "Memorandum Prepared by L. B. Currie, P. T. Ellsworth, and H. D. White (Cambridge, Mass., Jan. 1932)," *HOPE*, Fall 2002, 535.

26. Karl Brunner and Allan H. Meltzer, "What Did We Learn from the Monetary Experience of the United States in the Great Depression?" *Canadian Journal of Economics*, May 1968, 334–48; Friedman and Schwartz, *Monetary History*, 348; Allan Meltzer, *A History of the Federal Reserve*, v. 1 (Chicago: UCP, 2003), 280, 321. Fed officials often complained that rates were absurdly low and therefore no benefit could come from further easing credit conditions; Friedman and Schwartz, *Monetary History*, 372. On high real interest rates, see Harold L. Cole and Lee E. Ohanian, "Re-examining the Contributions of Money and Banking Shocks to the U.S. Great Depression," *NBER Macroeconomics Annual, 2000* (2001), 187; Meltzer, *Federal Reserve*, 412.

27. Meltzer, *Federal Reserve*, 364–65.

28. The Fed took notice of this fact; Meltzer, *Federal Reserve*, 373. On falling commodity prices, "Average Prices Down Slightly in November," *NYT*, Dec. 2, 1932; Willford I. King, "The Outlook for the Price Level," *JASA*, Dec. 1932, 431.

29. *Banking and Monetary Statistics, 1914–1941* (Washington: Federal Reserve Board, 1943), 451; Gerald Epstein and Thomas Ferguson, "Monetary Policy, Loan Liquidation, and Industrial Conflict: The Federal Reserve and the Open Market Operations of 1932," *JEH*, Dec. 1984, 957–83. Friedman and Schwartz also cite the adjournment of Congress on July 16, which eliminated Congressional pressure for easing, as a factor in ending the open market operations; *Monetary History*, 389.

30. "New Law Helping Fight on Deflation," *NYT*, March 20, 1932; Chang-Tai Hsieh and Christina D. Romer, "Was the Federal Reserve Constrained by the Gold Standard During the Great Depression? Evidence from the 1932 Open Market Purchase Program," *JEH*, March 2006, 140–76.

31. James Harvey Rogers, *America Weighs Her Gold* (New Haven: Yale University Press, 1931), 208–9.

32. Lori Montgomery, "Congress May Need to Fund Another Stimulus, Pelosi Says," *WP*, March 11, 2009.

33. "House Group Backs an Inflation Bill," *NYT*, April 16, 1932.

34. "Prosperity by Fiat," *NYT*, April 22, 1932.

35. "Dollar Stabilizing Bill Voted, 289–60," *WP*, May 3, 1932.

36. "House Passed the Goldsborough Bill," *Barron's*, May 9, 1932.

37. "Fisher for 'Reflation,'" *NYT*, July 9, 1932.

Notes

38. Herbert Hoover, "Special Message to the Congress on Budgetary Legislation," May 5, 1932.

39. "Currency Inflation Approved in Senate," *WP*, July 12, 1932.

40. Herbert Hoover, *The Memoirs of Herbert Hoover: The Great Depression, 1929–1941* (New York: Macmillan, 1952), 30.

41. "Anderson Advises World Gold Accord," *NYT*, May 7, 1933; Henry Hazlitt, "The Dollar Adrift," May 3, 1933, 495–96, and "Inflation: How Much?" May 31, 1933, 606, both *The Nation*; Hugh Bancroft, "Fighting Economic Law: Wage Scales and Purchasing Power," *Barron's*, Jan. 25, 1932, 5; Fred Rogers Fairchild, "Government Saves Us From Depression," *Yale Review*, Summer 1932, 661–83; John Oakwood, "How High Wages Destroy Buying Power," *Barron's*, Feb. 29, 1932; Lionel Robbins, *The Great Depression* (London: Macmillan, 1934), 186.

42. On the zero-bound problem, see Ben S. Bernanke, Vincent R. Reinhart, and Brian P. Sack, "Monetary Policy Alternatives at the Zero Bound: An Empirical Assessment," Finance and Economics Discussion Series 2004–48, Federal Reserve Board, Sept. 2004; Tony Yates, "Monetary Policy and the Zero Bound to Interest Rates: A Review," *Journal of Economic Surveys*, July 2004, 427–81.

43. "Inflation Favored By 46 Senators," *NYT*, April 23, 1933.

44. In March, the Federal Reserve staff estimated that the economy needed an interest rate of −5 percent to restore growth; Krishna Guha, "Fed Study Puts Ideal Interest Rate at −5%," *FT*, April 27, 2009.

45. Irving Fisher, "The Debt-Deflation Theory of Great Depressions," *Econometrica*, Oct. 1933, 347. On the disappointing reception to Fisher's theory, see Robert W. Dimand, "Irving Fisher's Debt-Deflation Theory of Great Depressions," *Review of Social Economy*, Spring 1994, 92–107. For a recent analysis supporting Fisher's argument, see James S. Fackler and Randall E. Parker, "Was Debt Deflation Operative During the Great Depression?" *EI*, Jan. 2005, 67–78.

46. Irving Fisher, *The Works of Irving Fisher*, v. 14, ed. William J. Barber (London: Pickering & Chatto, 1997), 50.

47. Elliot A. Rosen, *Roosevelt, the Great Depression, and the Economics of Recovery* (Charlottesville: University of Virginia Press, 2005), 33–35. The concept of effective money supply basically corresponds to what we call the gross national product today, a term that was unknown in 1933. The first estimate of GNP didn't appear until 1934. See *National Income, 1929–32*, Senate Document 124, 73rd Cong., 2nd sess. (Washington: USGPO, 1934). This document estimated that the economy contracted 40 percent between 1929 and 1932.

48. Jacob Viner, *Balanced Deflation, Inflation, or More Depression* (Minneapolis: University of Minnesota Press, 1933), 20–25.

49. Michael D. Bordo, Christopher J. Erceg, and Charles L. Evans, "Money, Sticky Wages, and the Great Depression," *AER*, Dec. 2000, 1447–63; Harold L. Cole and Lee E. Ohanian, "New Deal Policies and the Persistence of the Great Depression: A General Equilibrium Analysis," *JPE*, Aug. 2004, 779–816.

50. Daniel R. Fusfeld, *The Economic Thought of Franklin D. Roosevelt and the Origins of the New Deal* (New York: Columbia University Press, 1954), 192–95, 205–6; "Roosevelt Calls Monetary Aides," *NYT*, Aug. 8, 1933; John Morton Blum, *From the Morgenthau Diaries: Years of Crisis, 1928–1938* (Boston: Houghton Mifflin, 1959), 61; F. A. Pearson, W. I. Myers, and A. R. Gans, *Warren as Presidential Adviser* (Ithaca: Dept. of Agricultural Economics, Cornell University, 1957); Henry A. Wallace, "Further Facts on Raising the Price of Gold," *Journal of Farm Economics*, Aug. 1958, 709–18; Elmus Wicker, "Roosevelt's 1933 Monetary Experiment," *JAH*, March 1971, 864–79.

51. Blum, *Morgenthau Diaries*, 69; Jesse Jones, *Fifty Billion Dollars* (New York: Macmillan, 1951), 245–52; "Text of Dr. Sprague's Letter to President," *NYT*, Nov. 22, 1933.

52. "Gold Purchase Plan Is Wrong, Says Expert," *WP*, Dec. 27, 1933. A similar view was expressed by economist Gustav Stolper in "Warns of 'Danger' in 'Stable Dollar,'" *NYT*, Dec. 28, 1933.

53. Elliot Thurston, "Inflation Battle Rages In Open With President Pushing Cheap Dollar," *WP*, Nov. 23, 1933; "Yale Economists Score Gold Policy," *NYT*, Dec. 16, 1933.

54. Lauchlin Currie, "Money, Gold, and Income in the United States, 1921–32," *QJE*, Nov. 1933, 84; Frank G. Steindl, "The Monetary Economics of Lauchlin Currie," *JME*, June 1991, 445–61. Currie's important work during this period has not gotten the attention it deserves because he was accused of being a Communist spy in the 1940s. But the evidence against him is very thin; James M. Boughton and Roger J. Sandilands, "Politics and the Attack on FDR's Economics: From the Grand Alliance to the Cold War," *Intelligence and National Security*, Sept. 2003, 73–99; Roger J. Sandilands, "Guilt By Association? Lauchlin Currie's Alleged Involvement with Washington Economists in Soviet Espionage," *HOPE*, Fall 2000, 473–515.

55. In 1930 Keynes laid primary blame for the slump on the Federal Reserve's tight money policy; Keynes, *Writings*, 6:176.

56. Keynes, *Writings*, 21:289–97.

57. "3 Reply to Keynes on NRA Criticism," *NYT*, Jan. 1, 1934.

58. See, for example, Robert Barro, "Government Spending Is No Free Lunch," *WSJ*, Jan. 22, 2009; Gary S. Becker and Kevin M. Murphy, "There's No Stimulus Free Lunch," *WSJ*, Feb. 10, 2009.

59. See, for example, remarks by National Economic Council Director Lawrence Summers, March 13, 2009, and by CEA Chair Christina Romer, March 9, 2009, both at the Brookings Institution. Also see minutes of the Federal Open Market Committee meeting, Jan. 27–28, 2009, 13, at www.federalreserve.gov.
60. Elmer Thomas, "Money and Its Management," *AAAPSS*, Jan. 1934, 136.
61. "Sweep for the Farm Bill," *NYT*, April 29, 1933.
62. Senate Committee on Banking and Currency, *Gold Reserve Act of 1934*, 73rd Cong., 2nd sess. (Washington: USGPO, 1934), 230.
63. Ibid., 289. According to Warren's own theory, the general price level ought to have been twice as high as it was; Rufus S. Tucker, "Warren Theories Versus Facts," *New York Herald Tribune*, Jan. 11, 1934.
64. "1934 Letter to FDR," *Journal of Economic Studies*, nos. 3–4, 2004, 261.
65. "Prof. Fisher Urges Central Bank for U.S.," *WSJ*, Feb. 2, 1934.
66. Russell Leffingwell, "The Gold Problem and Currency Revaluation," *Proceedings of the Academy of Political Science*, April 1934, 79–80. Excerpts from this speech were extensively quoted in "Morgan Partner for Cheap Money," *NYT*, March 22, 1934.
67. John Maynard Keynes, "Sees Need for $400,000,000 Monthly to Speed Recovery," *NYT*, June 10, 1934. Roosevelt rejected the advice; Blum, *Morgenthau Diaries*, 404.
68. Lauchlin Currie, *The Supply and Control of Money in the United States* (Cambridge: HUP, 1935), 33. In 1963 Friedman and Schwartz (*Monetary History*, 299) concluded that the broad money supply fell by more than a third between August 1929 and March 1933.
69. Quoted in "Economists Warn Against Inflation," *NYT*, Dec. 28, 1934.

CHAPTER 2   THE TRIUMPH OF KEYNESIAN ECONOMICS

1. Mark Skousen, *Vienna & Chicago: Friends or Foes?* (Washington: Regnery, 2005).
2. Bruce Bartlett, "Keynes Is God," *Rutgers Daily Targum*, Nov. 10, 1972; "The Popularity of Keynes," *Wertfrei*, Spring 1974, 14–16; *The Keynesian Revolution Revisited* (Greenwich, CT: Committee for Monetary Research and Education, 1977).
3. For a history of the industrial policy movement, see Otis L. Graham Jr., *Losing Time: The Industrial Policy Debate* (Cambridge: HUP, 1992).
4. Bruce Bartlett, "Keynes as a Conservative," *Modern Age*, Spring/Summer 1984, 128–33; "Industrial Policy: Crisis for Liberal Economists," *Fortune*,

Nov. 14, 1983, 83–86; "America's New Ideology: 'Industrial Policy,' Is Splitting Economists," *American Journal of Economics and Sociology*, Jan. 1985, 1–7.

5. Keynes, *Writings*, 2:148–49.

6. Frank W. Fetter, "Lenin, Keynes and Inflation," *Economica*, Feb. 1977, 77–80.

7. "Bolshevist Lenine's [*sic*] View of Money," *Commercial and Financial Chronicle*, May 3, 1919, 1763. This quote is also referenced in "Lenin Pontificates," *NYT*, April 26, 1919.

8. Constantino Bresciani-Turroni, *The Economics of Inflation* (London: George Allen & Unwin, 1937), 5; Thomas Mann, "Inflation: The Witches' Sabbath," *Encounter*, Feb. 1975, 63; Niall Ferguson and Brigitte Granville, "'Weimar on the Volga': Causes and Consequences of Inflation in 1990s Russia Compared with 1920s Germany," *JEH*, Dec. 2000, 1084.

9. Niall Ferguson, "Keynes and the German Inflation," *English Historical Review*, April 1995, 368–91; Robert Skidelsky, *John Maynard Keynes: The Economist as Savior, 1920–1937* (New York: Viking Penguin, 1994), 116–29; Keynes, *Writings*, 4:22–23, 36, 45–52; 27:183–84. On the monetarist underpinnings of the *Tract*, see Filippo Cesarano, "Keynes's Revindication of Classical Monetary Theory," *HOPE*, Fall 2003, 494–98; Milton Friedman, "The Keynes Centenary: A Monetarist Reflects," *The Economist*, June 4, 1983, 17–19; Thomas M. Humphrey, "Keynes on Inflation," *FRBRER*, Jan.–Feb. 1981, 5–10; D. E. Moggridge and Susan Howson, "Keynes on Monetary Policy, 1910–1946," *OEP*, July 1974, 232–33; Susan Howson, "'A Dear Money Man': Keynes on Monetary Policy, 1920," *EJ*, June 1973, 456–64.

10. See, for example, George Selgin, *Less Than Zero: The Case for a Falling Price Level in a Growing Economy* (London: Institute of Economic Affairs, 1997).

11. Keynes, *Writings*, 4:9, 17.

12. Keynes, *Writings*, 4:36; Reuven Brenner, "Unemployment, Justice, and Keynes's 'General Theory,'" *JPE*, Aug. 1979, 837–50.

13. D. E. Moggridge, *British Monetary Policy, 1924–1931: The Norman Conquest of $4.86* (New York: CUP, 1972); the title refers to Montagu Norman, governor of the Bank of England from 1920 to 1944.

14. Keynes, *Writings*, 9:218.

15. Keynes, *Writings*, 20:318–19; Daniel K. Benjamin and Levis A. Kochin, "Searching for an Explanation of Unemployment in Interwar Britain," *JPE*, June 1979, 441–78.

16. Keynes, *Writings*, 6:163–65.

17. Keynes, *Writings*, 6:37–45.

18. Keynes, *Writings*, 13:360. See also "Keynes Says Prices Must Be Kept Up," *NYT*, June 16, 1931.

19. Keynes, *Writings*, 13:362.

20. Keynes, *Writings*, 9:156–57.

21. Keynes, *Writings*, 9:338.

22. J. R. Vernon, "World War II Fiscal Policies and the End of the Great Depression," *JEH*, Dec. 1994, 853.

23. Keynes originally planned to call his book *The Monetary Theory of Employment*; Charles H. Hession, *John Maynard Keynes* (New York: Macmillan, 1984), 269.

24. Keynes, *Writings*, 7:9.

25. Keynes, *Writings*, 7:264.

26. Keynes, *Writings*, 7:267–68.

27. This implication of Keynes's theory was better explained in J. R. Hicks, "Mr. Keynes and the 'Classics': A Suggested Interpretation," *Econometrica*, April 1937, 147–59. It is my view, which I think Hicks agreed with, that the notion of a "liquidity trap" is the one indisputably important theoretical innovation in *The General Theory*, although Keynes himself may not have realized it. See J. R. Hicks, "A Rehabilitation of 'Classical' Economics," *EJ*, June 1957, 278–89.

28. Keynes, *Writings*, 21:337.

29. Keynes, *Writings*, 7:129, 220.

30. Alvin H. Hansen, "Under-Employment Equilibrium," *Yale Review*, Summer 1936, 828–30; Alvin H. Hansen, "Mr. Keynes on Underemployment Equilibrium," *JPE*, Oct. 1936, 686.

31. Wassily W. Leontief, "The Fundamental Assumption of Mr. Keynes' Monetary Theory of Unemployment," *QJE*, Nov. 1936, 192.

32. Jacob Viner, "Mr. Keynes on the Causes of Unemployment," *QJE*, Nov. 1936, 149.

33. Franco Modigliani, "Liquidity Preference and the Theory of Interest and Money," *Econometrica*, Jan. 1944, 76–77; Paul A. Samuelson, "A Brief Survey of Post-Keynesian Developments," in Robert Lekachman, ed., *Keynes' General Theory: Reports of Three Decades* (New York: St. Martin's Press, 1964), 332.

34. John Morton Blum, *From the Morgenthau Diaries: Years of Crisis, 1928–1938* (Boston: Houghton Mifflin, 1959), 380–97; Julian E. Zelizer, "Forgotten Legacy of the New Deal: Fiscal Conservatism and the Roosevelt Administration, 1933–1938," *PSQ*, June 2000, 345–52; Mark Leff, "Taxing the 'Forgotten Man': The Politics of Social Security Finance in the New Deal," *JAH*, Sept. 1983, 359–81.

35. Blum, *Morgenthau Diaries*, 367–75; Melvin Brockie, "Theories of the 1937–38 Crisis and Depression," *EJ*, June 1950, 292–97; Marriner S. Eccles, *Beckoning Frontiers* (New York: Knopf, 1951), 287–323; Milton Friedman and Anna J. Schwartz, *A Monetary History of the United States, 1867–1960* (Princeton: PUP,

1963), 543–45; E. Carey Brown, "Fiscal Policy in the 'Thirties: A Reappraisal," *AER*, Dec. 1956, 857–79; Will Lissner, "New Deal Policies Blamed for Slump," *NYT*, Jan. 23, 1938; Kenneth D. Roose, "The Recession of 1937–38," *JPE*, June 1948, 239–48.

36. Charles A. Beard, *American Foreign Policy in the Making, 1932–1940* (New Haven: Yale University Press, 1946), 178.

37. Jesse Burkhead, "The Balanced Budget," *QJE*, May 1954, 191–216; Lewis H. Kimmel, *Federal Budget and Fiscal Policy, 1789–1958* (Washington: Brookings, 1959); James D. Savage, *Balanced Budgets and American Politics* (Ithaca: Cornell University Press, 1988); Keynes, *Writings*, 21:386.

38. Basil Rauch, *Roosevelt: From Munich to Pearl Harbor* (New York: Creative Age Press, 1950), 89; Arthur A. Ekirch Jr., *Ideologies and Utopias: The Impact of the New Deal on American Thought* (Chicago: Quadrangle, 1969), 139.

39. John T. Flynn, "Recovery Through War Scares," *TNR*, Nov. 2, 1938, 360.

40. Wayne S. Cole, *Roosevelt and the Isolationists, 1932–45* (Lincoln: University of Nebraska Press, 1983); Robert A. Divine, *The Illusion of Neutrality* (Chicago: UCP, 1962); Hazel Erskine, "The Polls: Is War a Mistake?" *Public Opinion Quarterly*, Spring 1970, 136.

41. John T. Flynn, "Hooray for War Profits!" *TNR*, Nov. 1, 1939, 368.

42. Keynes, *Writings*, 22:149.

43. Robert M. Collins, *The Business Response to Keynes, 1929–1964* (New York: Columbia University Press, 1981), 12; Robert Lekachman, *The Age of Keynes* (New York: Random House, 1966), 153; Christina Romer, "What Ended the Great Depression?" *JEH*, Dec. 1992, 757–84; Elmus R. Wicker, "The World War II Policy of Fixing a Pattern of Interest Rates," *JF*, June 1969, 447–58.

44. Keynes, *Writings*, 27:385.

45. Keynes, *Writings*, 27:444.

46. Skidelsky, *Economist as Savior*, 344, 425, 546; he (224) says that with Keynes, expediency was "raised to a high principle of statecraft." See also Robert Skidelsky, *John Maynard Keynes: Hopes Betrayed, 1883–1920* (New York: Viking Penguin, 1986), 154; Elizabeth Johnson, "John Maynard Keynes: Scientist or Politician?" *JPE*, Jan.–Feb. 1974, 101.

47. Don Patinkin, "Keynes and Economics Today," *AER*, May 1984, 99.

48. Barry Eichengreen, "Keynes and Protection," *JEH*, June 1984, 363–73; Keynes, *Writings*, 9:298, 20:120–22, 21:233–46; Skidelsky, *Hopes Betrayed*, 227–28. See also "Keynes Advises Economic Isolation," *NYT*, June 19, 1933; R. F. Harrod, *The Life of John Maynard Keynes* (London: Macmillan, 1952), 610.

49. F. A. Hayek, review of *The Life of John Maynard Keynes*, in *Journal of Modern History*, June 1952, 198.

Notes

50. John H. Williams, "An Economist's Confessions," *AER*, March 1952, 10; Keynes, *Writings*, 14:122.

51. Robert Skidelsky, *John Maynard Keynes: Fighting for Britain, 1937–1946* (London: Macmillan, 2000), 19, 26.

52. Joseph A. Schumpeter, *History of Economic Analysis* (New York: OUP, 1954), 1121.

53. David McCord Wright, "The Future of Keynesian Economics," *AER*, June 1945, 287; Gottfried Haberler, "The Place of the General Theory of Employment, Interest, and Money in the History of Economic Thought," *RES*, Nov. 1946, 193.

54. George Gilder, *Wealth and Poverty* (New York: Basic Books, 1981), 32, 34; Mark Skousen, "Roaches Outlive Elephants: An Interview with Peter F. Drucker," *Forbes*, Aug. 19, 1991, 74. See also Peter F. Drucker, "Keynes: Economics as a Magical System," *Virginia Quarterly Review*, Fall 1946, 532–46; "Toward the Next Economics," *TPI*, special issue, 1980, 4–18. Indeed, Keynes had little use for trade unions, saying that they had "selfish and sectional pretensions" that needed to be "bravely opposed." Keynes, *Writings*, 9:309.

55. John Kenneth Galbraith, "Keynes, Roosevelt, and the Complimentary Revolutions," *Challenge*, Jan.–Feb. 1984, 7. See also John Kenneth Galbraith, "How Keynes Came to America," in Milo Keynes, ed., *Essays on John Maynard Keynes* (New York: CUP, 1975), 132–41; Dudley Dillard, "The Pragmatic Basis of Keynes's Political Economy," *JEH*, Nov. 1946, 121–52. Many right-wingers continue to argue that the New Deal epitomized an extreme leftist approach to the economy: for example, Gary Dean Best, *Pride, Prejudice, and Politics: Roosevelt versus Recovery, 1933–1938* (New York: Praeger, 1991); Burton Folsom Jr., *New Deal or Raw Deal?* (New York: Threshold Editions, 2008). However, those on the left have long recognized that the New Deal's greatest achievement was fundamentally conservative—preventing socialism from becoming a viable force in American politics; Barton J. Bernstein, "The New Deal: The Conservative Achievements of Liberal Reform," in Barton J. Bernstein, ed., *Towards a New Past* (New York: Vintage Books, 1968), 263–88; Seymour Martin Lipset and Gary Marks, *It Didn't Happen Here: Why Socialism Failed in the United States* (New York: Norton, 2000), 205–19; Ronald Radosh, "The Myth of the New Deal," in Ronald Radosh and Murray N. Rothbard, eds., *A New History of Leviathan* (New York: Dutton, 1972), 146–87. At least some conservatives are now coming around to this view as well: Conrad Black, *Franklin Delano Roosevelt* (New York: PublicAffairs, 2003), 1123–24.

56. In the words of Elizabeth Johnson, "Although Keynes thought of himself as a radical, one can see that he took a conservative, even an archaic view of society," Johnson, "Keynes: Scientist or Politician," 109.

57. Harrod, *Life of Keynes*, 331–33.

58. Keynes, *Writings*, 9:297, 19:639–40, 21:495; Skidelsky, *Hopes Betrayed*, 154–57.

59. For a recent right-wing attack on Keynes that attempts to paint him as a communist sympathizer, see Ralph Raico, "Was Keynes a Liberal?" *Independent Review*, Fall 2008, 165–88.

60. Carl B. Turner, *An Analysis of Soviet Views on John Maynard Keynes* (Durham: Duke University Press, 1969). On the negative reaction to publication of *The General Theory* by those on the political left, see Skidelsky, *Economist as Savior*, 575. Keynes was always very hostile to socialism despite its popularity among the British intellectual class in the 1930s; see Skidelsky, *Economist as Savior*, 438; Keynes, *Writings*, 9:290–1, 28:42. On the Ricardian underpinnings of Marxism, see Schumpeter, *History of Economic Analysis*, 390.

61. Keynes, *Writings*, 28:34; D. E. Moggridge, *Maynard Keynes: An Economist's Biography* (New York: Routledge, 1992), 470; Skidelsky, *Economist as Savior*, 520, 523; Keynes, *Writings*, 9:258, 267, 309.

62. Keynes, *Writings*, 7:162; Roberto Marchionatti, "On Keynes' Animal Spirits," *Kyklos*, no. 3, 1999, 415–39.

63. Keynes, *Writings*, 7:380.

64. Keynes, *Writings*, 7:380–81.

65. Keynes, *Writings*, 7:378, 22:123–24.

66. A. F. W. Plumptre, "Keynes in Cambridge," *Canadian Journal of Economics and Political Science*, Aug. 1947, 371. See also Harrod, *Life of Keynes*, 334; John A. Hall and Michael R. Smith, "The Political and Economic Consequences of Mr. Keynes," *Canadian Journal of Sociology*, Spring 2002, 245–67.

67. Bruce Bartlett, "The Harsh Impact on Consumption of Lost Home Equity," *Forbes.com*, Feb. 6, 2009.

68. Vikas Bajaj and Michael M. Grynbaum, "Investors Buy Federal Debt at Zero Yield," *NYT*, Dec. 18, 2008.

69. Bruce Bartlett, "What Would Keynes Do?" *Forbes.com*, Dec. 5, 2008; "How To Get the Money Moving," *NYT*, Dec. 24, 2008.

CHAPTER 3 INFLATION

1. L. J. Griffin, M. Wallace, and D. Devine, "The Political Economy of Military Spending: Evidence from the United States," *Cambridge Journal of Economics*, March 1982, 1–14; Alex Mintz and Alexander Hicks, "Military Keynesianism in the United States, 1949–1976: Disaggregating Military

Expenditures and Their Determination," *American Journal of Sociology*, Sept. 1984, 411–17.

2. For example, even former Federal Reserve Board chairman Alan Greenspan saw no signs of the recession in January 2008 although it began in December 2007; Krishna Guha, "Greenspan Sees No Clear Proof of Recession Among U.S. Data," *FT*, Jan. 25, 2008.

3. Even those close to Keynes had concerns about the overgenerality of *The General Theory* in terms of its analysis of inflation and unemployment. See D. G. Champernowne, "Unemployment, Basic and Monetary: The Classical Analysis and the Keynesian," *Review of Economic Studies*, June 1936, 201–16; John Hicks, *The Crisis in Keynesian Economics* (New York: Basic Books, 1974), 60–61; A. C. Pigou, "Mr. J. M. Keynes' General Theory of Employment, Interest and Money," *Economica*, May 1936, 115–32; D. H. Robertson, "Some Notes on Mr. Keynes' General Theory of Employment," *QJE*, Nov. 1936, 168–91.

4. Robert Leeson, "Keynes and the 'Keynesian' Phillips Curve," *HOPE*, Fall 1999, 497.

5. Alan S. Blinder and Janet L. Yellen, *The Fabulous Decade* (New York: Century Foundation, 2001); Anton Burger and Martin Zagler, "U.S. Growth and Budget Consolidation in the 1990s: Was There a Non-Keynesian Effect?" *International Economics and Economic Policy*, July 2008, 225–35; CEA, *ERP*, 2001, 79–93.

6. Jacob Viner, "Mr. Keynes on the Causes of Unemployment," *QJE*, Nov. 1936, 149.

7. Keynes, *Writings*, 21:390.

8. Keynes, *Writings*, 21:404–409, 2:151, 22:43.

9. Keynes, *Writings*, 22:44–46.

10. Keynes, *Writings*, 22:46.

11. Keynes, *Writings*, 9:367–439; F. A. Hayek, *The Collected Works of F. A. Hayek*, v. 10, ed. Bruce Caldwell (Chicago: UCP, 1997), 164–72.

12. Robert Skidelsky, *John Maynard Keynes: Fighting for Britain, 1937–1946* (London: Macmillan, 2000), 58–60.

13. Byrd L. Jones, "The Role of Keynesians in Wartime Policy and Postwar Planning, 1940–1946," *AER*, May 1972, 125–33.

14. Skidelsky, *Fighting for Britain*, 67.

15. Lionel Robbins, *The Economic Problem in Peace and War* (London: Macmillan, 1950), 29–56; Derek H. Aldcroft, "The Effectiveness of Direct Controls in the British Economy, 1946–1950," *Scottish Journal of Political Economy*, June 1963, 226–42; T. W. Hutchison, *Economics and Economic Policy in Britain, 1946–1966* (London: George Allen & Unwin, 1968), 55–67; Robert Bacon and Walter Eltis, *Britain's Economic Problem: Too Few Producers* (London: Macmillan, 1978);

Samuel Brittan, "How British Is the British Sickness?" *JLE*, Oct. 1978, 245–68; Barry Supple, "British Economic Decline Since 1945," in Roderick Floud and Donald McCloskey, eds., *The Economic History of Britain Since 1700*, 2nd ed. (New York: CUP, 1994), 3:318–46.

16. Alvin H. Hansen, "The Postwar Economy," in Seymour E. Harris, ed., *Postwar Economic Problems* (New York: McGraw-Hill, 1943), 12–13. See also Paul A. Samuelson, "Unemployment Ahead," *TNR*, Sept. 18, 1944, 333–35; George Soule, "That Post-War Depression," *TNR*, July 20, 1942, 74–76.

17. Alvin H. Hansen, "Economic Progress and Declining Population Growth," *AER*, March 1939, 1–15; Alan Sweezy, "Secular Stagnation?" in Harris, *Postwar Economic Problems*, 67–82; Robert W. Fogel, "Reconsidering Expectations of Economic Growth After World War II from the Perspective of 2004," *IMF Staff Papers*, special issue, 2005, 7.

18. Before Keynes, economists assumed that a free market economy would always tend toward full employment. Keynes argued that it was possible for the economy to stabilize for long periods at a high level of unemployment. See William Guthrie and Vincent J. Tarascio, "Keynes on Economic Growth, Stagnation, and Structural Change: New Light on a 55-Year Controversy," *HOPE*, Summer 1992, 381–412.

19. Gabriel Kolko, *The Politics of War* (New York: Random House, 1968), 245.

20. Wendy Asbeek Brusse, "Liberalizing Intra-European Trade," in Richard T. Griffiths, ed., *Explorations in OEEC History* (Paris: OECD, 1997), 123–37; J. Bradford DeLong and Barry Eichengreen, "The Marshall Plan: History's Most Successful Structural Adjustment Program," in Rudiger Dornbusch, Wilhelm Nölling, and Richard Layard, eds., *Postwar Economic Reconstruction and Lessons for the East Today* (Cambridge: MIT Press, 1993), 189–230; Ronald I. McKinnon, "The Marshall Plan's True Purpose," *WSJ*, July 16, 1991.

21. Herb Gintis, "American Keynesianism and the War Machine," in David Mermelstein, ed., *Economics: Mainstream Readings and Radical Critiques* (New York: Random House, 1970), 245–48; Paul A. Samuelson, *Economics: An Introductory Analysis*, 7th ed. (New York: McGraw-Hill, 1967), 767–68.

22. Robert L. Heilbroner, "Will Our Prosperity Last?" *Harper's*, Dec. 1948, 54; *U.S. News & World Report*, May 19, 1950, 7.

23. Daniel Dombey, "Crisis Cushioned," *FT*, Feb. 19, 2008; Paul Krugman, "Taming the Beast," *NYT*, March 24, 2008; Martin Feldstein, "Defense Spending Would Be Great Stimulus," *WSJ*, Dec. 24, 2008.

24. Stephen K. Bailey, *Congress Makes a Law: The Story Behind the Employment Act of 1946* (New York: Columbia University Press, 1950), 14–28; James E. Murray, "A Program to Prevent 'Boom or Bust,'" *NYT*, Dec. 29, 1946; G. J. Santoni,

"The Employment Act of 1946: Some History Notes," *FRBSLR*, Nov. 1986, 5–15.

25. George S. Tavlas, "The Chicago Tradition Revisited: Some Neglected Monetary Contributions: Senator Paul Douglas (1892–1976)," *JMCB*, Nov. 1977, 529–35; Arthur F. Burns, "Economic Research and the Keynesian Thinking of Our Times," in *The Frontiers of Economic Knowledge* (Princeton: PUP, 1954), 3–25; Arthur F. Burns, "Keynesian Economics Once Again," *RES*, Nov. 1947, 252–67; Wyatt C. Wells, *Economist in an Uncertain World: Arthur F. Burns and the Federal Reserve, 1970–1978* (New York: Columbia University Press, 1994), 12–16.

26. JEC, *Federal Tax Policy for Economic Growth and Stability*, 84th Cong., 1st sess. (Washington: USGPO, 1956); Sen. Rep. 1310, 84th Cong., 2nd sess. (Washington: USGPO, 1956); JEC, *Federal Expenditure Policy for Economic Growth and Stability*, 85th Cong., 1st sess. (Washington: USGPO, 1958).

27. Milton Friedman, *Dollars and Deficits* (Englewood Cliffs, NJ: Prentice-Hall, 1968), 73; CEA, *ERP*, 1954, iv; A. E. Holmans, "The Eisenhower Administration and the Recession, 1953–5," *OEP*, Feb. 1958, 34–54.

28. Quoted in Christopher Cerf and Victor Navasky, *The Experts Speak* (New York: Villard, 1998), 61.

29. Franklyn D. Holzman, "Creeping Inflation," *RES*, Aug. 1959, 324. On the view that moderate inflation was no problem, see also Sumner H. Slichter, "Argument for 'Creeping' Inflation," *NYTM*, March 8, 1959, 23ff.

30. Gardner Ackley, "Administered Prices and the Inflationary Process," *AER*, May 1959, 419–30; John Kenneth Galbraith, *The Affluent Society* (Boston: Houghton Mifflin, 1958), 210–25, 226–38. The report of the Radcliffe Committee in Britain in 1959 argued strongly against the importance of monetary policy and influenced Keynesian economists; John G. Gurley, "The Radcliffe Report and Evidence," *AER*, Sept. 1960, 672–700; Nicholas Kaldor, "The Radcliffe Report," *RES*, Feb. 1960, 14–19. A similar view was expressed in JEC, *Employment, Growth, and Price Levels*, Sen. Rep. 1043, 86th Cong., 2nd sess. (Washington: USGPO, 1960), and reported in Richard D. Mooney, "Report Criticizes U.S. Fiscal Policy," *NYT*, Dec. 29, 1959.

31. James L. Sundquist, *Politics and Policy: The Eisenhower, Kennedy, and Johnson Years* (Washington: Brookings, 1968), 431–41, 456–66; Richard Nixon, *Six Crises* (Garden City, NY: Doubleday, 1962), 309–10; Walter Heller, *New Dimensions of Political Economy* (Cambridge: HUP, 1967), 12.

32. "Soviet Closing Output Gap, Allen Dulles Warns U.S.," *NYT*, Nov. 14, 1959; Abram Bergson, *The Real National Income of Soviet Russia Since 1928* (Cambridge: HUP, 1961); Calvin B. Hoover, "Soviet Economic Growth,"

Foreign Affairs, Jan. 1957, 257–70; JEC, *Comparisons of the United States and Soviet Economies*, 86th Cong., 2nd sess. (Washington: USGPO, 1960).

33. Senate Commerce Committee, *The Speeches of Senator John F. Kennedy: Presidential Campaign of 1960*, Sen. Rep. 994, pt. 1, 87th Cong., 1st sess. (Washington: USGPO, 1961), 113, 124, 280, 288, 602, 605, 616, 820–22, 893, 1035, 1141; A. H. Raskin, "Goldberg Studies Automation Move," *NYT*, Jan.15, 1961. The JEC and CEA both issued reports concluding that if aggregate demand were maintained then there was no reason to fear a net loss of jobs in the future; CEA, *ERP*, 1964, 165–90; JEC, *Higher Unemployment Rates, 1957–60: Structural Transformation or Inadequate Demand*, 87th Cong., 1st sess. (Washington: USGPO, 1961). For surveys of the automation debate during this period, see Bruce Bartlett, "Is Industrial Innovation Destroying Jobs?" *Cato Journal*, Fall 1984, 625–43; Amy Sue Bix, *Inventing Ourselves Out of Jobs? America's Debate over Technological Unemployment, 1929–1981* (Baltimore: Johns Hopkins University Press, 2000).

34. Julian E. Zelizer, *Taxing America: Wilbur D. Mills, Congress, and the State, 1945–1975* (New York: CUP, 1998), 180; Bernard D. Nossiter, "Business Tax Break Urged," *WP*, Jan. 28, 1961.

35. Sar Levitan, *Federal Aid to Depressed Areas* (Baltimore: Johns Hopkins University Press, 1964), 50–51.

36. William J. Tobin, *Public Works and Unemployment: A History of Federally Funded Programs* (Washington: U.S. Department of Commerce, Economic Development Administration, 1975), 116; Nancy Teeters, "The 1972 Budget: Where It Stands and Where It Might Go," *BPEA*, no. 1, 1971, 233.

37. GAO, Letter to Senator Carl Hayden, Rep. no. B-146910, June 3, 1964; Letter to Senator A. Willis Robertson, Rep. no. B-153449, May 3, 1965; "Information Relating to Local Employment Created by the Accelerated Public Works Program," Rep. no. B-153449, Feb. 1966.

38. John Kenneth Galbraith, *A Journey Through Economic Time* (Boston: Houghton Mifflin, 1994), 172; Heller, *New Dimensions of Political Economy*, 32; John S. Odell, *U.S. International Monetary Policy* (Princeton: PUP, 1982), 106–109; Theodore Sorenson, *Kennedy* (New York: Harper & Row, 1965), 406–8.

39. Kennedy himself did a good job of discussing his options in a special message to Congress on Feb. 6, 1961.

40. John Kenneth Galbraith, *Letters to Kennedy*, ed. James Goodman (Cambridge: HUP, 1998), 43–45.

41. On failure of the interest equalization tax, see John R. Griffith Jr., "The Effect of the Interest Equalization Tax and the Interest Equalization Tax Extension Act on Purchases of Long-Term Bonds of Selected Countries Marketed in the United

States: 1959 to March 1966," *JF*, June 1969, 538–39. Kennedy's jawboning dimin-
ished the steel industry's profitability and thus its investment in new technology,
which contributed heavily to its long-term decline; Richard M. Duke *et al.*, *The
United States Steel Industry and Its International Rivals*, Staff Report, Bureau of
Economics, Federal Trade Commission (Washington: USGPO, 1978), 251–66;
William H. Peterson, "Steel Price Administration: Myth and Reality," in Helmut
Schoeck and James W. Wiggins, eds., *Central Planning and Neomercantilism*
(Princeton: Van Nostrand, 1964), 155–78. The Fed reluctantly supported the
Treasury on "Operation Twist," which sought to raise short-term interest rates
in order to support the dollar while reducing long-term rates, which would stim-
ulate investment. More of the Treasury's debt financing was shifted into short-
term Treasury bills and long-term bond sales were reduced. It didn't work very
well; Donald F. Kettl, *Leadership at the Fed* (New Haven: Yale University Press,
1986), 98–101; Myron H. Ross, " 'Operation Twist': A Mistaken Policy?" *JPE*,
April 1966, 195–99.

42. Timothy Naftali, ed., *John F. Kennedy: The Great Crises*, v. 1 (New York: Norton,
2001), 238, 247.

43. John Kenneth Galbraith, *The New Industrial State* (Boston: Houghton Mifflin,
1967), 229. One explanation for why conservative businessmen so strongly support defense spending while opposing government outlays on domestic programs
is self-interest; see Earl A. Thompson, "Taxation and National Defense," *JPE*,
July–Aug. 1974, 755–82.

44. John F. Kennedy, "Address to the Economic Club of New York," Dec. 14, 1962.

45. A. W. Phillips, "The Relation Between Unemployment and the Rate of Change
of Money Wage Rates in the United Kingdom, 1861–1957," *Economica*, Nov.
1958, 283–99.

46. Paul A. Samuelson and Robert M. Solow, "Analytical Aspects of Anti-Inflation
Policy," *AER*, May 1960, 177–94.

47. Thomas M. Humphrey, "The Early History of the Phillips Curve," *FRBRER*,
Sept.–Oct. 1985, 24.

48. Sydney Weintraub, "The Keynesian Theory of Inflation: The Two Faces of
Janus?" *IER*, May 1960, 154.

49. Albert E. Burger, "A Historical Analysis of the Credit Crunch of 1966,"
FRBSLR, Sept. 1969, 13–30; Kettl, *Leadership at the Fed*, 107–109; John W.
Sloan, "President Johnson, the Council of Economic Advisers, and the Failure to
Raise Taxes in 1966 and 1967," *PSQ*, Winter 1985, 89–98.

50. On extension of the surtax, see Nigel Bowles, *Nixon's Business* (College Station:
Texas A&M University Press, 2005), 38–43; Allen J. Matusow, *Nixon's Economy*
(Lawrence: University Press of Kansas, 1998), 34–45. On Federal Reserve policy,

see Burton A. Abrams, "How Richard Nixon Pressured Arthur Burns: Evidence from the Nixon Tapes," *JEP*, Fall 2006, 177–88; Richard F. Janssen and John Pierson, "Easier Money Policies Are Key to Plan to Spur Economy, White House Aides Say," *WSJ*, Nov. 9, 1970; William Poole, "Burnsian Monetary Policy: Eight Years of Progress?" *JF*, May 1979, 473–84; Sanford Rose, "The Agony of the Federal Reserve," *Fortune*, July 1974, 90ff.; William Safire, *Before the Fall* (Garden City, NY: Doubleday, 1975), 492–96; Hugh Rockoff, *Drastic Measures: A History of Wage and Price Controls in the United States* (New York: CUP, 1984), 200–33.

51. CBO, *Incomes Policies in the United States* (Washington: USGPO, 1977), 61–80; George P. Shultz and Kenneth W. Dam, *Economic Policy Beyond the Headlines* (New York: Norton, 1977), 65–85; Alan S. Blinder and William J. Newton, "The 1971–1974 Controls Program and the Price Level," *JPE*, July 1981, 1–23.

52. Alan S. Blinder, "Temporary Income Taxes and Consumer Spending," *JPE*, Feb. 1981, 26–53; Alan S. Blinder and Angus Deaton, "The Time Series Consumption Function Revisited," *BPEA*, no. 2, 1985, 465–511; Franco Modigliani and Charles Steindel, "Is a Tax Rebate an Effective Tool for Stabilization Policy?" *BPEA*, no. 1, 1977, 175–203.

53. U.S. Treasury Department, *Federal-State-Local Fiscal Relations: Report to the President and Congress* (Washington: USGPO, 1985), 372; Edward M. Gramlich, "State and Local Budgets the Day After It Rained: Why Is the Surplus So High?" *BPEA*, no. 1, 1978, 191–216; GAO, "Antirecession Assistance Is Helping but Distribution Formula Needs Reassessment," Rep. no. GGD-77-76, July 20, 1977; "Antirecession Assistance—An Evaluation," Rep. no. PAD-78-20, Nov. 29, 1977.

54. Chase Econometrics, *Local Public Works Program: Evaluation of the National Impact of the Local Public Works Program* (Washington: U.S. Department of Commerce, 1980), ii; Program Evaluation Division, *Local Public Works Program: Report on the Characteristics of LPW Employees* (Washington: U.S. Department of Commerce, 1980), 10, 50–1, 60; Daniel P. Kessler and Lawrence F. Katz, "Prevailing Wage Laws and Construction Labor Markets," *Industrial and Labor Relations Review*, Jan. 2001, 259–74.

55. Gramlich, "State and Local Budgets," 208–9.

56. Clyde Farnsworth, "Rise in Public Works Spending Would Not Affect Jobless This Year, Congressional Expert Asserts," *NYT*, Jan. 25, 1977; James C. Hyatt, "The Public Works Controversy," *WSJ*, Feb. 14, 1977.

57. Stacey L. Schreft, "Credit Controls: 1980," *FRBRER*, Nov.–Dec. 1990, 25–55; John Herbers, "$100 Billion Is Found Approved but Unused in Public Works Plans," *NYT*, June 30, 1980.

58. Ronald Reagan, "Remarks on Signing the Surface Transportation Assistance Act of 1982," Jan. 6, 1983; Bruce Bartlett, "Sure Enough, Gas Tax Wasn't a Jobs Bill," *WSJ*, Jan. 26, 1984; Bill Paul, "Road Repair Bill Is Doubtful Job-Creator in an Industry Shrunk by a Lack of Work," *NYT*, Dec. 1, 1982.

59. John Herbers, "Study Says More U.S. Aid May Hurt Public Works," *NYT*, Dec. 20, 1982; Richard Corrigan, "If Jobs Programs Don't Work, Why All the Clamor in Congress?" *National Journal*, Jan. 29, 1983, 214–17.

60. Diane Granat, "House Appropriations Panel Doles Out Cold Federal Cash, Chafes at Budget Process," *Congressional Quarterly*, June 18, 1983, 1209–15; Iver Peterson, "3-Month-Old Emergency Act Has Created Few Jobs as Yet," *NYT*, July 5, 1983; Patricia Cohen, "Is the Jobs Bill Creating Jobs?" *Washington Monthly*, Dec. 1983, 26–29.

61. GAO, "Emergency Jobs Act of 1983: Funds Spent Slowly, Few Jobs Created," Rep. no. GAO/HRD-87-1, Dec. 1986; "Antirecessionary Job Creation: Lessons from the Emergency Jobs Act of 1983," Rep. no. GAO/T-HRD-92-13, Feb. 1992.

62. Julius Margolis, "Public Works and Economic Stability," *JPE*, Aug. 1949, 293–303.

63. William J. Baumol, "Pitfalls in Contracyclical Policies: Some Tools and Results," *RES*, Feb. 1961, 21–26.

64. Sumner Slichter, "The Economics of Public Works," in Arthur Smithies and J. Keith Butters, eds., *Readings in Fiscal Policy* (Homewood, IL: Richard D. Irwin, 1955), 38–50.

65. Milton Friedman, "The Supply of Money and Changes in Prices and Output," in JEC, *The Relationship of Prices to Economic Stability and Growth*, 85th Cong., 2nd sess. (Washington: USGPO, 1958); Thomas Mayer, "The Keynesian Legacy: Does Countercyclical Policy Pay Its Way?" in Thomas D. Willett, ed., *Political Business Cycles* (Durham: Duke University Press, 1988), 129–44; Allan Meltzer, "Limits of Short-Run Stabilization Policy," *EI*, Jan. 1987, 1–14.

66. CEA, *ERP*, 1983, 41; David B. Gordon and Eric M. Leeper, "Are Countercyclical Fiscal Policies Counterproductive?" NBER Working Paper no. 11869, Dec. 2005.

67. Prakash Loungani, "How Accurate Are Private Sector Forecasts? Cross-Country Evidence from Consensus Forecasts of Output Growth," IMF Working Paper WP/00/77, April 2000; Stephen K. McNees, "How Accurate Are Macroeconomic Forecasts?" *New England Economic Review*, July–Aug. 1988, 15–36; Stephen K. McNees, "How Large Are Economic Forecast Errors?" *New England Economic Review*, July–Aug. 1992, 25–42; Scott Schuh, "An Evaluation of Recent Macroeconomic Forecast Errors," *New England Economic Review*, Jan.–Feb.

Notes

2001, 35–56; Charles Wolf, "Scoring the Economic Forecasters," *TPI*, Summer 1987, 48–55; Joseph Minarik, "Countercyclical Fiscal Policy: In Theory, and in Congress," *NTJ*, Sept. 1991, 251–56; Paul Portney, "Congressional Delays in U.S. Fiscal Policymaking," *Journal of Public Economics*, April-May 1976, 237–47.

68. "Balanced-Budget Politics," *NYT*, Jan. 29, 1997.

69. Ann F. Friedlaender, "The Federal Highway Program as a Public Works Tool," in Albert Ando, E. Carey Brown, and Ann F. Friedlaender, eds., *Studies in Economic Stabilization* (Washington: Brookings, 1968), 61–116; Ronald L. Teigen, "The Effectiveness of Public Works as a Stabilization Device," in W. L. Smith and R. L. Teigen, eds., *Readings in Money, National Income, and Stabilization Policy* (Homewood, IL: Richard D. Irwin, 1974), 305–10; George Vernez and Roger Vaughn, *Assessment of Countercyclical Public Works and Public Services Employment Programs* (Santa Monica, CA: Rand, 1978), 49; Sherman Maisel, "Timing and Flexibility of a Public Works Program," *RES*, May 1949, 147–52; Leland S. Burns and Leo Grebler, "Is Public Construction Countercyclical?" *Land Economics*, Nov. 1984, 367–77.

70. Urban Institute, "Effects of Economic Cycles" *Policy and Research Report*, Summer 1983, 1–3.

71. Alan Fechter, *Public Employment Programs* (Washington: AEI, 1975); George E. Johnson, "Structural Unemployment Consequences of Job Creation Policies," in John L. Palmer, ed., *Creating Jobs* (Washington: Brookings, 1978), 123–52; George E. Johnson and James D. Tomola, "The Fiscal Substitution Effect of Alternative Approaches to Public Service Employment Policy," *Journal of Human Resources*, Winter 1977, 3–26; Allen L. Webster, "Alternative Methods of Measuring Displacement Within Public Employment Programs," *Review of Regional Economics and Business*, April 1982, 16–22; Michael Wiseman, "Public Employment as Fiscal Policy," *BPEA*, no. 1, 1976, 67–104.

72. George Vernez, Roger Vaughn, Burke Burright, and Sinclair Coleman, *Regional Cycles and Employment Effects of Public Works Investments* (Santa Monica, CA: Rand, 1977), xvi.

73. Keynes, *Writings*, 27:122.

74. Jennifer Steinhauer, "In Budget Crises, California and Other States Reluctantly Halt Road Projects," *NYT*, Dec. 23, 2008; Nicholas Confessore, "$4 Billion in Stimulus, $41.8 Billion in Requests," *NYT*, March 5, 2009.

75. CBO, Letter to the Honorable Nancy Pelosi, Feb.13, 2009.

76. Michael M. Phillips, "Shovels Are There, but the Readiness May Not Be," *WP*, March 17, 2009; Donald Marron statement, House Committee on Transportation and Infrastructure, March 27, 2007, 7; Erik Sofge, "Why Shovel-Ready

Infrastructure Is Wrong (Right Now)," www.popularmechanics.com, Feb. 5, 2009.

77. Jennifer LaFleur and Michael Grabell, "Stimulus Infrastructure Funding Short-Changes States with High Unemployment," www.propublica.org, Feb. 15, 2009.

78. Christina Romer and Jared Bernstein, "The Job Impact of the American Recovery and Investment Plan," published by the Obama transition office on Jan. 9, 2009; CBO, Letter to the Honorable Charles E. Grassley, March 2, 2009.

CHAPTER 4   THE CONSERVATIVE COUNTERREVOLUTION

1. "The Great New Monetary Experiment," *Business Week,* July 13, 1981, 48. This theory was less controversial by 1981 than it seemed: see, for example, Martin Feldstein and Kathleen Feldstein, "Tight Money and Tax Cuts: A Mix That Works," *WP,* July 21, 1981.

2. Robert J. Samuelson, *The Great Inflation and Its Aftermath* (New York: Random House, 2008), 105–17.

3. "Nixon Reportedly Says He Is Now a Keynesian," *NYT,* Jan. 7, 1971. Nixon is often misquoted as saying, "We are all Keynesians now." That quotation in fact comes from economist Milton Friedman and originally appeared in *Time,* Dec. 31, 1965. In a letter to the editor on Feb. 4, 1966, Friedman said the quote was somewhat out of context. What he said was, "In one sense, we are all Keynesians now; in another, nobody is any longer a Keynesian."

4. Harry G. Johnson, "The Keynesian Revolution and the Monetarist Counter-Revolution," *AER,* May 1971, 1–14.

5. Milton Friedman and Rose D. Friedman, *Two Lucky People: Memoirs* (Chicago: UCP, 1998), 112–13; George Tavlas, "Was the Monetarist Tradition Invented?" *JEP,* Fall 1998, 211–22; J. Ronnie Davis, *The New Economics and the Old Economists* (Ames: Iowa State University Press, 1971), 38–63; see also Davis, "Chicago Economists, Deficit Budgets, and the Early 1930s," *AER,* June 1968, 476–82, and "The Last Remake of the New Economics and the Old Economists: Comment," *SEJ,* Jan. 1979, 919–25; Tavlas, "Chicago, Harvard, and the Doctrinal Foundations of Monetary Economics," *JPE,* Feb. 1997, 153–77.

6. Milton Friedman, "The Goldwater View of Economics," *NYTM,* Oct. 11, 1964, 35ff; Alan Otten, "Barry's Boys," *WSJ,* July 17, 1964; Frank C. Porter, "Blunt Views from a Barry Aide," *WP,* Sept. 11, 1964; M. J. Rossant, "A Talk with a Goldwater Man," *NYT,* Oct. 8, 1964.

Notes

7. Milton Friedman, "The Role of Monetary Policy," *AER*, March 1968, 1–17; Friedman, "Inflation and Unemployment," *JPE*, June 1977, 451–72; Friedman, *Unemployment versus Inflation* (London: Institute of Economic Affairs, 1975).

8. "The New Attack on Keynesian Economics," *Time*, Jan. 10, 1969; Alfred L. Malabre Jr., "Milton Friedman's Ideas Gain Wider Acceptance Among Policy-Makers," *WSJ*, Nov. 4, 1969; Hobart Rowen, "Friedman's Views Gaining Credence," *WP*, Dec. 29, 1968.

9. Melville J. Ulmer, "The Collapse of Keynesianism," *TNR*, May 5, 1973, 18–21.

10. Franco Modigliani, "The Monetarist Controversy or, Should We Forsake Stabilization Policies?" *AER*, March 1977, 1.

11. On inflation and the individual income tax, see Henry Aaron, *Inflation and the Income Tax* (Washington: Brookings, 1976); CBO, *Indexing the Individual Income Tax for Inflation* (Washington: USGPO, 1980); George von Furstenberg, "Individual Income Taxation and Inflation," *NTJ*, March 1975, 117–25. On the increase in marginal tax rates, see Appendix VI and Robert J. Barro and Chaipat Sahasakul, "Measuring the Average Marginal Tax Rate from the Individual Income Tax," *Journal of Business*, Oct. 1983, 419–52; Jane Gravelle, *The Economic Effects of Taxing Capital Income* (Cambridge: MIT Press, 1994), 20; John Seater, "Marginal Federal Personal and Corporate Income Tax Rates in the U.S., 1909–1975," *JME*, Nov. 1982, 361–81. On capital gains, see Robert Eisner, "Capital Gains and Income: Real Changes in the Value of Capital in the United States, 1946–77," in Dan Usher, ed., *The Measurement of Capital* (Chicago: UCP, 1980), 175–342; Martin Feldstein and Joel Slemrod, "Inflation and the Excess Taxation of Capital Gains on Corporate Stock," *NTJ*, June 1978, 107–18. On corporations, see Solomon Fabricant, "Accounting for Business Income Under Inflation: Current Issues and Views in the United States," *RIW*, March 1978, 1–24; Nicholas J. Gonedes, "Evidence on the 'Tax Effects' of Inflation under Historical Cost Accounting Methods," *Journal of Business*, April 1981, 227–70; John B. Shoven and Jeremy I. Bulow, "Inflation Accounting and Nonfinancial Corporate Profits: Physical Assets," *BPEA*, no. 3, 1975, 557–98; John B. Shoven and Jeremy I. Bulow, "Inflation Accounting and Nonfinancial Corporate Profits: Financial Assets and Liabilities," *BPEA*, no. 1, 1976, 15–57.

12. U.S. Treasury Department, *Report to Congress on the Capital Gains Tax Reductions of 1978* (Washington: USGPO, 1985), 11.

13. Milton Friedman, "Real and Pseudo Gold Standards," *JLE*, Oct. 1961, 66–79.

14. Robert Mundell, *The Dollar and the Policy Mix: 1971* (Princeton: International Finance Section, Department of Economics, Princeton University, 1971), 24–25.

15. Arthur B. Laffer, "Economist of the Century," *WSJ*, Oct. 15, 1999; David Meiselman and Arthur B. Laffer, *The Phenomenon of Worldwide Inflation* (Washington: AEI, 1975).

16. Robert Mundell, "Inflation from an International Point of View," in Meiselman and Laffer, *Phenomenon of Worldwide Inflation*, 143. On the importance of this conference, see Howard R. Vane and Chris Mulhearn, "Interview with Robert A. Mundell," *JEP*, Fall 2006, 102–3. On the inflationary effect of tax cuts, see the statements by Alan Blinder, John Brittain, Edward Denison, Otto Eckstein, Martin Feldstein, John Kenneth Galbraith, Edward Gramlich, and Joseph A. Pechman in House Ways and Means Committee, *Tax Reductions: Economists' Comments on H.R. 8333 and S. 1860 (The Kemp-Roth Bills)*, 95th Cong., 2nd sess. (Washington: USGPO, 1978); CEA, *ERP*, 1981, 493–99.

17. Jude Wanniski, "It's Time to Cut Taxes," *WSJ*, Dec. 11, 1974; James P. Gannon, "Tax Cut to Stimulate Economy Is Urged at White House Meeting of Economists," *WSJ*, Dec. 20, 1974.

18. Arthur B. Laffer, Stephen Moore, and Peter J. Tanous, *The End of Prosperity* (New York: Simon & Schuster, 2008), 23–24; Dick Cheney discussed this meeting in a *Fortune* interview on its website, Nov. 26, 2007; John Robert Greene, *The Presidency of Gerald R. Ford* (Lawrence: University Press of Kansas, 1995), 73–74.

19. Jude Wanniski, "The Mundell-Laffer Hypothesis—A New View of the World Economy," *TPI*, Spring 1975, 49–50.

20. Jude Wanniski, *The Way the World Works* (New York: Basic Books, 1978); Arthur B. Laffer, "The Iniquitous 'Wedge,'" *WSJ*, July 28, 1976; Paul Craig Roberts, "The Economic Case for Kemp-Roth," *WSJ*, Aug. 1, 1978.

21. Irving Kristol, *Neoconservatism* (New York: Free Press, 1995), 34–37; Robert L. Bartley, "Thirty Years of Progress—Mostly," *WSJ*, Nov. 20, 2002.

22. Edwin Dale Jr., "A New Theory: Inflation Triggers Recession," *NYT*, July 18, 1976.

23. "Mr. Callaghan Talks Business," *NYT*, Oct. 10, 1976.

24. Leonard Silk, "Germany Intends to Keep Economy 'in Good Shape,'" *NYT*, Jan. 24, 1977; "Is Keynes Dead?" *Business Week*, June 20, 1977, 74–75; "Keynes Is Dead," *WSJ*, Jan. 31, 1977; Alfred L. Malabre Jr., "May His Ideas Rest in Peace," *WSJ*, Nov. 17, 1977.

25. Anthony M. Santomero and John J. Seater, "The Inflation-Unemployment Trade-Off: A Critique of the Literature," *JEL*, June 1978, 533.

26. Alan S. Blinder, "The Fall and Rise of Keynesian Economics," *Economic Record*, Dec. 1988, 278.

27. Martin Feldstein, "The Retreat from Keynesian Economics," *TPI*, Summer 1981, 93.

28. Edmund S. Phelps, "Cracks in the Demand Side: A Year of Crisis in Theoretical Macroeconomics," *AER*, May 1982, 378.

29. On the history of changes in the capital gains tax rate, see Leonard Burman, *The Labyrinth of Capital Gains Tax Policy* (Washington: Brookings, 1999): 26–27; data on capital gains tax rates and realizations in Appendix V; Martin Feldstein, "American Economic Policy in the 1980s: A Personal View," in Martin Feldstein, ed., *American Economic Policy in the 1980s* (Chicago: UCP, 1994), 14.

30. Charles C. Holt and John P. Shelton, "The Lock-In Effect of the Capital Gains Tax," *NTJ*, Dec. 1962, 337–52; Harley H. Hinrichs, "An Empirical Measure of Investors' Responsiveness to Differentials in Capital Gains Tax Rates Among Income Groups," *NTJ*, Sept. 1963, 228.

31. Martin Feldstein statement, Senate Finance Committee, *Revenue Act of 1978*, 95th Cong., 2nd sess. (Washington: USGPO, 1978), 3:687–90; Martin Feldstein, Joel Slemrod, and Shlomo Yitzhaki, "The Effects of Taxation on the Selling of Corporate Stock and the Realization of Capital Gains," *QJE*, June 1980, 777–91; Gary L. Ciminero, *Economic Impact Analysis of a Capital Gains Tax Reduction* (New York: Merrill Lynch Economics, 1978); Michael K. Evans, *The Economic Effects of Reducing Capital Gains Taxes* (Bala Cynwyd, PA: Chase Econometric Associates, 1978); JCT, *General Explanation of the Revenue Act of 1978* (Washington: USGPO, 1979), 252; CBO, *How Capital Gains Tax Rates Affect Revenues: The Historical Evidence* (Washington: USGPO, 1988), 43; Lawrence B. Lindsey, "Capital Gains Rates, Realizations, and Revenues," in Martin Feldstein, ed., *The Effects of Taxation on Capital Accumulation* (Chicago: UCP, 1987), 69–100; Treasury Department, *Capital Gains Tax Reductions*, 178, 184. Indeed, the Treasury eventually changed its revenue-estimating methodology to show that capital gains tax cuts can raise revenue; Kenneth Gideon statement, Senate Finance Committee, *Tax Incentives for Increasing Savings and Investments*, 101st Cong., 2nd sess. (Washington: USGPO, 1990), 209–37.

32. Michael K. Evans, "The Bankruptcy of Keynesian Econometric Models," *Challenge*, Jan.–Feb. 1980, 13–19; and "Confessions of an Economic Forecaster," *NYT*, Feb. 17, 1980.

33. John F. Manley, "Congressional Staff and Public Policy-Making: The Joint Committee on Internal Revenue Taxation," *Journal of Politics*, Nov. 1968, 1046–67. For a review of the revenue-estimating process, see Michael D. Bopp, "The Roles of Revenue Estimating and Scoring in the Federal Budget Process," *Tax Notes*, Sept. 21, 1992, 1629–52; Emil M. Sunley and Randall D. Weiss, "The Revenue Estimating Process," *American Journal of Tax Policy*, Fall 1992, 261–98.

34. *Congressional Record*, Nov. 14, 1989, S15534 (daily ed.).

35. CBO, *Temporary Measures to Stimulate Employment: An Evaluation of Some Alternatives* (Washington: USGPO, 1975), 69.

36. Paul Craig Roberts, "The Breakdown of the Keynesian Model," *TPI*, Summer 1978, 20–33.

37. Senate Finance Committee, *Incentives for Economic Growth*, 95th Cong., 1st sess. (Washington: USGPO, 1977), 242. Interestingly, economist Kenneth Judd later confirmed Long's casual observation that the Investment Tax Credit probably paid for itself: Judd, "The Welfare Cost of Factor Taxation in a Perfect-Foresight Model," *JPE*, Aug. 1987, 675–709.

38. Juan Cameron, "The Economic Modelers Vie for Washington's Ear," *Fortune*, Nov. 20, 1978, 102–5; Michael K. Evans to Bruce R. Bartlett, May 21, 1981, in possession of the author. Of course, Evans was being totally disingenuous. He knew that because the Finance Committee had no further interest in his work, he was free to do what he wanted with it and had no intention of giving it away for free. Much of the research, however, ended up in Michael K. Evans, *The Truth About Supply-Side Economics* (New York: Basic Books, 1983).

39. Robert E. Lucas, "Econometric Policy Evaluation: A Critique," in Karl Brunner and Allan Meltzer, eds., *The Phillips Curve and Labor Markets* (New York: North-Holland, 1976), 19–46; Robert E. Lucas and Thomas J. Sargent, "After Keynesian Macroeconomics," *FRBMQR*, Spring 1979, 1–16; Keynes, *Writings*, 7:297–98, 14:295–301. See also Robert Leeson, "'The Ghosts I Called I Can't Get Rid of Now': The Keynes-Tinbergen-Friedman-Phillips Critique of Keynesian Macroeconomics," *HOPE*, Spring 1998, 51–94.

40. The memo is reprinted in Bruce Bartlett, *Reaganomics: Supply-Side Economics in Action* (Westport, CT: Arlington House, 1981), 213–14.

41. JEC, *The 1977 Economic Report of the President*, 95th Cong., 1st sess. (Washington: USGPO, 1977), 161.

42. Walter W. Heller, "'Supply-Side' Tax Reductions," *NYT*, Dec. 17, 1980.

43. *Congressional Record*, Sept. 24, 1963, 17907. It should be noted that Kennedy's official revenue estimates, like Reagan's, all showed significant revenue losses; see Treasury Secretary Henry Fowler statement, House Committee on Banking and Currency, *Meetings with Department and Agency Officials*, 90th Cong., 1st sess. (Washington: USGPO, 1967), 2–17.

44. CEA, *ERP*, 1965, 65–66; Arthur M. Okun, "Measuring the Impact of the 1964 Tax Reduction," in Walter W. Heller, ed., *Perspectives on Economic Growth* (New York: Random House, 1968), 25–49; Lawrence B. Klein, "Econometric Analysis of the Tax Cut of 1964," in James Duesenberry et al., *The Brookings Model: Some Further Results* (Chicago: Rand McNally, 1969), 459–72.

45. Published in House Budget Committee and JEC, *Economic Stabilization Policies: The Historical Record, 1962–76*, Joint Committee Print, 95th Cong., 2nd sess. (Washington: USGPO, 1978).

46. CBO, *Understanding Fiscal Policy* (Washington: USGPO, 1978), 25.

47. Victor A. Canto, Douglas H. Joines, and Robert I. Webb came closest to proving that the Kennedy tax cut paid for itself by including higher revenues that accrued to state and local governments with those received by the federal government in "The Revenue Effects of the Kennedy Tax Cuts," in Canto, Joines, and Arthur B. Laffer, eds., *Foundations of Supply-Side Economics: Theory and Evidence* (New York: Academic Press, 1983), 72–103.

48. Paul Evans, "Kemp-Roth and Saving," *Federal Reserve Bank of San Francisco Weekly Letter*, May 8, 1981; Paul Craig Roberts, "The Tax Cut Will Help Savings," *Fortune*, Aug. 24, 1981, 44–45; Michael K. Evans, "The Source of Personal Saving in the U.S.," *WSJ*, March 23, 1981.

49. JEC, *The 1977 Economic Report of the President*, 95th Cong., 1st sess. (Washington: USGPO, 1977), 478.

50. Hobart Rowen, "Treasury Chief Favors Uniform, Lower Income Tax Rate," *WP*, Jan. 23, 1977.

51. CBO, *An Analysis of the Roth-Kemp Tax Cut Proposal* (Washington: USGPO, 1978), 43; Douglas Brinkley, ed., *The Reagan Diaries* (New York: HarperCollins, 2007), 58. However, all of the administration's official revenue forecasts clearly showed revenue losses from the tax cut consistent with standard revenue-estimating methodology.

52. Peter M. Gutmann, "The Subterranean Economy," *Financial Analysts Journal*, Nov.–Dec. 1977, 26–27, 34. Gutmann's work was the subject at three congressional hearings in 1979 and spawned a vast literature well summarized in Friedrich Schneider and Dominik H. Enste, "Shadow Economies: Size, Causes, and Consequences," *JEL*, March 2000, 77–114. Among articles showing that tax rate reductions can significantly reduce tax evasion are James Alm, "Compliance Costs and the Tax Avoidance-Tax Evasion Decision," *PFQ*, Jan. 1988, 31–66; Charles T. Clotfelter, "Tax Evasion and Tax Rates: An Analysis of Individual Returns," *RES*, Aug. 1983, 363–73; Reinhard Neck, Friedrich Schneider, and Markus F. Hofreither, "The Consequences of Progressive Income Taxation for the Shadow Economy: Some Theoretical Considerations," in Dieter Bös and Bernhard Felderer, eds., *The Political Economy of Progressive Taxation* (New York: Springer-Verlag, 1989), 149–76; Roger N. Waud, "Tax Aversion and the Laffer Curve," *Scottish Journal of Political Economy*, Aug. 1986, 213–27.

53. See Henry S. Farber, "Individual Preferences and Union Wage Determination: The Case of the United Mine Workers," *JPE*, Oct. 1978, 923–42; Werner Z.

Hirsch and Anthony M. Rufolo, "Effects of State Income Taxes on Fringe Benefit Demand of Policemen and Firemen," *NTJ*, June 1986, 211–19; James E. Long and Frank A. Scott, "The Income Tax and Nonwage Compensation," *RES*, May 1982, 211–19; James E. Long and Frank A. Scott, "The Impact of the 1981 Tax Act on Fringe Benefits and Federal Tax Revenues," *NTJ*, June 1984, 185–94; Frank A. Sloan and Killard W. Adamache, "Taxation and the Growth of Nonwage Compensation," *PFQ*, April 1986, 115–37; Susan Vroman and Gerard Anderson, "The Effect of Income Taxation on the Demand for Employer-Provided Health Insurance," *Applied Economics*, Feb. 1984, 33–43; Stephen A. Woodbury, "Substitution Between Wage and Nonwage Benefits," *AER*, March 1983, 166–82; Stephen A. Woodbury and Daniel S. Hammermesh, "Taxes, Fringe Benefits and Faculty," *RES*, May 1992, 287–96.

54. Victor A. Canto and Marc A. Miles, "The Missing Equation: The Wedge Model Alternative," *Journal of Macroeconomics*, Spring 1981, 247–89; Charles T. Clotfelter, "Tax-Induced Distortions and the Business-Pleasure Borderline: The Case of Travel and Entertainment," *AER*, Dec. 1983, 1053–65; James Gwartney and James Long, "Tax Rates, Tax Shelters, and the Efficiency of Capital Formation," in Dwight R. Lee, ed., *Taxation and the Deficit Economy* (San Francisco: Pacific Research Institute, 1986), 107–39; James Gwartney and James Long, "Income Tax Avoidance and an Empirical Estimation of the Laffer Curve," Office of the Assistant Secretary for Economic Policy, U.S. Treasury Department, July 1984; James E. Long, "The Income Tax and Self-Employment," *NTJ*, March 1982, 31–42; James E. Long, "Income Taxation and the Allocation of Market Labor," *Journal of Labor Research*, Summer 1982, 259–76; James E. Long, "Tax Rates and Tax Losses: A Preliminary Analysis Using Aggregate Data," *PFQ*, Oct. 1984, 457–72; James E. Long, "Marginal Tax Rates and IRA Contributions," *NTJ*, June 1990, 143–53. Note that lowering the top rate at this time automatically lowered the capital gains rate because 60 percent of gains were excluded from taxation, with the balance taxed at ordinary income tax rates.

55. Darwin G. Johnson, "Sensitivity of Federal Expenditures to Unemployment," *PFQ*, Jan. 1981, 3–21; Office of Income Security Policy, "The Cyclical Behavior of Income Transfer Programs: A Case Study of the Current Recession," Technical Analysis Paper no. 7, Office of the Assistant Secretary for Planning and Evaluation; Department of Health, Education and Welfare, Oct. 1975.

56. House Ways and Means Committee, *Economists' Comments*, 64.

57. On the inclusion of state and local government effects, see Michael R. Baye and Darrell F. Parker, "The Consumption Tax and Supply Side Economics: Some Short-Term Revenue Effects," *Cato Journal*, Fall 1981, 629–32.

58. JEC, *The 1978 Midyear Review of the Economy*, 95th Cong., 2nd sess. (Washington: USGPO, 1978), 129.

59. Arthur B. Laffer, "An Equilibrium Rational Macroeconomic Framework," in Nake M. Kamrany and Richard H. Day, eds., *Economic Issues of the Eighties* (Baltimore: Johns Hopkins University Press, 1979), 54–55. There are some typos in this publication that Laffer personally corrected for me.

60. Arthur B. Laffer, "Government Exactions and Revenue Deficiencies," *Cato Journal*, Spring 1981, 21. Feldstein cites this quotation in refutation of the statement by Martin Anderson that the Reagan Administration never predicted higher revenues from its tax cut. Of course, Laffer was not an administration official, although he was a member of President Reagan's Economic Policy Advisory Board, a group of private economists who met with him occasionally to give informal advice. Martin Anderson, *Revolution* (New York: Harcourt Brace Jovanovich, 1988), 140–63; Martin Feldstein, "American Economic Policy in the 1980s: A Personal View," in Martin Feldstein, ed., *American Economic Policy in the 1980s* (Chicago: UCP, 1994), 25.

61. House Ways and Means Committee, *Economists' Comments*, 96. Although Ture's estimate of the revenue effects of Kemp-Roth was reasonable, he was not always so conservative. In 1976, Ture estimated that an earlier Kemp tax cut, the Jobs Creation Act, would pay for itself immediately and raise net revenue every year thereafter; see *Reducing Unemployment: The Humphrey-Hawkins and Kemp-McClure Bills* (Washington: AEI, 1976), 30–32.

62. House Budget Committee and Senate Budget Committee, *Leading Economist's Views of Kemp-Roth*, Joint Committee Print, 95th Cong., 2nd sess. (Washington: USGPO, 1978), 76.

63. Stockman's *mea culpa* appeared in William Greider, "The Education of David Stockman," *Atlantic Monthly*, Dec. 1981, 27–54.

64. *Congressional Record*, March 1, 1978, E919 (daily ed.).

65. Senate Finance Committee, *Individual and Business Tax Reduction Proposals*, 95th Cong., 2nd sess. (Washington: USGPO, 1978), 101–4.

66. *Congressional Record*, Aug. 10, 1978, H8358 (daily ed.); David A. Stockman, "Why the Economic Doctors Failed," *WP*, March 2, 1980; Stockman, "Our Grand New Platform," *WP*, July 15, 1980.

67. White House, *A Program for Economic Recovery* (Washington: USGPO, 1981), 16.

68. JEC, *The 1981 Economic Report of the President*, 97th Cong., 1st sess. (Washington: USGPO, 1981), 3:17–21.

69. House Ways and Means Committee, *Tax Aspects of the President's Economic Program*, 97th Cong., 1st sess. (Washington: USGPO, 1981), 449.

70. House Ways and Means Committee, *Tax Aspects of the President's Economic Program*, 97th Cong., 1st sess. (Washington: USGPO, 1981), 469.

71. Ibid., 430.

72. Senate Finance Committee, *Nomination of David A. Stockman*, 97th Cong., 1st sess. (Washington: USGPO, 1981), 24–25.

73. David A. Stockman, *The Triumph of Politics* (New York: Harper & Row, 1986), 67, 94–95.

74. Richard B. McKenzie, "An Introduction to the Personal Tax 'Cuts,'" *WSJ*, Jan. 8, 1982, and "Supply-Side Economics and the Vanishing Tax Cut," *FRBAER*, May 1982, 20–24; Stephen A. Meyer and Robert J. Rossana, "Did the Tax Cut Really Cut Taxes?" *FRBPBR*, Nov.–Dec. 1981, 3–12; "Why Only a Popgun Tax Cut?" *NYT*, Feb. 26, 1981; "Kemp-Roth: Too Large and Too Small," *NYT*, April 27, 1981; Dimitri Andrianacos and Ali T. Akarca, "Long-Run Impact of Tax Rate Changes on Government Receipts," *PFQ*, Jan. 1998, 80–94; Charles T. Clotfelter, "Tax Cut Meets Bracket Creep: The Rise and Fall of Marginal Tax Rates," *PFQ*, April 1984, 131–52; Stephen A. Meyer, "Tax Cuts: Reality or Illusion?" *FRBPBR*, July–Aug. 1983, 3–15; Sylvia Nasar, "After Tax Changes of 80's, Burden Is No Lighter," *NYT*, Oct. 1, 1992; John A. Tatom, "The 1981 Personal Income Tax Cuts: A Retrospective Look at Their Effects on the Federal Tax Burden," *FRBSLR*, Dec. 1984, 5–17.

75. For a typical example of this thinking, see Hobart Rowen, "Deficits Prove Supply-Side Theory False," *WP*, Dec. 20, 1981.

76. Lawrence B. Lindsey, "Individual Taxpayer Response to Tax Cuts: 1982–1984," *Journal of Public Economics*, July 1987, 173–206; Rosemarie M. Neilsen, Frank J. Sammartino, and Eric Toder, "CBO Replies to Lindsey," *Tax Notes*, May 4, 1987, 496–501.

77. Lawrence B. Lindsey, *The Growth Experiment: How the New Tax Policy Is Transforming the U.S. Economy* (New York: Basic Books, 1990), 76.

78. Paul Craig Roberts, "How the Defeat of Inflation Wrecked the U.S. Budget," *LAT*, Jan. 27, 1987, and "What Really Happened in 1981," *Independent Review*, Fall 2000, 279–81.

79. Arthur Okun said that to bring the basic inflation rate down by one percent would cost 10 percent of a year's GNP in "Efficient Disinflationary Policies," *AER*, May 1978, 348–52.

80. White House, *Program for Economic Recovery*, 25.

81. OMB, *Budget of the United States Government, Fiscal Year 1982* (Washington: USGPO, 1981), 3, 59.

82. M. A. Akhtar and Ethan S. Harris, "The Supply-Side Consequences of U.S. Fiscal Policy in the 1980s," *Federal Reserve Bank of New York Quarterly Review*, Spring 1992, 1–20.

83. Paul Samuelson, "The '80s Are an Economic Success Story," *Christian Science Monitor*, Oct. 4, 1989; CEA, *ERP*, 1994, 88.

CHAPTER 5   THE RISE AND FALL OF
SUPPLY-SIDE ECONOMICS

1. See Frank Ackerman, *Hazardous to Our Wealth* (Boston: South End Press, 1984); Robert D. Atkinson, *Supply-Side Follies* (New York: Rowman & Littlefield, 2006); Jonathan Chait, *The Big Con* (Boston: Houghton Mifflin, 2007); Bryan D. Jones and Walter Williams, *The Politics of Bad Ideas* (New York: Pearson/ Longman, 2008); Paul Krugman, *Peddling Prosperity* (New York: Norton, 1994); Robert Lekachman, *Greed Is Not Enough* (New York: Pantheon, 1982).

2. Ibn Khaldun, *The Muqaddimah*, trans. Franz Rosenthal (New York: Pantheon, 1958), 2: 89.

3. Jean David Boulakia, "Ibn Khaldun: A Fourteenth-Century Economist," *JPE*, Sept.–Oct. 1971, 1105–18. In private correspondence, Mundell told me that he was familiar with Khaldun before seeing the Boulakia manuscript because he and Khaldun were born exactly 600 years apart.

4. Jonathan Swift, "An Answer to a Paper Called a Memorial of the Poor Inhabitants, Tradesmen, and Laborers of the Kingdom of Ireland," in Herbert Davis, ed., *Jonathan Swift: Irish Tracts* (Oxford: Blackwell, 1964), 17–25; Bruce Bartlett, "Jonathan Swift: Father of Supply-Side Economics?" *HOPE*, Fall 1992, 745–48.

5. James Ring Adams, "Supply-Side Roots of the Founding Fathers," *WSJ*, Nov. 17, 1981; James Ring Adams, *Secrets of the Tax Revolt* (New York: Harcourt Brace Jovanovich, 1984); Robert Keleher, "Supply-Side Effects of Fiscal Policy: Some Preliminary Hypotheses," Federal Reserve Bank of Atlanta Research Paper no. 9, June 1979; Robert Keleher, "Historical Origins of Supply-Side Economics," *FRBAER*, Jan. 1982, 12–19, and "Supply-Side Economics: Guiding Principles for the Founding Fathers," *FRBAER*, Sept. 1982, 42–54.

6. Adam Smith, *The Wealth of Nations* (New York: Modern Library, 1937), 835.

7. Baron de Montesquieu, *The Spirit of the Laws* (New York: Hafner Publishing Co., 1949), 216.

8. Bruce Bartlett, *Reaganomics: Supply-Side Economics in Action* (Westport, CT: Arlington House, 1981), 1. See also George Gilder, *Wealth and Poverty* (New York: Basic Books, 1981), 40; Salim Rashid, "Historical Notes on the Origins of Supply-Side Economics and Its Ethical Roots: Say's Law, Smith's Law, or Moral Law?" *Quarterly Review of Economics and Business*, Winter 1986, 22–34.

9. Jean-Baptiste Say, *A Treatise on Political Economy*, 6th ed., trans. C. R. Prinsep and Clement C. Biddle (Philadelphia: Grigg & Elliott, 1834), 143.

10. John Stuart Mill, *Essays on Some Unsettled Questions of Political Economy*, 2nd ed. (London: Longmans, Green, Reader & Dyer, 1874), 49; William J. Baumol, "Say's (at Least) Eight Laws, or What Say and James Mill May Have Really Meant," *Economica*, May 1977, 145–61; Robert Clower and Axel Leijonhufvud, "Say's Principle, What it Means and Doesn't Mean," *Intermountain Economic Review*, Fall 1973, 1–16; W. H. Hutt, *A Rehabilitation of Say's Law* (Athens: Ohio University Press, 1974); A. S. Skinner, "Say's Law: Origins and Content," *Economica*, May 1967, 153–66; Thomas Sowell, *Say's Law: An Historical Analysis* (Princeton: PUP, 1972).

11. Say, *Treatise*, 453–54.

12. *Congressional Globe*, Appendix, 27th Cong., 2nd sess., 1842, 772.

13. "Affairs at the Capital," *NYT*, July 20, 1861, 5; Harold U. Faulkner, *Politics, Reform and Expansion, 1890–1900* (New York: Harper & Row, 1959), 106; Douglas A. Irwin, "Higher Tariffs, Lower Revenues? Analyzing the Fiscal Aspects of 'The Great Tariff Debate of 1888,' " *JEH*, March 1998, 59–72.

14. Michael Cooper, "Cigarettes Up to $7 a Pack With New Tax," *NYT*, July 1, 2002.

15. Edwin Cannan, "Equity and Economy in Taxation," *EJ*, Dec. 1901, 469–79; Martin Bronfenbrenner, "Diminishing Returns in Federal Taxation?" *JPE*, Oct. 1942, 699–715; Simon Kuznets, "National Income and Taxable Capacity," *AER*, March 1942, 37–76; F. W. Paish, "Economic Incentive in Wartime," *Economica*, Aug. 1941, 239–48; Carl Shoup, "Problems in War Finance," *AER*, March 1943, 74–97; Colin Clark, "Public Finance and Changes in the Value of Money," *EJ*, Dec. 1945, 371–89; John Maynard Keynes to Colin Clark, March 9, 1945, reprinted in *The State of Taxation* (London: Institute of Economic Affairs, 1977), 23; Keynes, *Writings*, 21:145.

16. Ludwig von Mises, *Human Action* (New Haven: Yale University Press, 1949), 734.

17. C. Northcote Parkinson, *The Law and the Profits* (Boston: Houghton Mifflin, 1960), 95; Richard B. McKenzie, "The Micro and Macro Economic Effects of Changes in the Statutory Tax Rates," *Review of Social Economy*, April 1973, 20.

18. Jude Wanniski, "Taxes and a Two-Santa Theory," *National Observer*, March 6, 1976; Jude Wanniski, "Taxes and the Kennedy Gamble," *WSJ*, Sept. 23, 1976; Herbert Stein, *The Fiscal Revolution in America* (Chicago: UCP, 1969), 9–10.

19. Lawrence L. Murray, "Bureaucracy and Bi-partisanship in Taxation: The Mellon Plan Revisited," *BHR*, Summer 1978, 200–25.

20. Andrew Mellon, *Taxation: The People's Business* (New York: Macmillan, 1924), 13.

21. Benjamin G. Rader, "Federal Taxation in the 1920s: A Re-examination," *The Historian*, May 1971, 434; Robert B. Ekelund Jr. and Mark Thornton, "Schumpeterian Analysis, Supply-Side Economics and Macroeconomic Policy in the 1920s," *Review of Social Economy*, Dec. 1986, 221–37; James Gwartney and Richard Stroup, "Tax Cuts: Who Shoulders the Burden?" *FRBAER*, March 1982, 19–27; Gabriel G. Rudney, "Income Under Low and High Tax Rate Systems: 1929 vs. 1973," Office of Tax Analysis Paper 17, U.S. Treasury Department, Sept. 1976.

22. Gene Smiley and Richard H. Keehn, "Federal Personal Income Tax Policy in the 1920s," *JEH*, June 1995, 302.

23. Victor A. Canto and Robert I. Webb, "The Effect of State Fiscal Policy on State Relative Economic Performance," *SEJ*, July 1987, 186–202; William J. Hunter and Charles E. Scott, "The Impact of Income Tax Progressivity on Tax Revenue," *PFQ*, April 1987, 188–98; W. Robert Reed, "The Robust Relationship Between Taxes and U.S. State Income Growth," *NTJ*, March 2008, 57–79; Ronald E. Grieson, "Theoretical Analysis and Empirical Measurements of the Effects of the Philadelphia Income Tax," *Journal of Urban Economics*, July 1980, 123–37; John Gruenstein, "Jobs in the City: Can Philadelphia Afford to Raise Taxes?" *FRBPBR*, May–June 1980, 3–11; Robert Inman, "Can Philadelphia Escape Its Fiscal Crisis With Another Tax Increase?" *FRBPBR*, Sept.–Oct. 1992, 5–20.

24. Two members of the JEC's Democratic staff during this era have written about the difficult transition from Keynesianism to supply-side economics on their side of the aisle: Mark Bisnow, *In the Shadow of the Dome* (New York: William Morrow, 1990), 229–40; Kent H. Hughes, *Building the Next American Century* (Baltimore: Johns Hopkins University Press, 2005), 58–62, 114–22.

25. JEC, *1980 Joint Economic Report*, Sen. Rep. 96–618, 96th Cong., 1st sess. (Washington: USGPO, 1980), 1.

26. JEC, *Forecasting the Supply Side of the Economy*, 96th Cong., 2nd sess. (Washington: USGPO, 1980); Otto Eckstein, *The DRI Model of the U.S. Economy* (New York: McGraw-Hill, 1983), 55–76.

27. Leonard Silk, "Major Change in Theory Seen," *NYT*, March 5, 1980.

28. Steven Rattner, "Economic Panel Splits on Policy," *NYT*, Feb. 27, 1981.

29. Robert J. Barro, "Economic Growth in a Cross Section of Countries," *QJE*, May 1991, 407–43; Charles T. Carlstrom and Jagadeesh Gokhale, "Government Consumption, Taxation, and Economic Activity," *Federal Reserve Bank of Cleveland Economic Review*, 3rd quarter 1991, 18–29; Eric Engen and Jonathan Skinner, "Taxation and Economic Growth," *NTJ*, Dec. 1996, 617–42; Stefan Fölster and Magnus Henrekson, "Growth Effects of Government Expenditure and Taxation in Rich Countries," *European Economic Review*, Aug. 2001,

Notes

1501–20; Kevin B. Grier and Gordon Tullock, "An Empirical Analysis of Cross-National Economic Growth, 1951–80," *JME*, Sept. 1989, 259–76; Pär Hansson and Magnus Henrekson, "A New Framework for Testing the Effect of Government Spending on Growth and Productivity," *PC*, Dec. 1994, 381–401; Bernhard Heitger, "Convergence, the 'Tax-State' and Economic Dynamics," *Weltwirtschaftliches Archiv*, no. 2, 1993, 254–73; Georgios Karras, "Employment and Output Effects of Government Spending: Is Government Size Important?" *EI*, July 1993, 354–69; Robert G. King and Sergio Rebelo, "Public Policy and Economic Growth: Developing Neoclassical Implications," *JPE*, Oct. 1990, 2:S126–50; Reinhard B. Koester and Roger C. Kormendi, "Taxation, Aggregate Activity and Economic Growth: Cross-Country Evidence on Some Supply-Side Hypotheses," *EI*, July 1989, 367–86; Daniel Landau, "Government Expenditure and Economic Growth: A Cross-Country Study," *SEJ*, Jan. 1983, 783–92; Daniel Landau, "Government Expenditures and Economic Growth in the Developed Countries: 1952–76," *PC*, no. 3, 1985, 459–77; Young Lee and Roger H. Gordon, "Tax Structure and Economic Growth," *Journal of Public Economics*, June 2005, 1027–43; Michael L. Marlow, "Private Sector Shrinkage and the Growth of Industrialized Economies," *PC*, no. 2, 1986, 143–54; Keith Marsden, *Big, Not Better? Evidence from 20 Countries That Slim Governments Work Better* (London: Centre for Policy Studies, 2008); Ricardo Martin and Mohsen Fardmanesh, "Fiscal Variables and Growth: A Cross-Sectional Analysis," *PC*, March 1990, 239–51; Edgar A. Peden, "Productivity in the United States and Its Relationship to Government Activity: An Analysis of 57 Years, 1929–1986," *PC*, Feb. 1991, 153–73; Edgar A. Peden and Michael D. Bradley, "Government Size, Productivity, and Economic Growth: The Post-War Experience," *PC*, June 1989, 229–45; Gerald Scully, *Constitutional Environments and Economic Growth* (Princeton: PUP, 1992); Gerald Scully, "Optimal Taxation, Economic Growth and Income Inequality," *PC*, June 2003, 299–312; David B. Smith, *Living With Leviathan: Public Spending, Taxes and Economic Performance* (London: Institute of Economic Affairs, 2006).

30. For recent surveys, see *Recent Tax Policy Trends and Reforms in OECD Countries* (Paris: OECD, 2004); Ken Messere, Flip de Kam, and Christopher Heady, *Tax Policy: Theory and Practice in OECD Countries* (New York: OUP, 2003).

31. Ved P. Ghandi, *Supply-Side Tax Policy: Its Relevance to Developing Countries* (Washington: IMF, 1987); Asa Johansson *et al.*, "Tax and Economic Growth," OECD Economics Department Working Paper no. 620, July 11, 2008; Vito Tanzi, *Taxation in an Integrating World* (Washington: Brookings, 1995); Vito Tanzi and Howell H. Zee, "Tax Policy for Emerging Markets: Developing Countries," *NTJ*, June 2000, 299–322; Vito Tanzi and Howell Zee, *Tax Policy for Developing*

Countries (Washington: IMF, 2001); Wayne Thirsk, *Tax Reform in Developing Countries* (Washington: World Bank, 1997); Howell Zee, "Personal Income Tax Reform: Concepts, Issues, and Comparative Country Developments," IMF Working Paper WP/05/87, April 2005.

32. Charles L. Ballard, John B. Shoven, and John Whalley, "General Equilibrium Computations of the Marginal Welfare Costs of Taxes in the United States," *AER,* March 1985, 128–38; Charles L. Ballard, John B. Shoven, and John Whalley, "The Total Welfare Cost of the United States Tax System: A General Equilibrium Approach," *NTJ,* June 1985, 125–40; Edgar K. Browning, "On the Marginal Welfare Cost of Taxation," *AER*, March 1987, 11–23; Dale W. Jorgenson and Kun-Young Yun, "The Excess Burden of Taxation in the United States," *Journal of Accounting, Auditing and Finance*, Fall 1991, 487–508; Charles E. Stuart, "Welfare Costs per Dollar of Additional Tax Revenue in the United States," *AER*, June 1984, 352–62.

33. Arnold C. Harberger, "Taxation, Resource Allocation, and Welfare," in *Taxation and Welfare* (Chicago: UCP, 1974), 25–62.

34. Martin Feldstein, "Tax Avoidance and the Deadweight Loss of the Income Tax," *RES*, Nov. 1999, 674–80.

35. Ian W. Parry, "Tax Deductions and the Marginal Welfare Cost of Taxation," *International Tax and Public Finance*, Sept. 2002, 531–52.

36. GAO, *Summary of Estimates of the Federal Tax System*, Rep. no. GAO-05-878, Aug. 2005.

37. David Altig *et al.*, "Simulating Fundamental Tax Reform in the United States," *AER*, June 2001, 574–95; Andrew Atkeson, V.V. Chari, and Patrick J. Kehoe, "Taxing Capital Income: A Bad Idea," *FRBMQR*, Summer 1999, 3–17; Alan Auerbach, Laurence J. Kotlikoff, and Jonathan Skinner, "The Efficiency Gains from Dynamic Tax Reform," *IER*, Feb. 1983, 81–100; Steven P. Cassou and Kevin J. Lansing, "Growth Effects of Shifting from a Graduated-Rate Tax System to a Flat Tax," *EI*, April 2004, 194–213; Elizabeth M. Caucutt, Selahattin Imrohoroglu, and Krishna B. Kumar, "Does the Progressivity of Taxes Matter for Economic Growth?" Federal Reserve Bank of Minneapolis Discussion Paper no. 138, Dec. 2000; Christophe Chamley, "Optimal Taxation of Capital Income in General Equilibrium with Infinite Lives," *Econometrica*, May 1986, 607–22; Juan Carlos Conesa and Dirk Krueger, "On the Optimal Progressivity of the Income Tax Code," *JME*, Oct. 2006, 1425–50; Clemens Fuest, Andreas Peichl, and Thilo Schaefer, "Is a Flat Tax Reform Feasible in a Grown-up Democracy of Western Europe? A Simulation Study for Germany," *International Tax and Public Finance*, Oct. 2008, 620–36; Craig S. Hakkio, Mark Rush, and Timothy J. Schmidt, "The Marginal Income Tax Rate Schedule from 1930 to 1990,"

JME, Aug. 1996, 117–38; Burkhard Heer and Mark Trede, "Efficiency and Distribution Effects of a Revenue-Neutral Income Tax Reform," *Journal of Macroeconomics*, March 2003, 87–107; Michael Keen, Yitae Kim, and Ricardo Varsano, "The 'Flat Tax(es)': Principles and Evidence," *International Tax and Public Finance*, Dec. 2008, 712–51; Wenli Li and Pierre-Daniel Sarte, "Growth Effects of Progressive Taxes," Finance and Economics Discussion Series 2002-3, Federal Reserve Board, Jan. 2002; J. A. Mirrlees, "An Exploration in the Theory of Optimal Income Taxation," *Review of Economic Studies*, April 1971, 175–208; Fabio Padovano and Emma Galli, "Tax Rates and Economic Growth in the OECD Countries (1950–1990)," *EI*, Jan. 2001, 44–57; Frida Widmalm, "Tax Structure and Growth: Are Some Taxes Better Than Others?" *PC*, June 2001, 199–219.

38. Joseph A. Pechman, "The Future of the Income Tax," *AER*, March 1990, 1.
39. *A New Tax Framework: A Blueprint for Averting a Fiscal Crisis* (Washington: Committee for Economic Development, 2005); *Replacing the Income Tax: Principles for a New Tax System* (Washington: Center for Strategic and International Studies, 1996); National Commission on Economic Growth and Tax Reform, *Unleashing America's Potential* (New York: St. Martin's, 1996); President's Advisory Panel on Federal Tax Reform, *Simple, Fair, and Pro-Growth: Proposals to Fix America's Tax System*, Nov. 2005; U.S. Treasury Department, *Blueprints for Basic Tax Reform* (Washington: USGPO, 1977); U.S. Treasury Department, *Tax Reform for Fairness, Simplicity, and Economic Growth* (Washington: USGPO, 1984); U.S. Treasury Department, *Integration of the Individual and Corporate Tax Systems: Taxing Business Income Once* (Washington: USGPO, 1992); U.S. Treasury Department, *Restructuring the U.S. Tax System for the 21st Century: An Option for Fundamental Reform*, Office of Tax Policy, Dec. 10, 1992.
40. Jonas Agell and Mats Persson, "On the Analytics of the Dynamic Laffer Curve," *JME*, Oct. 2001, 397–414; Zsolt Becsi, "The Shifty Laffer Curve," *FRBAER*, 3rd quarter 2000, 53–64; Bruce Bender, "An Analysis of the Laffer Curve," *EI*, July 1984, 414–20; James M. Buchanan and Dwight R. Lee, "Politics, Time, and the Laffer Curve," *JPE*, Aug. 1982, 816–19; Don Fullerton, "On the Possibility of an Inverse Relationship Between Tax Rates and Government Revenues," *Journal of Public Economics*, Oct. 1982, 3–22; Firouz Gahvari, "The Nature of Government Expenditures and the Shape of the Laffer Curve," *Journal of Public Economics*, Nov. 1989, 251–60; Austan Goolsbee, "Evidence on the High-Income Laffer Curve from Six Decades of Tax Reform," *BPEA*, no. 2, 1999, 1–47; R. Hemming and J. A. Kay, "The Laffer Curve," *Fiscal Studies*, March 1980, 83–90; James M. Malcomson, "Some Analytics of the Laffer Curve," *Journal of Public Economics*,

April 1986, 263–79; Alfonso Novales and Jesús Ruiz, "Dynamic Laffer Curves," *Journal of Economic Dynamics & Control*, Dec. 2002, 181–206; Alan Peacock, "The Rise and Fall of the Laffer Curve," in Dieter Bös and Bernhard Felderer, eds., *The Political Economy of Progressive Taxation* (New York: Springer-Verlag, 1989), 25–40; Amal Sanyal, Ira N. Gang, and Omkar Goswami, "Corruption, Tax Evasion and the Laffer Curve," *PC*, Oct. 2000, 61–78; Douglas R. Shaller, "The Tax-Cut-But-Revenue-Will-Not-Decline Hypothesis and the Classical Macromodel," *SEJ*, April 1983, 1147–54; Uriel Spiegel and Joseph Templeman, "A Non-Singular Peaked Laffer Curve: Debunking the Traditional Laffer Curve," *American Economist*, Fall 2004, 61–66; Mathias Trabandt and Harald Uhlig, "How Far Are We From the Slippery Slope? The Laffer Curve Revisited," Centre for Economic Policy Research Discussion Paper 5657, May 2006; James A. Yunker, "A Supply-Side Analysis of the Laffer Hypothesis," *Public Finance*, no. 3, 1986, 372–91.

41. Data in Appendix III. See also Donald Bruce, M. H. Tuttle, and Charles B. Garrison, "Changes in Income Concentration: Taxes or Macroeconomic Conditions?" *EI*, Jan. 2003, 147–62. There was also an increase in the share of taxes by the wealthy following a cut in the top rate in the United Kingdom; data in Appendix IV. The experiences of Australia, New Zealand, and Canada also show that reductions in tax rates on the wealthy increased their share of the total tax burden; see Anthony B. Atkinson and Andrew Leigh, "The Distribution of Top Incomes in Australia," *Economic Record*, Sept. 2007, 247–61; Anthony B. Atkinson and Andrew Leigh, "Top Incomes in New Zealand, 1921–2005: Understanding the Effects of Marginal Tax Rates, Migration Threat, and the Macroeconomy," *RIW*, June 2008, 149–65; Sinclair Davis, *Who Pays the Lion's Share of Personal Income Tax?* (Sydney: Centre for Independent Studies, 2004); Patrice Martineau, "Federal Personal Income Tax: Slicing the Pie," Statistics Canada Analysis in Brief, April 2005; Mary-Anne Sillamaa and Michael R. Veall, "The Effect of Marginal Tax Rates on Taxable Income: A Panel Study of the 1986 Tax Flattening in Canada," *Journal of Public Economics*, June 2001, 341–56.

42. Caroline Van Rijckeghem, "Social Security Tax Reform and Unemployment: A General Equilibrium Analysis for France," IMF Working Paper WP/97/59, May 1997.

43. "IMF Seminar Discusses Revenue Implications of Trade Liberalization," IMF News Brief No. 99/8, Feb. 25, 1999. A World Bank study came to similar conclusions: "Above a certain level of the official tariff rate, further increases in the official tariff rate produces no increase (and there is some evidence of a decrease) in the collected rate." Lant Pritchett and Geeta Sethi, "Tariff Rates, Tariff Revenue,

and Tariff Reform: Some New Facts," World Bank Policy Research Working Paper 1143, May 1993.

44. Richard Disney, "The Impact of Tax and Welfare Policies on Employment and Unemployment in OECD Countries," IMF Working Paper WP/00/164, Oct. 2000.

45. Anna Ivanova, Michael Keen, and Alexander Klemm, "The Russian Flat Tax Reform," IMF Working Paper WP/05/16, Jan. 2005.

46. Tamás K. Papp, "Tax Rate Cuts and Tax Compliance—the Laffer Curve Revisited," IMF Working Paper WP/08/07, Jan. 2008.

47. Reference was often made to a series of studies done at the Harvard Business School in the early 1950s showing virtually no impact on business executives of even extremely high wartime tax rates; see Thomas H. Sanders, *Effects of Taxation on Executives* (Cambridge: Harvard Business School, 1951). For a summary of mid-1970s knowledge on taxes and labor supply, see L. Godfrey, *Theoretical and Empirical Aspects of the Effects of Taxation on the Supply of Labour* (Paris: OECD, 1975). In the 1970s, reference was often made to Denison's law, which showed that the rate of saving was essentially a constant regardless of the tax or economic regime; see Paul A. David and John L. Scadding, "Private Savings: Ultrarationality, Aggregation, and 'Denison's Law,'" *JPE*, March–April 1974, 1:225–49; Edward F. Denison, "A Note on Private Saving," *RES*, Aug. 1958, 261–67.

48. Marco Bianchi, Björn R. Gudmundsson, and Gylfi Zoega, "Iceland's Natural Experiment in Supply-Side Economics," *AER*, Dec. 2001, 1564–79; Emanuela Cardia, Norma Kozhaya, and Francisco J. Ruge-Murcia, "Distortionary Taxation and Labor Supply," *JMCB*, June 2003, 351–73; CBO, *The Effect of Tax Changes on Labor Supply in CBO's Microsimulation Tax Model*, April 2007; James Gwartney and Richard Stroup, "Labor Supply and Tax Rates: A Correction of the Record," *AER*, June 1983, 446–51; Jerry A. Hausman, "Labor Supply," in Henry Aaron and Joseph A. Pechman, eds., *How Taxes Affect Economic Behavior* (Washington: Brookings, 1981), 27–64; Jerry A. Hausman, "Taxes and Labor Supply," in Alan J. Auerbach and Martin Feldstein, eds., *Handbook of Public Economics*, v. 1 (New York: North-Holland, 1985), 213–63; Susumu Imai and Michael P. Keane, "Intertemporal Labor Supply and Human Capital Accumulation," *IER*, May 2004, 601–41; Assar Lindbeck, "Tax Effects Versus Budget Effects on Labor Supply," *EI*, Oct. 1982, 473–89; Costas Meghir and David Phillips, *Labour Supply and Taxes* (London: Institute for Fiscal Studies, 2008); Mark H. Showalter and Norman K. Thurston, "Taxes and Labor Supply of High-Income Physicians," *Journal of Public Economics*, Oct. 1997, 73–97; Robert K. Triest, "The Effect of Income Taxation on Labor Supply in the United

States," *Journal of Human Resources*, Summer 1990, 491–516; On saving, see B. Douglas Bernheim, "Taxation and Saving," in Alan J. Auerbach and Martin Feldstein, eds., *Handbook of Public Economics*, v. 3 (New York: Elsevier, 2002), 1173–1249; James M. Poterba, *Public Policies and Household Saving* (Chicago: UCP, 1994); Vito Tanzi and Howell H. Zee, "Taxation and the Household Saving Rate: Evidence from OECD Countries," *Banca Nazionale del Lavoro Quarterly Review*, March 2000, 31–43.

49. Edward C. Prescott, "Prosperity and Depression," *AER*, May 2002, 1–15; Edward C. Prescott, "The Transformation of Macroeconomic Policy and Research," *JPE*, April 2006, 203–35; Edward C. Prescott, "Why Do Americans Work So Much More Than Europeans?" *FRBMQR*, July 2004, 2–13; Steven J. Davis and Magnus Henrekson, "Tax Effects on Work Activity, Industry Mix and Shadow Economy Size: Evidence from Rich-Country Comparisons," NBER Working Paper no. 10509, May 2004; Tine Dhont and Freddy Heylen, "Why Do Europeans Work (Much) Less? It Is Taxes and Government Spending," *EI*, April 2008, 197–207; Ingemar Hansson and Charles Stuart, "The Effects of Taxes on Aggregate Labor: A Cross-Country General-Equilibrium Study," *Scandinavian Journal of Economics,* Sept. 1993, 311–26; Lee Ohanian, Andrea Raffo, and Richard Rogerson, "Work and Taxes: Allocation of Time in OECD Countries," *Federal Reserve Bank of Kansas City Economic Review*, 3rd quarter 2007, 37–58; Richard Rogerson, "Structural Transformation and the Deterioration of European Labor Market Outcomes," *JPE*, April 2008, 235–59. Scandinavian countries tend to be exceptions to this analysis; however it appears that changes in government spending in those countries may explain this anomaly: Richard Rogerson, "Taxation and Market Work: Is Scandinavia an Outlier?" *Economic Theory*, July 2007, 59–85. Raw data appear in Appendix II.

50. Martin Anderson, *Welfare* (Stanford: Hoover Institution, 1978), 43–58; Michael J. Boskin, "The Effects of Taxes on the Supply of Labor: With Special Reference to Income Maintenance Programs," *NTAP, 1971* (1972), 684–98; John F. Cogan, *Negative Income Taxation and Labor Supply: New Evidence from the New Jersey-Pennsylvania Experiment* (Santa Monica, CA: Rand, 1978); Arthur B. Laffer, "Disincentives Drag Non-Whites," *LAT*, Aug. 28, 1978.

51. Linda Giannarelli and Eugene Steuerle, "The True Tax Rates Faced By Welfare Recipients," *NTAP, 1995* (1996), 123–29; Andrew Lyon, "Individual Marginal Tax Rates Under the U.S. Tax and Transfer System," in David F. Bradford, ed., *Distributional Analysis of Tax Policy* (Washington: AEI, 1995), 214–47; Robert A. Moffitt, "Welfare Programs and Labor Supply," in Alan J. Auerbach and Martin Feldstein, eds., *Handbook of Public Economics*, v. 4 (New York: Elsevier, 2002), 2393–2430.

52. Donald Bruce and Tami Gurley, "Taxes and Entrepreneurial Entry: An Empirical Investigation Using Longitudinal Tax Return Data," *NTAP, 2004* (2005), 336–43; Robert Carroll *et al.*, "Income Taxes and Entrepreneurs' Use of Labor," *Journal of Labor Economics*, April 2000, 324–51; Julie Berry Cullen and Roger H. Gordon, "Taxes and Entrepreneurial Risk-Taking: Theory and Evidence for the U.S.," *Journal of Public Economics*, Aug. 2007, 1479–1505; William Gentry and R. Glenn Hubbard, "Tax Policy and Entrepreneurial Entry," *AER*, May 2000, 283–87.

53. Gerald Auten, Robert Carroll, and Geoffrey Gee, "The 2001 and 2003 Tax Rate Reductions: An Overview and Estimate of the Taxable Income Response," *NTJ*, Sept. 2008, 345–64; Robert Carroll and Warren Hrung, "What Does the Taxable Income Elasticity Say About Dynamic Responses to Tax Changes?" *AER*, May 2005, 426–31; CBO, "Analyzing the Economic and Budgetary Effects of a 10 Percent Cut in Income Tax Rates," Economic and Budget Issue Brief, Dec. 1, 2005; Martin Feldstein, "The Effect of Marginal Tax Rates on Taxable Income: A Panel Study of the 1986 Tax Reform Act," *JPE*, June 1995, 551–72; Jon Gruber and Emmanuel Saez, "The Elasticity of Taxable Income: Evidence and Implications," *Journal of Public Economics*, April 2002, 1–32; Peter N. Ireland, "Supply-Side Economics and Endogenous Growth," *JME*, June 1994, 559–71; Wojciech Kopczuk, "Tax Bases, Tax Rates and the Elasticity of Reported Income," *Journal of Public Economics*, Dec. 2005, 2093–119; Lawrence B. Lindsey, "Individual Taxpayer Response to Tax Cuts, 1982–1984," *Journal of Public Economics*, July 1987, 173–206; N. Gregory Mankiw and Matthew Weinzierl, "Dynamic Scoring: A Back-of-the-Envelope Guide," *Journal of Public Economics*, Sept. 2006, 1415–33; Emmanuel Saez, "The Effect of Marginal Tax Rates on Income: A Panel Study of 'Bracket Creep,'" *Journal of Public Economics*, May 2003, 1231–58.

54. Edgar K. Browning, "Elasticities, Tax Rates, and Tax Revenue," *NTJ*, March 1989, 45–58; Martin Feldstein and Daniel Feenberg, "The Effects of Increased Tax Rates on Taxable Income and Economic Efficiency: A Preliminary Analysis of the 1993 Tax Rate Increase," *Tax Policy and the Economy*, v. 10, 1996, 89–117; Austan Goolsbee, "What Happens When You Tax the Rich? Evidence from Executive Compensation," *JPE*, April 2000, 352–78; Christina D. Romer and David H. Romer, "The Macroeconomic Effects of Tax Changes: Estimates Based on a New Measure of Fiscal Shocks," NBER Working Paper no. 13264, July 2007; Frank Sammartino and David Weiner, "Recent Evidence on Taxpayer Response to the Rate Increases of the 1990s," *NTJ*, Sept. 1997, 683–705.

55. Seth H. Giertz, "Recent Literature on Taxable-Income Elasticities," CBO Technical Paper 2004-16, Dec. 2004, 14, and "The Elasticity of Taxable Income Over the 1980s and 1990s," *NTJ*, Dec. 2007, 743–68.

56. Paul Krugman, "The Danger of New Tax Cuts," *Fortune*, Feb. 6, 1995, 45.

57. Lawrence Chimerine, "Return of the Supply-Siders," *WP*, July 23, 1996.

58. NBC News, "Meet the Press," Jan. 27, 2002.

59. House Ways and Means Committee, *Trade Agreements Resulting from the Uruguay Round of Multilateral Trade Negotiations*, 103rd Cong., 2nd sess. (Washington: USGPO, 1994), 52. *Washington Post* columnist Hobart Rowen, a long-time critic of supply-side economics, agreed with Kantor: "Because one of the great achievements of the new GATT treaty is to sharply reduce tariffs, the Treasury will initially lose revenue. But the economy will expand as a result of the GATT and eventually more than make up those losses" "The Raid on GATT," *WP*, Sept. 29, 1994. On the Clinton Administration's hostility to dynamic scoring for taxes, see Laura D'Andrea Tyson, "Dynamic Scoring: Not Ready for Prime Time," *WSJ*, Jan. 12, 1995.

60. Robert A. Bennett, "Supply-Side's Intellectual Guru," *NYT*, Jan. 12, 1986.

61. The popular press certainly saw it that way; Jack Egan, "Supply-Side Godfather," *U.S. News & World Report*, Oct. 25, 1999, 49; Michael M. Phillips, "Mundell Wins Nobel Prize in Economics: Columbia University Figure Is a Father of the Euro and Supply-Side School," *WSJ*, Oct. 14, 1999.

62. Robert E. Lucas, "Supply-Side Economics: An Analytical Review," *OEP*, April 1990, 314, and "Macroeconomic Priorities," *AER*, March 2003, 1–14.

63. Louis Uchitelle, "How Both Sides Joined the Supply Side," *NYT*, Aug. 25, 1996; Stiglitz shared the Nobel Prize in economics in 2001.

64. Gerard Baker, "The White House Fights the Last Economic War," *FT*, Dec. 13, 2001.

65. Floyd Norris, "Japan's Budget Deficit Has Soared. It's Time for a Tax Cut," *NYT*, Aug. 17, 2001.

66. Paul Gigot, "Bush Has a Tax Credit for You and You, and…" *WSJ*, April 21, 2000.

67. Of course, tax credits can be designed to have marginal effects and some do. For example, the research and development tax credit applies to R&D above a base level, and the Earned Income Tax Credit is phased-out as one's income rises, which creates high de facto tax rates for those in the phase-out range; see Nada Eissa and Hilary W. Hoynes, "Behavioral Responses to Taxes: Lessons from the EITC and Labor Supply," *Tax Policy and the Economy*, v. 20, 2006, 73–110. This is another reason to oppose tax credits—there is always pressure to phase them out for those with high incomes. Such phase-outs have created a crazy quilt of very high effective tax rates for taxpayers in particular income ranges; see JCT, *Present Law and Analysis Relating to Individual Effective Marginal Tax Rates*, Report no. JCS-3-98 (Washington: USGPO, 1998). It's not known to what extent

taxpayers are aware of many of these high effective rates and respond to them; Charles R. Enis and Leroy F. Christ, "Implications of Phase-Outs on Individual Marginal Tax Rates," *Journal of the American Taxation Association*, Spring 1999, 45–72.

68. Scott A. Hodge, "Tax Credits—Just Say No," *Tax Notes*, Jan. 8, 2007, 86–87.

69. On the failure of consumers to respond to tax rebates, see Alan Blinder, "Temporary Income Taxes and Consumer Spending," *JPE*, Feb. 1981, 26–53; Franco Modigliani and Charles Steindel, "Is a Tax Rebate an Effective Tool for Stabilization Policy?" *BPEA*, no. 1, 1977, 175–209; James Poterba, "Are Consumers Forward Looking? Evidence from Fiscal Experiments," *AER*, May 1988, 413–18; Charles Steindel, "The Effect of Tax Changes on Consumer Spending," *Current Issues in Economics and Finance*, Federal Reserve Bank of New York, Dec. 2001, 1–6; Peter S. Yoo, "The Tax Man Cometh: Consumer Spending and Tax Payments." *FRBSLR*, Jan.–Feb. 1996, 37–44.

70. Ron Suskind, "What Bush Meant," *Esquire* web site, Sept. 19, 2008 (emphasis in original).

71. Of 142 million total returns, 50.6 million had either a negative income tax liability or no tax liability in 2001; in the aggregate, all returns under $30,000 had no tax liability; JCT, "Updated Distribution of Certain Federal Tax Liabilities by Income Class for Calendar Year 2001," Rep. no. JCX-65-01, Aug. 2, 2001.

72. Julian Barnes, "Retailers Split Over Setting Sights on Tax Rebates," *NYT*, Aug. 22, 2001; Anitha Reddy, "Retailers Zero In on Tax Refund Checks," *WP*, July 13, 2001.

73. Matthew D. Shapiro and Joel Slemrod, "Consumer Response to Tax Rebates," *AER*, March 2003, 381–96; Matthew D. Shapiro and Joel Slemrod, "Did the 2001 Tax Rebate Stimulate Spending? Evidence from Taxpayer Surveys," *Tax Policy and the Economy*, v. 17, 2003, 83–109.

74. David S. Johnson, Jonathan A. Parker, and Nicholas S. Souleles, "Household Expenditure and the Income Tax Rebates of 2001," *AER*, Dec. 2006, 1589–1610.

75. Bruce Bartlett, "Stop Those Checks," *NYT*, March 24, 2008.

76. Mathew D. Shapiro and Joel Slemrod, "Did the 2008 Tax Rebate Stimulate Spending?" paper presented at the January 2009 American Economic Association annual meeting. According to an Associated Press/Ipsos poll in February, 77 percent of respondents said they would either save the rebate or use it to pay down debt; only 19 percent said they would spend it. A CNN/Opinion Research poll in March found 73 percent of people saying they would save the rebate or pay down debt, with 21 percent saying they would spend it. A CBS/New York Times poll in April found 78 percent of people saying they would save the rebate or pay

down debt and 18 percent saying they would spend it. Polls accessed at www. pollingreport.com.

77. Christopher L. House and Matthew D. Shapiro, "Phased-in Tax Cuts and Economic Activity," *AER*, Dec. 2006, 1835–49. For a fuller criticism of Bush's tax policies from a supply-side perspective, see Bruce Bartlett, *Impostor: How George W. Bush Bankrupted America and Betrayed the Reagan Legacy* (New York: Doubleday, 2006), 44–63.

78. Robert Shogan, "Bush Ends His Waiting Game, Attacks Reagan," *LAT*, April 14, 1980.

79. Republicans in Congress were just as bad; see, for example, the statements by Senators Robert Bennett, John Cornyn, and Judd Gregg in the *Congressional Record*, May 15, 2007, S6082-85 (daily ed.).

80. George W. Bush, "President Discusses Homeland Security and the Economy with Cabinet," Nov. 13, 2002.

81. George W. Bush, "President Bush Taking Action to Strengthen America's Economy," Jan. 7, 2003.

82. George W. Bush, "President Discusses 2007 Budget and Deficit Reduction in New Hampshire," Feb. 8, 2006.

83. George W. Bush, "Press Conference by the President," Sept. 20, 2007.

84. CEA, *ERP*, 2003, 57–58.

CHAPTER 6   STARVING THE BEAST DIDN'T WORK

1. Charles Edward Barnes, "In a Tiger Trap," *WP*, Dec. 22, 1907.

2. John Kenneth Galbraith, *Ambassador's Journal: A Personal Account of the Kennedy Years* (Boston: Houghton Mifflin, 1969), 381; and *A Journey Through Economic Time* (Boston: Houghton Mifflin, 1994), 174.

3. JEC, *January 1965 Economic Report of the President*, 89th Cong., 1st sess. (Washington: USGPO, 1965), 13.

4. Michael Harrington, "'Reactionary Keynesianism,'" *Encounter*, March 1966, 51.

5. House Ways and Means Committee, *Revenue Act of 1963*, House Rep. no. 749, 88th Cong., 1st sess. (Washington: USGPO, 1963), c5-28; Donald F. Swanson, "Andrew Mellon on Tax Cuts," *TNR*, March 23, 1963, 22.

6. Paul Blustein, "Recent Budget Battles Leave the Basic Tenets of Welfare State Intact," *WSJ*, Oct. 21, 1985.

7. M. Susan Murnane, "Selling Scientific Taxation: The Treasury Department's Campaign for Tax Reform in the 1920s," *Law and Social Inquiry*, Fall 2004,

819–56; Roy G. Blakey and Gladys C. Blakey, "The Revenue Act of 1932," *AER*, Dec. 1932, 620–40; E. Carey Brown, "Fiscal Policy in the 'Thirties: A Reappraisal," *AER*, Dec. 1956, 857–79.

8. For a recent review of Eisenhower's opposition to tax cuts, see Marc Linder, "Eisenhower-Era Marxist-Confiscatory Taxation: Requiem for the Rhetoric of Rate Reduction for the Rich," *Tulane Law Review*, March 1996, 905–1040.

9. Allen J. Matusow, *Nixon's Economy: Booms, Busts, Dollars, & Votes* (Lawrence: University Press of Kansas, 1998), 39–40.

10. John R. Greene, *The Presidency of Gerald R. Ford.* (Lawrence: University Press of Kansas, 1995), 72–81.

11. Jude Wanniski, "Taxes and a Two-Santa Theory," *National Observer*, March 6, 1976.

12. James R. Adams, *Secrets of the Tax Revolt* (New York: Harcourt Brace Jovanovich, 1984).

13. Senate Finance Committee, *Individual and Business Tax Reduction Proposals*, 95th Cong., 2nd sess. (Washington: USGPO, 1978), 172.

14. Milton Friedman, "The Limitations of Tax Limitation," *Policy Review*, Summer 1978, 11.

15. Milton Friedman, "The Kemp-Roth Free Lunch," *Newsweek*, Aug. 7, 1978.

16. Irving Kristol, "Populist Remedy for Populist Abuses," *WSJ*, Aug. 10, 1978.

17. Dennis Farney, "Tip O'Neill's Unpleasant Duty," *WSJ*, April 5, 1979.

18. James M. Buchanan and Richard E. Wagner, *Democracy in Deficit: The Political Legacy of Lord Keynes* (New York: Academic Press, 1977).

19. Geoffrey Brennan and James M. Buchanan, *The Power to Tax: Analytical Foundations of a Fiscal Constitution* (New York: CUP, 1980); Geoffrey Brennan and James M. Buchanan, "The Logic of Tax Limits: Alternative Constitutional Constraints on the Power to Tax," *NTJ*, June 1979, 11–22; Geoffrey Brennan and James M. Buchanan, "Towards a Tax Constitution for Leviathan," *Journal of Public Economics*, Dec. 1977, 255–73; James M. Buchanan, "Taxation in Fiscal Exchange," *Journal of Public Economics*, July–Aug. 1976, 17–29.

20. Burton A. Abrams and William R. Dougan, "The Effects of Constitutional Restraints on Government Spending," *PC*, May 1986, 101–16; John G. Matsusaka, "Fiscal Effects of the Voter Initiative: Evidence from the Last 30 Years," *JPE*, June 1995, 587–623; Carolyn Sherwood-Call, "Tax Revolt or Tax Reform? The Effects of Local Government Limitation Measures in California," *Federal Reserve Bank of San Francisco Economic Review*, Spring 1987, 57–67.

21. Alberto Alesina and Guido Tabellini, "A Positive Theory of Fiscal Deficits and Government Debt," *Review of Economic Studies*, July 1990, 403–14; Torsten Persson and Lars E. O. Svensson, "Why a Stubborn Conservative Would Run a

Deficit: Policy With Time-Inconsistent Preferences," *QJE*, May 1989, 325–45; Per Pettersson-Lidbom, "An Empirical Investigation of the Strategic Use of Debt," *JPE*, June 2001, 570–83; Guido Tabellini and Alberto Alesina, "Voting on the Budget Deficit," *AER*, March 1990, 37–49.

22. White House, *America's New Beginning: A Program for Economic Recovery* (Washington: USGPO, 1981).

23. Murray Weidenbaum, *Rendezvous With Reality* (New York: Basic Books, 1988), 19; Milton Friedman, "Closet Keynesianism," *Newsweek*, July 27, 1981, 60.

24. Jerry Tempalski, "Revenue Effects of Major Tax Bills," Office of Tax Analysis Working Paper no. 81, U.S. Treasury Department, July 2003.

25. Daniel Patrick Moynihan, "Reagan's Bankrupt Budget," *TNR*, Dec. 31, 1983, 18–21; and "Reagan's Inflate-the-Deficit Game," *NYT*, July 21, 1985.

26. David A. Stockman, *The Triumph of Politics* (New York: Harper & Row, 1986), 267–68.

27. Martin Anderson, *Revolution* (New York: Harcourt Brace Jovanovich, 1988), 140–63; William A. Niskanen, *Reaganomics* (New York: OUP, 1988), 19; Paul Craig Roberts, "'The Stockman Recession': A Reaganite's Account," *Fortune*, Feb. 22, 1982, 56ff; and *The Supply-Side Revolution* (Cambridge: HUP, 1984), 119–20.

28. Tom Wicker, "The Mondale Trap," *NYT*, Feb. 7, 1986; Jeffrey H. Birnbaum and Alan S. Murray, *Showdown at Gucci Gulch* (New York: Random House, 1987), 35. On the same page, Birnbaum and Murray report that a few minutes later Mondale turned to House Ways and Means Committee chairman Dan Rostenkowski, pointed to the crowd, and said, "Look at 'em. We're going to tax their ass off."

29. Robert Eisner, "What Went Wrong?" *JPE*, May-June 1971, 629–41.

30. Beryl W. Sprinkel, "More Taxes Feed More Spending," *WSJ*, Nov. 10, 1983.

31. George M. von Furstenberg, R. Jeffrey Green, and Jin-Ho Jeong, "Have Taxes Led Government Expenditures? The United States as a Test Case," *Journal of Public Policy*, Aug. 1985, 321–48; George M. von Furstenberg, "Taxes: A License to Spend or a Late Charge?" in Rudolph Penner, ed., *The Great Fiscal Experiment* (Washington: AEI, 1991), 155–91; George M. von Furstenberg, R. Jeffrey Green, and Jin-Ho Jeong, "Tax and Spend, or Spend and Tax," *RES*, May 1986, 179–88.

32. Neela Manage and Michael L. Marlow, "The Causal Relation Between Federal Expenditures and Receipts," *SEJ*, Jan. 1986, 625; Michael Marlow and Neela Manage, "Expenditures and Receipts: Testing for Causality in State and Local Government Finances," *PC*, June 1987, 243–55; Michael L. Marlow and William Orzechowski, "Controlling Leviathan Through Tax Reduction," *PC*, Sept. 1988, 237–45.

Notes

33. William Anderson, Myles S. Wallace, and John T. Warner, "Government Spending and Taxation: What Causes What?" *SEJ*, Jan. 1986, 630–39; Ben Baack and Edward John Ray, "The Political Economy of the Origin and Development of the Federal Income Tax," in Robert Higgs, ed., *Emergence of the Modern Political Economy* (Greenwich, CT: JAI Press, 1985), 121–38; CBO, "The Relationship Between Federal Taxes and Spending: An Examination of Recent Research," July 1987.

34. James C. W. Ahiakpor and Saleh Amirkhalkhali, "On the Difficulty of Eliminating Deficits with Higher Taxes: Some Canadian Evidence," *SEJ*, July 1989, 24–31; Paul R. Blackley, "Causality Between Revenues and Expenditures and the Size of the Federal Budget," *PFQ*, April 1986, 139–56; Charles W. Calomiris and Kevin A. Hassett, "Marginal Tax Rate Cuts and the Public Tax Debate," *NTJ*, March 2002, 119–31; David Joulfaian and Rajen Mookerjee, "The Government Revenue-Expenditure Nexus: Evidence from a State," *PFQ*, Jan. 1990, 92–103; Rati Ram, "Additional Evidence on Causality between Government Revenue and Government Expenditure," *SEJ*, Jan. 1988, 763–69.

35. Henning Bohn, "Budget Balance Through Revenue or Spending Adjustments?" *JME*, June 1991, 333–59; Kevin D. Hoover and Steven M. Sheffrin, "Causation, Spending, and Taxes: Sand in the Sandbox or Tax Collector for the Welfare State?" *AER*, March 1992, 225–48; Dwight R. Lee and Richard K. Vedder, "Friedman Tax Cuts vs. Buchanan Deficit Reduction as the Best Way of Constraining Government," *EI*, Oct. 1992, 722–32.

36. Richard Vedder, Lowell Gallaway, and Christopher Frenze, *Federal Tax Increases and the Budget Deficit, 1947–1986: Some Empirical Evidence* (Washington: JEC, 1987). The latest version of this study, however, shows that spending rises by only seven cents for each dollar of tax increase; Richard Vedder and Jonathan Leirer, *Taxes and Deficits: An Observation on the Relationship Between Taxes and Spending* (Washington: JEC, 2007).

37. George H. W. Bush, "Remarks at the Intel Corporation, Portland, Oregon," May 14, 1988.

38. *Congressional Record*, May 18, 1993, S5987.

39. Ronald Reagan, "Hurry Up and Wait," *WSJ*, July 8, 1993.

40. Richard Wolffe, "Bush Admits Dispute With Greenspan on Tax Cuts," *FT*, Jan. 25, 2000.

41. David E. Rosenbaum, "Embracing Deficits to Deter Spending," *NYT*, Feb. 9, 2003.

42. OMB, *A Blueprint for New Beginnings* (Washington: USGPO, 2001), 172; Allen Schick, "The Deficit That Didn't Just Happen," *Brookings Review*, Spring 2002, 48; Kimberley Strassel, "Bush on His Record," *WSJ*, Dec. 20, 2008.

43. Ron Suskind, *The Price of Loyalty* (New York: Simon & Schuster, 2004), 300; Hans Nichols, "Leadership Lines Up with Deficit Doves," *The Hill*, Feb. 5, 2003.

44. James A. Baker, "A 'Reformed Drunk' on Tax Relief," *WSJ*, April 18, 2003.

45. Stephen Moore, "Don't Know Much About History," *WSJ*, June 12, 2006.

46. David Firestone, "Conservatives Now See Deficits as a Tool to Fight Spending," *NYT*, Feb. 11, 2003; Holman W. Jenkins, "Republicans Learn to Love (Well, Like) the Deficit," *WSJ*, Nov. 5, 2003; Robert D. Novak, "The GOP's Pain-Free Path," *WP*, July 18, 2005; George F. Will, "Campaign by Tax Cut," *WP*, June 1, 2003.

47. Steve Chapman, "Supersizing the Federal Government," *Chicago Tribune*, Dec. 15, 2005.

48. Niskanen comment in Jeffrey Frankel and Peter Orszag, eds., *American Economic Policy in the 1990s* (Cambridge: MIT Press, 2002), 184–87; William A. Niskanen, "Starve the Beast Does Not Work," *Cato Policy Report*, March-April 2004, 2.

49. William G. Gale and Peter R. Orszag, "Bush Administration Tax Policy: Starving the Beast?" *Tax Notes*, Nov. 15, 2004, 999; Daniel N. Shaviro, "The New Age of Big Government," *Regulation*, Spring 2004, 36–42; William A. Niskanen, "Limiting Government: The Failure of 'Starve the Beast,'" *Cato Journal*, Fall 2006, 553–58; Christina D. Romer and David H. Romer, "Do Tax Cuts Starve the Beast? The Effect of Tax Changes on Government Spending," NBER Working Paper no. 13548, Oct. 2007.

50. Robert J. Barro, "There's a Lot to Like About Bush's Tax Plan," *Business Week*, Feb. 24, 2003, 28; Gary S. Becker, Edward P. Lazear, and Kevin M. Murphy, "The Double Benefit of Tax Cuts," *WSJ*, Oct. 7, 2003; Milton Friedman, "What Every American Wants," *WSJ*, Jan. 15, 2003.

51. Joshua Bolten, "Budget for the Future," *WSJ*, Feb. 6, 2006.

52. *OECD Revenue Statistics, 1965–2007* (Paris: OECD, 2008), 19.

53. Peter Beinart, "Unbalanced," *TNR*, May 26, 2003, 6.

54. Paul Krugman, "The Tax-Cut Con," *NYTM*, Sept. 14, 2003, 54–61; "Support the Troops," *NYT*, Nov. 11, 2003; "Red Ink Realities," *NYT*, Jan. 27, 2004; "Deficits and Deceit," *NYT*, March 4, 2005. The Bush administration systematically lied about the true cost of the drug coverage program; Bruce Bartlett, *Impostor: How George W. Bush Bankrupted America and Betrayed the Reagan Legacy* (New York: Doubleday, 2006), 67–72.

55. Jonathan Baron and Edward J. McCaffery, "Starving the Beast: The Psychology of Budget Deficits," Working Paper, Center for the Study of Law and Politics, USC Law School and California Institute of Technology, 2006; Martin A. Sullivan, "Getting Serious About Starving the Beast," *Tax Notes*, May 16, 2005, 822–28.

56. www.npr.org/news/specials/polls/taxes2003/index.html; www.nationaljournal.com; www.rasmussenreports.com.
57. Jonathan Rauch, "Stoking the Beast," *Atlantic Monthly*, June 2006, 27.

CHAPTER 7 DEALING WITH TOMORROW'S ECONOMIC CRISIS

1. Greg Ip, "Long Study of Great Depression Has Shaped Bernanke's Views," *WSJ*, Dec. 7, 2005.
2. Ben S. Bernanke, "On Milton Friedman's Ninetieth Birthday," Nov. 8, 2002, www.federalreserve.gov/newsevents/speech/2002speech.htm.
3. For good surveys of the impending crisis, see Alan Auerbach, Jason Furman, and William G. Gale, "Facing the Music: The Fiscal Outlook as the Bush Years End," *Tax Notes*, June 2, 2008, 981–92; Peter S. Heller, *Who Will Pay?* (Washington: IMF, 2003); Laurence J. Kotlikoff and Scott Burns, *The Coming Generational Storm* (Cambridge: MIT Press, 2004); Roger Lowenstein, *While America Aged* (New York: Penguin, 2008); Peter G. Peterson, *Running on Empty* (New York: Farrar, Straus & Giroux, 2004).
4. OMB, *Budget of the United States Government, Fiscal Year 2009: Analytical Perspectives* (Washington: USGPO, 2008), 195.
5. www.fms.treas.gov/fr/index.html.
6. These data can be found in the stewardship chapter in the analytical perspectives supplement to the federal budget published by OMB, available at www.whitehouse.gov/omb.
7. The actuaries for Social Security and Medicare calculate the present value of future GDP in perpetuity at $1.3 quadrillion.
8. Data in Table IV.B6 of the annual Social Security Trustees reports, at www.ssa.gov/OACT/TR/index.html.
9. Data in Tables III.B10, III.C15, and III.C23 of the annual Medicare Trustees reports, available at www.cms.hhs.gov/reportstrustfunds.
10. Medicare covers virtually everyone over the age of 65 regardless of income. Medicaid is a health program limited to the poor of any age.
11. CBO, "The Long-Term Budget Outlook," Dec. 2007; www.gao.gov/special.pubs/longterm/simulations.html.
12. Laurence J. Kotlikoff, "Is the United States Bankrupt?" *FRBSLR*, July–Aug. 2006, 235–49; Daniel N. Shaviro, *Taxes, Spending, and the U.S. Government's March Toward Bankruptcy* (New York: CUP, 2007); Richard Barley, "Triple Threat to Government Debt," *WSJ*, Feb. 14, 2009; Franceso Guerra, Aline van

Duyn, and Daniel Pimlott, "U.S.'s Triple-A Credit Rating 'Under Threat,'" *FT*, Jan. 11, 2008; Päivi Munter, "U.S., Germany, France and U.K. Face Junk Debt Status Within 30 Years, Warns S&P," *FT*, March 21, 2005.

13. *United States v. Ptasynski*, 462 U.S. 74 (1983). See also Joseph J. Darby, "Confiscatory Taxation," *American Journal of Comparative Law*, supplement, 1990, 545–55; Gale Ann Norton, "The Limitless Federal Taxing Power," *Harvard Journal of Law and Public Policy*, Summer 1985, 591–625.

14. Charles M. Tiebout, "A Pure Theory of Local Expenditures," *JPE*, Oct. 1956, 416–24.

15. According to Citizens Against Government Waste, a budgetary watchdog group, total pork barrel spending in 2008 came to just $17.2 billion (www.cagw.org). The total budget was $3 trillion.

16. On the Fed as a political institution, see Robert J. Shapiro, "Politics and the Federal Reserve," *TPI*, Winter 1982, 119–39; John T. Woolley, *Monetary Politics: The Federal Reserve and the Politics of Monetary Policy* (New York: CUP, 1984).

17. Thomas Laubach, "New Evidence on the Interest Rate Effects of Budget Deficits and Debt," Finance and Economics Discussion Series 2003–12, Federal Reserve Board, April 2003; Eric M. Engen and R. Glenn Hubbard, "Federal Government Debt and Interest Rates," *NBER Macroeconomics Annual, 2004* (2005), 83–138.

18. John B. Shoven and Gopi Shah Goda, "Adjusting Government Policies for Age Inflation," NBER Working Paper no. 14231, Aug. 2008.

19. See Census Bureau, "Voting and Registration in the Election of November 2004," Rep. no. P20-556, March 2006; Census Bureau, "Voting and Registration in the Election of November 2006," Rep. no. P20-557, June 2008.

20. Statement before the Senate Budget Committee, Jan. 18, 2007, n. 6.

21. David Koitz and Michelle Harlan, "Major Deficit-Reduction Measures Enacted in Recent Years," CRS Report for Congress no. 94–719 EPW, Sept. 8, 1994.

22. Alberto Alesina and Roberto Perotti, "Fiscal Adjustments in OECD Countries: Composition and Macroeconomic Effects," *IMF Staff Papers*, June 1997, 210–48; Alberto Alesina and Roberto Perotti, "Fiscal Expansions and Adjustments in OECD Countries," *Economic Policy*, Oct. 1995, 207–48; Boris Cournède and Frédéric Gonand, "Restoring Fiscal Sustainability in the Euro Area: Raise Taxes or Curb Spending?" OECD Economics Department Working Paper no. 520, Oct. 2006.

23. *OECD Economic Outlook*, May 2007, 235; GAO, "Deficit Reduction: Experiences of Other Nations," Rep. no. GAO/AIMD-95-30, Dec. 1994.

24. For years, the IMF and OECD have told the United States that higher taxes are inevitable if it doesn't sharply reduce entitlement costs; Elizabeth Becker, "I.M.F.

Notes

Chief Sees Potential Hazard in U.S. Fiscal Policies," *NYT*, Sept. 21, 2004; Martin Mühleisen and Christopher Towe, eds., *U.S. Fiscal Policies and Priorities for Long-Run Sustainability* (Washington: IMF, 2004); *OECD Economic Survey: United States*, 2007, 59–73.

25. *Treasury Bulletin*, March 2009, 40; Justin Murray and Marc Labonte, "Foreign Holdings of Federal Debt," CRS Report for Congress no. RS22331, March 12, 2008.

26. James K. Jackson, "Foreign Ownership of U.S. Financial Assets: Implications of a Withdrawal," CRS Report for Congress no. RL34319, Jan. 14, 2008; "China's Premier Seeks Guarantee from U.S. on Debt," *NYT*, March 14, 2009; Anthony Faiola, "China Worried About U.S. Debt," *WP*, March 14, 2009; "Barclays Says 40% of Japan's Investors See Risk of U.S. Default," Bloomberg News, Jan. 30, 2009; Henny Sender, "Mideast Sovereign Wealth Funds Fret Over US Treasuries," *FT*, Feb. 17, 2009.

27. "The Unpleasant Arithmetic of Budget and Trade Deficits," *Federal Reserve Bank of Minneapolis Annual Report, 1986*, available at www.minneapolisfed.org; B. Douglas Bernheim, "Budget Deficits and the Balance of Trade," *Tax Policy and the Economy*, v. 2, 1988, 1–31; CBO, "Long-Term Economic Effects of Chronically Large Federal Deficits," Economic and Budget Issue Brief, Oct. 13, 2005.

28. Interview on *U.S. News & World Report* website, Oct. 20, 2008.

29. Bruce Bartlett, "Taxes, Bailouts and Class Warfare," *Forbes.com*, March 20, 2009; Bob Inglis and Arthur B. Laffer, "An Emissions Plan Conservatives Could Warm To," *NYT*, Dec. 28, 2008.

30. David Hume, *Essays: Moral, Political, and Literary* (Indianapolis: Liberty Fund, 1985; originally published 1742), 345.

31. It's worth noting that the premier liberal philosopher of his generation, John Rawls, thought that a flat rate consumption tax is the fairest form of taxation; *A Theory of Justice*, revised ed. (Cambridge: HUP, 1999), 246.

32. Keynes, *Writings*, 19:295.

33. This is the main problem with the so-called FairTax, which has been promoted by a number of people as a complete replacement for all federal taxes. For criticism, see Bruce Bartlett, "Why the FairTax Won't Work," *Tax Notes*, Dec. 24, 2007, 1241–54.

34. Alfred G. Buehler, "The Spendings Tax," *Public Finance*, no. 1, 1950, 8–22; Randolph Paul, *Taxation in the United States* (Boston: Little, Brown, 1954), 291–94; Kenyon E. Poole, "Problems of Administration and Equity Under a Spendings Tax," *AER*, March 1943, 63–73; U.S. Treasury Department, *Annual Report of the Secretary of the Treasury, 1943* (Washington: USGPO, 1944), 93–94, 410–20.

Notes

35. Seminal contributions to this analysis include Irving Fisher and Herbert W. Fisher, *Constructive Income Taxation* (New York: Harper & Brothers, 1942); Nicholas Kaldor, *An Expenditure Tax* (London: George Allen & Unwin, 1955).

36. This discussion refers to what is a called a credit-invoice VAT. Another type is a subtraction-method VAT, under which businesses subtract all purchases from other businesses, including any VAT paid, from their gross sales and calculate the tax on the net. The two methods are mathematically equivalent.

37. A German business executive, Wilhelm von Siemens, is often credited with inventing the VAT; Clara K. Sullivan, *The Tax on Value Added* (New York: Columbia University Press, 1965), 12. Other early contributions include T.S. Adams, "Fundamental Problems of Federal Income Taxation," *QJE*, Aug. 1921, 527–56; Gerhard Colm, "The Ideal Tax System," *Social Research*, Aug. 1934, 319–42; Paul Studenski, "Toward a Theory of Business Taxation," *JPE*, Oct. 1940, 621–54. A group of American tax experts sent to Japan after World War II recommended a VAT for that country, but after the proposal was enacted it was repealed before taking effect; Martin Bronfenbrenner, "The Japanese Value-Added Sales Tax," *NTJ*, Dec. 1950, 298–313; Sullivan, *Tax on Value Added*, 126–47.

38. The VAT's border adjustment is often viewed as a sort of penalty on imports and a subsidy to exports; in fact, the VAT is neutral with respect to trade, neither benefiting exports nor penalizing imports; see Harry Johnson and Mel Krauss, "Border Taxes, Border Tax Adjustments, Comparative Advantage, and the Balance of Payments," *Canadian Journal of Economics*, Nov. 1970, 595–602; Martin Feldstein and Paul Krugman, "International Trade Effects of Value-Added Taxation," in Assaf Razin and Joel Slemrod, eds., *Taxation in the Global Economy* (Chicago: UCP, 1990), 263–78.

39. In his State of the Union address in 1972, he asked the ACIR to study the idea of using a VAT to reduce property taxes. The commission concluded that it was not a good idea; ACIR, *The Value-Added Tax and Alternative Sources of Federal Revenue* (Washington: USGPO, 1973).

40. For evidence that more efficient taxation leads to higher taxation, see Gary S. Becker and Casey B. Mulligan, "Deadweight Costs and the Size of Government," *JLE*, Oct. 2003, 293–340; Stanley Fischer and Lawrence H. Summers, "Should Governments Learn to Live With Inflation?" *AER*, May 1989, 382–87; Randall G. Holcombe and Jeffrey A. Mills, "Is Revenue-Neutral Tax Reform Revenue Neutral?" *PFQ*, Jan. 1994, 65–85.

41. On whether a VAT is a money machine, the evidence is decidedly mixed: Liam Ebrill, Michael Keen, Jean-Paul Bodin, and Victoria Summers, *The Modern VAT* (Washington: IMF, 2001), 25–39; Diana Furchtgott-Roth, "OECD Countries

and the VAT: The Historical Experience," Research Study no. 49, American Petroleum Institute, Feb. 1990; Michael Keen and Ben Lockwood, "Is the VAT a Money Machine?" *NTJ*, Dec. 2006, 905–28; Michael Keen and Ben Lockwood, "The Value-Added Tax: Its Causes and Consequences," IMF Working Paper WP/07/183, July 2007; J. A. Stockfisch, "Value-Added Taxes and the Size of Government: Some Evidence," *NTJ*, Dec. 1985, 547–52.

42. Bruce Bartlett, "Not VAT Again!" *WSJ*, April 16, 1993; and "Revenue-Raising: It's VAT Time Again," *WSJ*, Aug. 2, 1984.

43. I first put forward this conclusion in Bruce Bartlett, "A New Money Machine for the U.S.," *LAT*, Aug. 29, 2004. See also Bruce Bartlett, "Agenda for Tax Reform," *Tax Notes*, Dec. 13, 2004; 1531–39; "Feed the Beast," *NYT*, April 6, 2005; "Tax Advice for Mr. Bush: Consider the VAT," *Fortune*, Dec. 13, 2004, 77.

44. William D. Andrews, "A Consumption-Type or Cash Flow Personal Income Tax," *Harvard Law Review*, April 1974, 1113–88. Bradford did his main work in this subject while deputy assistant secretary of the Treasury for tax analysis during the Ford administration: U.S. Treasury Department, *Blueprints for Basic Tax Reform* (Washington: USGPO, 1977). The Meade Committee report in Britain was also important: Institute for Fiscal Studies, *The Structure and Reform of Direct Taxation* (London: George Allen & Unwin, 1978). A tax commission in Sweden recommended an expenditure-based system in 1972: Sven-Olof Lodin, *Progressive Expenditure Tax—An Alternative?* (Stockholm: LiberFölag, 1978).

45. Virtually all flat tax schemes derive from Robert E. Hall and Alvin Rabushka, "A Proposal to Simplify Our Tax System," *WSJ*, Dec. 10, 1981. The Hall-Rabushka flat tax is essentially a subtraction-method VAT.

46. Martin D. Ginsburg, "Life Under a Personal Consumption Tax: Some Thoughts on Working, Saving, and Consuming in Nunn-Domenici's Tax World," *NTJ*, Dec. 1995, 585–602; Laurence S. Seidman, *The USA Tax: A Progressive Consumption Tax* (Cambridge: MIT Press, 1997); Alvin C. Warren, "The Proposal for an 'Unlimited Savings Allowance,'" *Tax Notes*, Aug. 28, 1995, 1103–8.

47. Available at http://govinfo.library.unt.edu/taxreformpanel.

48. Al Ullman, "A Tax Without Loopholes," *WP*, Oct. 23, 1979; Jeffrey H. Birnbaum, "Tax Plan Backers Seek to Regroup After 2 Setbacks," *WSJ*, Oct. 21, 1985; "Beware the VAT," *WSJ*, March 25, 1993.

49. John Burgess, "Japanese Voters Deal Blow to Nakasone," *WP*, April 13, 1987; Anne Swardson, "Canada's Value-Added Tax: Cautionary Tale for Clinton," *WP*, April 16, 1993; John Shaw, "Australian Coalition Narrowly Reelected," *WP*, Oct. 4, 1998.

50. Steven M. Gillon, *The Pact: Bill Clinton, Newt Gingrich, and the Rivalry that Defined a Generation* (New York: OUP, 2008), 224, 268.

51. Report at www.csss.gov.

52. As Bill Clinton famously remarked when forced to adopt a deficit reduction plan in 1993, "You mean to tell me that the success of the program and my reelection hinges on the Federal Reserve and a bunch of f***ing bond traders?" Quoted in Bob Woodward, *The Agenda* (New York: Simon & Schuster, 1994), 84. In fact, the bond market did have extraordinary influence economic policy at that time: Douglas R. Sease and Constance Mitchell, "The World's Bond Buyers Gain Huge Influence Over U.S. Fiscal Plans," *WSJ*, Nov. 6, 1992.

53. Republican economist John Goodman claimed that passage of the 1993 tax increase would lower GDP by $244 billion by 1998, reduce capital formation by an astonishing $1.8 trillion, and eliminate 1.34 million jobs that otherwise would have been created. This forecast was completely wrong in every respect; John C. Goodman, "Forecast of the House-Senate Conference Committee 1993 Budget Bill," National Center for Policy Analysis Media Fact Sheet, Aug. 3, 1993.

54. Neil Brooks and Thaddeus Hwong, "The Social Benefits and Economic Costs of Taxation: A Comparison of High- and Low-Tax Countries," Canadian Centre for Policy Alternatives, Dec. 2006; Peter H. Lindert, *Growing Public: Social Spending and Economic Growth Since the Eighteenth Century* (New York: CUP, 2004); Harold L. Wilensky, "Trade-Offs in Public Finance: Comparing the Well-Being of Big Spenders and Lean Spenders," *International Political Science Review*, Oct. 2006, 333–58; Frederik Bergström and Robert Gidehag, *EU versus USA* (Stockholm: Timbro, 2004).

55. Vito Tanzi and Luger Schuknecht, *Public Spending in the 20th Century: A Global Perspective* (New York: CUP, 2000), 30–45. This is sometimes called "fiscal churning." See Filip Palda, "Fiscal Churning and Political Efficiency," *Kyklos*, no. 2, 1997, 189–206.

56. Roman Arjona, Maxime Ladaique, and Mark Pearson, "Social Protection and Growth," *OECD Economic Studies*, May 2002, 7–45; European Commission, *Public Finances in EMU—2008*, 127–65.

57. Between 1995 and 2002, ABC News asked people how much of each tax dollar was wasted. The mean response ranged between 46 cents and 56 cents. A Fox News poll in 2005 found that 71 percent of Americans objected more to how their taxes were being used than the amount they paid. Only 12 percent were mainly concerned about the amount they paid. Both polls at www.pollingreport.com.

58. Economists believe that the employers' share of the payroll tax is paid entirely by workers in the form of lower wages. In cases where this tax has been reduced, employers did in fact pass on the savings to workers in the form of higher wages.

See Jonathan Gruber, "The Incidence of Payroll Taxation: Evidence from Chile," *Journal of Labor Economics*, July 1997, S72-101.

59. Alan S. Blinder, Roger H. Gordon, and Donald E. Wise, "Reconsidering the Work Disincentive Effects of Social Security," *NTJ*, Dec. 1980, 431-42; Richard V. Burkhauser and John A. Turner, "Is the Social Security Payroll Tax a Tax?" *PFQ*, July 1985, 253-67; Richard Disney, "Are Contributions to Public Pension Programmes a Tax on Employment?" *Economic Policy*, July 2004, 267-311.

60. David Carey and Harry Tchilinguirian, "Average Effective Tax Rates on Capital, Labor and Consumption," OECD Economics Department Working Paper no. 258, Oct. 2000; CBO, *Corporate Income Tax Rates: International Comparisons*, Nov. 2005; European Commission, *Public Finances in EMU— 2008*, 169-205; Stephen Ganghof, "The Political Economy of High Income Taxation," *Comparative Political Studies*, Sept. 2007, 1059-84.

61. Victor R. Fuchs and Ezekiel J. Emanuel, "Health Care Reform: Why? What? When?" *Health Affairs*, Nov.-Dec. 2005, 1399-1414; Jane G. Gravelle and Jack Taylor, "Financing Long-Term Care for the Elderly," *NTJ*, Sept. 1989, 219-32; Samuel Y. Sessions and Philip R. Lee, "Using Tax Reform to Drive Health Care Reform," *Journal of the American Medical Association*, Oct. 22-29, 2008, 1929-31. Polls show that Americans would be willing to pay higher taxes to finance national health insurance: Robin Toner and Janet Elder, "Most Support U.S. Guarantee of Health Plans," *NYT*, March 2, 2007.

62. In truth, the VAT is not nearly as regressive as is generally believed. When viewed over a lifetime, consumption taxes are basically proportional to income because consumption is basically proportional to income. See Erik Caspersen and Gilbert Metcalf, "Is a Value Added Tax Regressive? Annual versus Lifetime Incidence Measures," *NTJ*, Dec. 1994, 731-46; Don Fullerton and Diane Lim Rogers, *Who Bears the Lifetime Tax Burden?* (Washington: Brookings, 1993); Gilbert E. Metcalf, "Life Cycle versus Annual Perspectives on the Incidence of a Value Added Tax," *Tax Policy and the Economy*, v. 8, 1994, 45-64; James M. Poterba, "Lifetime Incidence and the Distributional Burden of Excise Taxes," *AER*, May 1989, 325-30; John Sabelhaus, "What Is the Distributional Burden of Taxing Consumption?" *NTJ*, Sept. 1993, 331-44.

63. Stephen Cooney, "Comparing Automotive and Steel Industry Legacy Cost Issues," CRS Report for Congress no. RL33169, Nov. 28, 2005. In recent years, corporate executives have been among the strongest supporters of national health insurance: Jonathan Cohn, "What's the One Thing Big Business and the Left Have in Common?" *NYTM*, April 1, 2007, 45-49; Milt Freudenheim, "New Urgency in Debating Health Care," *NYT*, April 6, 2007; Jordan Rau, "Healthcare Reform's Unlikely Ally: Big Business," *LAT*, May 7, 2007; Catherine Arnst, "A

Secret Wish for Health Reform," *Business Week*, May 18, 2009, 23. On state and local governments: GAO, "State and Local Fiscal Challenges: Rising Health Care Costs Drive Long-Term and Immediate Pressures," Rep. no. GAO-09-210T, Nov. 2008.

64. CBO, "Accounting for Sources of Projected Growth in Federal Spending on Medicare and Medicaid," Economic and Budget Issue Brief, May 28, 2008; Ronald Lee and Jonathan Skinner, "Will Aging Baby Boomers Bust the Federal Budget?" *JEP*, Winter 1999, 117–40; Robert W. Fogel, "Forecasting the Cost of U.S. Health Care in 2040," NBER Working Paper no. 14361, Sept. 2008.

65. Jan M. Rosen, "Tax Watch; The Likely Form of New Taxes," *NYT*, Dec. 19, 1988.

66. James R. Hines Jr. and Lawrence H. Summers, "How Globalization Affects Tax Design," NBER Working Paper no. 14664, January 2009.

67. Jens Arnold, "Do Tax Structures Affect Aggregate Economic Growth? Empirical Evidence from a Panel of OECD Countries," OECD Economics Department Working Paper no. 643, Oct. 2008; Asa Johansson et al., "Tax and Economic Growth," OECD Economics Department Working Paper no. 620, July 2008.

68. *Progress and Poverty* (New York: Robert Schalkenbach Foundation, 1975; first published, 1880), 409.

69. Ebrill et al., *The Modern VAT*, 41.

70. Rates available at www.oecd.org/ctp/taxdatabase.

71. Ali Agha and Jonathan Houghton, "Designing VAT Systems: Some Efficiency Considerations," *RES*, May 1996, 303–8; Kent Matthews, "VAT Evasion and VAT Avoidance: Is There a European Laffer Curve for VAT?" *International Review of Applied Economics*, Jan. 2003, 105–14; Kent Matthews and Jean Lloyd-Williams, "Have VAT Rates Reached Their Limit? An Empirical Note," *Applied Economics Letters*, Feb. 2000, 111–15.

72. Michael J. Graetz, *100 Million Unnecessary Returns* (New Haven: Yale University Press, 2008).

73. Junko Kato, *Regressive Taxation and the Welfare State* (New York: CUP, 2003); Harold L. Wilensky, *Rich Democracies* (Berkeley: University of California Press, 2002), 384–85.

74. CBO, *Effects of Adopting a Value-Added Tax* (Washington: USGPO, 1992); Internal Revenue Service, *A Study of Administrative Issues in Implementing a Federal Value Added Tax*, Office of the Assistant Commissioner for Planning and Research, May 1993; JCT, *Factors Affecting the International Competitiveness of the United States*, Rep. no. JCS-6-91 (Washington: USGPO, 1991); GAO, *Value-Added Taxes: Lessons Learned from Other Countries on Compliance Risks, Administrative Costs, Compliance Burden, and Transition*, Rep. no. GAO-08-566, April 2008.

Index

Index

Index

Index

Index

Index

Index

Index

U.S. Treasury, 37, 44, 106, 168, 170–3, 176,
    178, 241n59
  triple-A credit rating, 170–1
U.S. Treasury Department, 26, 36, 88
U.S. Treasury securities, 6, 21–2, 24, 29, 35, 67,
    168, 172–3, 176, 217n41, 253n52
  foreign ownership of, 176
  bills, 6, 24, 67
  bonds, 172, 253n52
  notes, 35
University of Chicago, 30, 41, 78, 95, 98,
    100, 201
Uruguay Round, 135
USA Tax, 180

value-added tax (VAT), 2, 11, 179–88, 251n36,
    37, 38, 41, 254n62
  credit-invoice, 251n36
  and Europe, 179–80
  and Japan, 251n37
  as money machine, 180, 185, 251n41
  is neutral to trade, 251n38
  and politics, 181
  subtraction-method, 251n36
  and the U.S., 180
value of currency, 51
Vanity Fair, 49
velocity, 5, 20–1, 24, 30, 66
Vedder, Richard, 157
Versailles Treaty, 44, 76
Vietnam War, 69, 110
Viner, Jacob, 30–1, 53–4, 71
"voodoo economic policy," 140
von Furstenberg, George M., 156
von Mises, Ludwig, 41, 127

wage changes, 85–7
wage controls, 83, 86–7, 96
wage cuts, 29, 45–8, 50–1, 53
Wagner, Adolf, 171
Wagner's law, 171
Wall Street Journal, 4, 27, 101–2, 145, 147–8,
    155, 158–9, 188
Wanniski, Jude, 101–2, 128, 147
war spending
    See defense spending
Warburg, Paul M., 15
Warren, George F., 31
Washington Post, 4, 27, 144, 241n59
The Way the World Works, 102
The Wealth of Nations, 125
Wealth and Poverty, 61
Weidenbaum, Murray, 152
Weintraub, Sydney, 86
welfare, 114, 132, 134, 163, 187, 188–90
Wharton Econometric Forecasting Associates
    (WEFA), 107, 110, 134
White House, 11, 49–50, 77–8, 86, 101
Williams, John H., 60
Willis, H. Parker, 19, 35–6
Wilson, Woodrow, 28, 30, 128
Witteveen, Johannes, 103
World Bank, 76, 132, 187, 237n43
World Trade Organization, 76
World War I, 19, 44, 46, 56, 72, 76, 128
World War II, 56, 59, 64, 69, 72–6, 84, 97–8,
    127, 251n37
Wright, David McCord, 61

Yale Review, 53
Yale University, 32